T0291527

Business and Management Doctorates World-Wide

Business and Management Doctorates World-Wide: Developing the Next Generation

BY

NICOLA J. PALMER

Sheffield Hallam University, UK & University of York, UK

JULIE DAVIES

University College London, UK

AND

CLARE VINEY

Careers Research and Advisory Centre (CRAC) Limited, UK

United Kingdom – North America – Japan – India – Malaysia – China

Emerald Publishing Limited
Emerald Publishing, Floor 5, Northspring, 21-23 Wellington Street, Leeds LS1 4DL

First edition 2024

British Library Cataloguing in Publication Data
A catalogue record for this book is available from the British Library

ISBN: 978-1-78973-500-0 (Print)
ISBN: 978-1-78973-499-7 (Online)
ISBN: 978-1-78973-501-7 (Epub)

INVESTOR IN PEOPLE

Outline of the Book: A Flow Diagram

Chapter 1 Growth patterns of business and management doctorates around the world. Outlines growth patterns of business and management doctorates and their historical emergence, how the PhD and DBA have evolved, and discusses different models and influences on them.

Link: Highlights tensions between the strategic purpose and value of the doctorate from the perspective of providers, candidates, employers and/or funders within and beyond academia. Introduces different models globally and changing and challenging contexts.

Chapter 2 Recruitment, selection and retention in business and management doctorates around the world. Explores issues relating to programme choice, recruitment, selection, and retention. Discusses doctoral pricing and fees and their impact on institutional funding models.

Link: Analyses how institutional infrastructure and support, intrinsic motivation, and the financial and employment/student status of doctoral candidates can impact on retention and attrition rates. Looks at some of the recruitment barriers for under-represented groups and the effects on the research environment.

Chapter 3 The business school doctoral experience. Explores the concept of doctoral training, community building, supervision, doctoral assessment processes and practices, and quality assurance of the doctoral award.

Link: Highlights how the doctoral journey may differ from the multiple perspectives of providers, candidates, and employers and/or funders. There is a focus on issues of agency and structure which invariably impact the quality and vicissitudes of the business school doctoral experience.

Chapter 4 Employability, career management and post-doctoral outcomes in business and management. Examines employability, graduate outcomes, and career trajectories within and beyond academia, talent circulation, career management, and post-doctoral outcomes.

Link: Considers the potential for alignment between businesses and better business and management doctoral experiences, graduate outcomes, stronger links between industry and academia, and leading-edge creative practices.

Chapter 5 Research environment, culture, capacity, capabilities and connectivity. Recognises and explores components and the impact of a supportive research environment and culture on doctoral programmes and candidates.

Contents

About the Authors

Nicola J. Palmer has worked in Higher Education for over 25 years and in Doctoral Programmes Management for almost 15 years. She is an experienced Business School Doctoral Supervisor who, to date, has supervised 19 doctoral candidates to completion and examined over 20 candidates. She was one of the first doctoral supervisors to achieve UKCGE Research Supervisor Recognition and has won an Inspirational Research Supervisor award for her practice. Nicola served on the ESRC-initiated Northern Advanced Research Training Initiative (NARTI) Board 2014–2017 and the European Foundation for Management Development (EFMD) Doctoral Programmes Committee 2016–2022. She is an academic based in the Doctoral School at Sheffield Hallam University and the School for Business & Society at the University of York and is involved in the delivery of Research England funded projects on postgraduate research race equity and the transformation of doctoral supervision.

Julie Davies is a Professor in the Global Business School for Health at University College London, where she is Director of the MBA Health Programme. She earned her PhD in Strategic Management at Warwick University while working full time. Julie has worked in Business Schools for almost three decades and has facilitated Business School Deans' Development Programmes globally. Julie has completed the UKCGE Research Supervisor Recognition Programme and publishes research on impact and gender, hybrid leadership, ethnic minority micro-enterprises, and management education. She co-authored the *Routledge Book Leading a Business School*. Julie also served on EFMD's Doctoral Programmes Committee 2017–2022.

Clare Viney took up the role of Chief Executive Officer of CRAC in October 2016. She is a Strategic Leader with over 20 years' advocacy, policy and external affairs experience, and extensive experience in the not-for-profit sector. Clare is passionate about investing in future generations and those from diverse backgrounds and experiences, empowering people to realise their potential, and achieve their career and development goals. She currently sits on the UK R&D People and Culture Strategy Ministerial Coordination Group, QAA Advisory Committee on Degree Awarding Powers, and Technician Commitment Steering Board. CRAC manages the Vitae Programme in higher education, strengthening institutional provision for the professional development of researchers through research and innovation, training and resources, events, consultancy, and membership. Clare also served on EFMD's Doctoral Programmes Committee 2017–2019.

Foreword

Doctorates at business schools serve a variety of functions for society, academic disciplines, and the institutions that award the qualifications. The societal impact of Doctorates of Business Administration (DBA), other professional doctorates and PhDs has largely been neglected in the focus on providing business and management studies undergraduate degrees and programmes such as MBA. Yet, the future pipeline of academic faculty and highly qualified practising executives relies on a supply of business and management doctorates. Furthermore, holders of business doctorates are a source of research and new knowledge to inform practice as they shape the thinking, relevance and rigour of the most popular subject in universities globally – indeed, they are the custodians of their disciplines and creators of new knowledge that has a major that influence on our lives.

Business and Management Doctorates World-Wide: Developing the Next Generation by Nicola J. Palmer, Julie Davies, and Clare Viney offers valuable and differentiated insights and critical commentary on business school doctorates today. The authors seek to give an overview of the different types of business and management doctorate to present different models in the field. They draw upon a combined wealth of experience and acknowledging historical and contemporary influences. This volume skilfully engages with extensive published literature alongside experiential learning and navigates issues of structure and agency, highlighting tensions between the strategic purpose and value of the doctorate, barriers for under-represented groups, and effects on the research environment.

The authors draw attention to multiple stakeholder perspectives from business school educators, candidates and alumni, employers and policy makers to highlight the contributions to management scholarship and management practice of doctoral programmes in business schools.

As readers, we are encouraged to explore further the potential for alignment between businesses and better business and management doctoral experiences, graduate outcomes, links between industry and academia, and leading-edge creative practices. We are also challenged to broaden our own perspectives beyond familiarity with particular national systems to see the rich variety of doctorates.

In the following pages, you will find a comprehensive analysis of the current state of business and management doctorates not just on the European continent but around the globe. This complements the *EQUAL Guidelines for Doctoral Programmes in Business and Management* which present a common view of a doctorate in the field of business and management research, the largest in higher education.

We are confident that doctoral education in management, whether PhD, DBA, professional, executive, and other doctorates provided by business schools offers tremendous opportunities to bridge theory and practice in an applied discipline. This is particularly salient in a world that continues to question the rigour and relevance of business school research. We congratulate the authors on highlighting important aspects of management education and supporting progress in this popular and dynamic field.

Professor Mark Smith
Director of the Stellenbosch Business School,
Cape Town, South Africa
Friedemann Schulze-Fielitz
Director, EFMD Global Network Americas & Business
School Services

Preface

In this book, we provide reflections on the purpose of business doctorates and international comparisons of innovations in doctoral education within different national educational systems and research and industrial strategies.

A great deal has been written about the MBA, undergraduate business education, and changing models of business schools themselves. With an increase in doctoral candidates world-wide, concerns have been expressed about their employment prospects and the oversupply of graduates in the management field. It would appear that although management is an applied discipline, even professional doctorates in management are decoupled from the growing research impact and interdisciplinary agendas.

To complement recent texts about professional doctorate supervision and perspectives on DBA students as scholar-practitioners, we draw attention more broadly to the purpose of doctoral education in business schools, programme design and management, and candidate experiences. The book draws on the authors' practical experiences, observations, and research on business school doctorates and the development of researchers.

We note the importance of perspective when examining doctoral education. Doctoral researchers and supervisors in business schools need to take a broader helicopter view of changes in management disciplines and business functions. Of course, the successful completion of business and management doctorates around the world requires hard work, courage, and thrift and the ability to analyse detailed evidence while seeing the big picture and making theoretical abstractions. There is a need to foreground individuals in the doctoral environment as persisting in the face of incoming challenges. Our book's front cover reflects these elements.

We hope that you find some useful and thought-provoking insights in this book. We look forward to continuing conversations about the value of business doctorates, re-imagining different models, ecosystems and interdisciplinary, cross-sector, and international collaborations.

Nicola Palmer
Yorkshire

Julie Davies
London

Clare Viney
Cambridge

Acknowledgements

We would like to thank especially JAS as well as:

Elena Braccia
Nadine Burquel
Karen Clegg
Eva Cools
Ann Davis
Monique Donzel
Martin Eley
Vassili Joannidès de Lautour
Eline Loux
Yusra Mouzughi
Mark Saunders
Friedemann Schulze-Fielitz
Mark Smith
Howard Thomas
Christine Unterhitzenberger
Sofia Vala
Matthew Wood

Nicola would like to acknowledge her family, the resilience of a tired and failing laptop and the unconditional love and patience of a spaniel who found his way home.

To quote T. S. Eliot, it's been 'such a long journey' since Nicola, Clare, and I first met in Grenoble and great fun collaborating with fellow travellers who believe that doctorates can transform lives. I also owe a huge debt of gratitude to my family.

I would like to thank Nicola and Julie for allowing me to tag along on this journey! When I first met them at the EFMD Conference in Grenoble, I naively thought that the culture and practice in Business Schools might help Vitae unlock the secrets to helping ALL researchers realise their potential. Consistently, around 80% of researchers aspire to an academic career with over 60% expecting to achieve this, though we know that while the numbers of researchers have continued to increase, there has been little or no growth in the availability of academic positions. Therefore, the career aspirations of most researchers are unrealistic compared to the probability of achieving a long-term academic career.

xvi   *Acknowledgements*

We are a small team that sits at the heart of a diverse community in over 20 countries. All of the CRAC-Vitae research has been conducted by Dr Robin Mellors-Bourne and Dr Janet Metcalfe, I thank them for their curiosity, thoughtfulness, integrity, and passion.

Chapter 1

Growth Patterns of Business and Management Doctorates Around the World

Overview

The purpose of this chapter is to outline the historical emergence of business schools in Europe, the evolution of the PhD in business and management education from its origins in the USA, the development of the Doctorate in Business Administration (DBA) in different parts of the world including Organization for Economic Cooperation and Development (OECD) and non-OECD countries. We highlight debates about Western models of doctoral management adopted in non-Western contexts, specifically the influence of elite Anglophone business schools. In particular, we discuss the influence of media rankings and global mobility of candidates. Finally, the growth patterns of business and management doctorates worldwide are viewed in the context of rapid changes to online learning during the pandemic and a cold war geopolitical context in what has been called the Asian century (Woetzl & Seong, 2019).

An Overall Increase in Doctoral Qualifications Worldwide

A great deal has been written about the MBA, undergraduate business education, and changing models of business schools (see, e.g., Cheit, 1985; Glen, Suciu, & Baughn, 2014; Krishnamurthy, 2020; Navarro, 2008; Parker, 2018; Pfeffer & Fong, 2002). Less focus has been placed, however, on terminal degrees at doctoral level in business schools.

Since the appearance of the first business schools, which developed in Europe from trade or vocational commercial schools in the eighteenth century (Passant, 2016; Thomas, Thomas, & Wilson, 2013; Thomas & Wilson, 2011), the scale and continued growth of management education are unparalleled compared with other academic disciplines (De Meyer, 2013; Reddy, 2008; Thomas & Wilson, 2011). Over the last 50 years, the provision of doctorates in business and management has also enjoyed phenomenal global expansion.

The introduction of the PhD in business and management can be charted back to the USA in 1920 in what is now the University of Chicago Booth School

Business and Management Doctorates World-Wide: Developing the Next Generation, 1–34
Copyright © 2024 by Nicola J. Palmer, Julie Davies and Clare Viney
Published under exclusive licence by Emerald Publishing Limited
doi:10.1108/978-1-78973-499-720231001

of Business. The development of the DBA has followed a less straightforward path. In the USA, for example, its introduction was driven by administrative forces. The DBA was first offered at Harvard University in 1953 as the business school was not authorised to issue a PhD until 2018 (Bogle, personal communication with Julie Davies, July 15, 2019; Marakas, n.d.). The award is not offered by business schools globally as widely as the PhD. Notably in Germany, the DBA still lacks recognition by the national government as an equivalent award to the PhD even though the same DBA programme may be officially recognised in another country where the DBA awarding institution is based such as in the UK (Graf, 2014). This may not matter for those with DBAs in multinational firms based in Germany. There has been a tendency for the DBA to gain worldwide reach as a collaborative degree offered onsite in partner countries but awarded by Australian, North American, and UK universities.

Across all types of doctorates in all academic disciplines, growth in the rate of the qualification had reached a point where it was estimated that over one percent of the working-age population were qualified to doctoral level in more than one-third of OECD countries worldwide in 2015 (OECD, 2017). Between 2013 and 2017, the number of candidates graduating with a doctorate increased by approximately 8% across OECD countries (OECD, 2019). In business and management specifically, there has been growth in the provision of doctorates across the globe (Lean, Wilkins, Moizer, & Heffernan, 2022).

With the increase in doctoral candidates, concerns have been expressed about their employment prospects and over-supply of graduates in the management field (see, e.g., De Meyer, 2013; Ingeborgrud, Korseberg, & Lyby, 2021; Owen, 2009; Suomi, Kuoppakangas, Kivistö, Stenvall, & Pekkola, 2020).

Yet beyond OECD countries, it is important to recognise that geographically contextual conditions have impacted on doctoral education provision. There is an uneven playing field globally. The idea that 'globalization in doctoral education brings with it the legacies of imperialism, colonialism, and Western domination' (Nerad & Heggelund, 2011, p. 6) is mirrored when we look at business school doctoral education where globalisation is more widespread (Friga, Bettis, & Sullivan, 2003) or in many business schools where the doctoral education provision is less maturely developed (Bruner & Iannarelli, 2011; Suh, 2008). The influence of international excellence and the existence of a 'super league' of institutions that dominate the academic knowledge economy and the competitive environment warrants consideration.

Elite Reproduction and Academic Excellence

Pioneering business schools such as Wharton and Harvard Business School in the USA are noted as catalysts of global business school development. The private/non-profit business schools of INSEAD (France), IMD (Switzerland), and Harvard Business School (USA) have exerted some of the greatest influence on models of management education (Thomas et al., 2013).

Over time, business school performance has been increasingly measured (and shaped) by accreditation body and media rankings that primarily provide education quality assurance and enhanced business school reputations. Rankings methodologies have focused on variables that consumers of management education appear to value such as average earnings and alumni destinations (Thomas et al., 2013). Journalists including Jack (2022) have noted the influence of metrics such as *The Financial Times* (FT) business school rankings on multiple business school stakeholders. These affect potential candidate choice, employer recruitment and 'placement' of graduates following completion of their doctorates and hold implications for career trajectory and lifetime earnings. There are also unequal opportunities in faculty hiring, remuneration, and promotion (Pitt-Watson & Quigley, 2019). Notably, the international ranking of top performing business schools tends to be Western-led and linked to MBA programme characteristics. In relation to doctorates specifically, however, we also note implications for the quality of research training and research outputs. The proportion of female faculty and female candidates reported in the top 100 business schools ranked in the FT global MBA league tables indicates significant scope for better gender equity (Yarrow & Davies, 2023a) among candidates and faculty delivering MBA programmes. There are significant opportunities to mitigate gender inequalities in business education (Yarrow & Davies, 2023b) and to involve more women in business schools in research with impact (Davies, Yarrow, & Syed, 2020). This also applies to doctoral-level study in business schools.

Until recently there has been a sizeable, seemingly immovable, power differential between the international ranking levels of business schools located in Western countries (mainly in the USA and Europe) and the rest of the world (Vidaver-Cohen, 2007; Wedlin, 2006). Many institutions and countries worldwide, however, seek the reputation to be gained by climbing up the ranks of international schemes that originate from the West (and are driven by Western values of education quality). Latin American business schools, for instance, are reported to hold North American rankings in esteem (Orozco & Villaveces, 2015), whereas European rankings such as Eduniversal are influential in South Africa.

Ostensibly at least, business school education has become increasingly oriented towards internationalisation although local issues were accentuated during pandemic lockdowns. The drive to internationalisation is encouraged by business school accreditations such as AACSB and EQUIS which emphasise international mindsets. Growth in the doctoral education of graduates worldwide has involved international mobility of candidates and faculty members, especially pre-pandemic. This has impacted the global provision of business and management doctorates, contributing to a situation where 'on average across OECD countries, 25% of enrolled doctoral graduates are international students' (OECD, 2019, p. 1). International candidate mobility generally involves movements from less to more developed countries or between developed countries. In the case of business school doctoral education, this mobility of candidates is linked to faculty upskilling and goals of reproducing business models found outside low- and middle-income countries.

Research performance and 'academic excellence' are commonly measured through contributions to the world's leading business and management journals which are ranked, for example, in the *Academic Journal Quality Guide* and the *Financial Times* top 50 list of academic journals. There has been a rise in publications from business school academics in Asia (Collet & Vives, 2013). This tends to correlate with improvements in the quality of research training (Saunders, Wong, & Saunders, 2011).

It is common in top-ranking business schools for permanent academic contracts or tenure and promotions to depend on publishing in top-tier business and management journals. Additionally, there is a history of university and business school research assessments and research standing based on outputs in these journals. Pressures to publish are growing for business and management doctoral candidates in the UAE (Hill & Thabet, 2021). US-trained or US-based scholars of Middle Eastern or African origin can overcome traditional barriers to their career development by their exposure to conducting and publishing research in leading international journals (Lages, Pfajfar, & Shoham, 2015).

The impacts of privileging Western business school research ranking systems are not clearcut or wholesale in terms of the reproduction of an elite league of business schools. It has been reported, for instance, that 'unlike the USA and the Euro-area, where the top researchers are mainly born and research trained in their own country, the UK's leading business and management researchers tend to be non-locals trained outside the UK' (Saunders et al., 2011, p. 401). This may have changed following Brexit in 2016.

National models of training in doctoral education influence the development of doctoral education worldwide (Nerad & Heggelund, 2011). We can observe general patterns in the transfer of credit-bearing PhD training from the USA to Europe. This training has been linked to third-cycle higher education goals under the Bologna Process in Europe (Carter, Fazey, Gonzalez Geraldo, & Trevitt, 2010). National programmes have also been shaped by the implementation of transferable credit-bearing training as part of a commonly aligned and portable licence to practise and the development of *a European Code of Practice for Doctoral Studies in Management and Business* (EIASM & EDAMBA, 2020).

Bogle (personal communication with Julie Davies, July 15, 2019) contends that the UK was historically at the forefront of PhD training developments before the EU broadened PhD training with encouragement from the European Universities Association (EUA), the European Commission and university associations such as the *League of European Research Universities* (LERU). A UK model where training is located outside the PhD research programme, often linked to master's research training in the social sciences and business and management, has been acknowledged to have transferred to Australia. However, we can also observe exceptions in commonly acknowledged diffusion patterns of PhD training models. For example, Saunders et al. (2011) noted the adoption of the USA PhD training model by London Business School in the UK. Most recently, this has also happened at Warwick Business School.

Training for Research Excellence

Middle East and North African (MENA) universities have been impacted by regional factors not least 'the absence of intellectual freedom and the constraints imposed on the free expression of ideas in all MENA universities' (Forster, 2018, p. 1025) combined with strategic under-investment in university research and teaching. Subsequently, there have been attempts to align the provision of doctoral education across the region with European models (El Hassan, 2013) and the Americanisation of business education has been observed especially in the context of the United Arab Emirates (UAE) (Juusola, Kettunen, & Alajoutsi-järvi, 2015) whereby AACSB-accredited UAE institutions have recruited North American faculty with PhDs from AACSB-accredited universities to support the development of 'quality assured' in-country doctoral programmes.

The quality of US doctoral training is also appreciated in South Korea where almost 90% of business school faculty have been observed to hold US social science PhDs (Kim, 2007). Suh (2008) described an expectation in South Korea that a small number of leading universities will dominate global higher education and, thus, there is a need to achieve globalisation in education and research programmes to compete. It is noted that many private universities dominate the top ranks in business and economics disciplines' performance and have the highest school reputations among the general public in South Korea (Jin, 2019). Recruitment of international candidates and international faculty are viewed as a marker of offering the highest quality education in line with goals of achieving a place among 'best universities in the world'.

Furthermore, the US model of doctorates is noted to have influenced the design of doctoral programmes in China (Sun, 2010; Wang & Byram, 2019) whereby the 'numbers of PhD holders and the scale and quality of doctoral education is taken as an important indicator of the level of higher education and overall development of a country' (Wang & Byram, 2019, p. 256). This has driven the massification of doctoral education and China's position as one of the largest PhD-awarding countries worldwide (China Admissions, 2022, 2023). Degrees from China at all levels are increasingly recognised internationally and international demand has been supported by Chinese Government Scholarships and the 'Confucius China Studies Programme' (CCSP) aimed to provide financial assistance to Chinese citizens wishing to pursue their PhD abroad and to pump-prime doctoral research that focuses on China, respectively. Notably, the country is also beginning to attract international candidates from beyond developing countries – particularly from the USA and France. There is an interesting growth pattern to be observed; increasingly, Western-educated Chinese *PhD* graduates in management are starting their academic careers in *Chinese business schools* (Marini & Yang, 2021; Xu, 2009; Zweig & Yang, 2014). They are using their knowledge and experience of the Western system to inform Chinese business school doctorate programme design and delivery. In turn, through a diffusion strategy, these programmes are emerging as competitors of Western business school PhD offerings.

In a different part of the world, Jowi (2021, p. 159) notes the challenges of 'weak internal capacities for research and low numbers of staff with PhDs' across Sub-Saharan African universities. This has prompted a focus on securing rapid growth in PhD graduates. This development, however, is uneven with respect to doctoral enrolment and graduation rates. It is focused on upskilling staff to build academic capacity and it is limited to 'universities in a handful countries, especially South Africa, Nigeria, Kenya, and Ghana' (Jowi, 2021, p. 161). Creative solutions are sought to address resource challenges not least in terms of supervision and doctoral training including centres of excellence, collaborations, and partnerships within the region and beyond. A collaboration between Stellenbosch Faculty of Economics and Management (South Africa) and the University of Bath (UK) illustrates an attempt to build capacity through partnership and collaboration (University of Bath, 2021) rather than through traditional approaches whereby Western models are often imported that are 'more tailored towards functioning in a Western style environment' (Tshabangu-Soko & Caron, 2012, p. 37).

In 2021, a new doctoral training consortium was launched under the auspices of the South Africa-UK University Staff Doctoral Programme (USDP). Ten students at Stellenbosch University and the University of Fort Hare were selected to join the programme from 2021 to 2026 to study for a PhD degree in the field of public policy and inclusive development.

This partnership was designed to address some of South Africa's most challenging societal issues by helping to inform better policy making, support inclusive growth, and to generate new knowledge as part of South Africa's post-Apartheid Transformation agenda. It is a part-time, blended programme, which includes cohort-based research training, professional skills development, and international mobility for research visits, conferences, and summer schools. Customised support includes buy-out of teaching, and online interactive platforms. University of Bath (UK) academics in social science disciplines co-supervise, mentor and support cohort-building activities.

A two-day virtual orientation enables candidates to present their projects, work with their supervisors, and gain insights from colleagues at Bath, Fort Hare, and Stellenbosch as they prepare for the PhD journey and an academic career in different cultural contexts through interdisciplinary scholarship. The USDP project is aligned closely with priorities in South Africa's National Development Plan and reflects academic strengths and research profiles across the three partner universities. The African Doctoral Academy supports the programme and it is led by Stellenbosch's Faculty of Economic and Management Sciences. The Faculty of Management and Commerce hosts the project in Fort Hare and at Bath University, the Faculty of Humanities and Social Sciences leads on the partnership in close collaboration with the School of Management and other departments and academic units.

This PhD training support for academic staff in South Africa receives funding from the South African Department of Higher Education and Training (DHET) and the British Council. Only approximately 40% of academic staff employed in South African universities have a PhD. There are particular challenges for faculty who are undertaking doctoral research in terms of completion, especially in historically disadvantaged universities such as the University of Fort Hare and among disadvantaged people, including women, black, and working-class academics.

To address this issue, the USDP concept was launched by the South African government in the context of wider higher education reform for widening participation, encouraging both new international links and stronger connections between research-intensive and disadvantaged universities within the country. In 2017, a pilot call was launched for consortia with US universities, followed in 2018 by a second call for partnerships with the UK.

Building on Bath's and Stellenbosch's experience of delivering blended doctoral training for international cohorts, the Stellenbosch-Fort Hare-Bath project will allow sharing of good practice developed around the UK's Researcher Development Framework (RDF) (Vitae, n.d.) with South Africa's review of doctoral standards and PhD graduate attributes.

In recognition of its innovative approach, the project featured as a case study at the Africa-Europe Conference on Higher Education Collaboration: *Investing in people, by investing in higher education and skills in Africa*, which took place in Brussels in October 2019 and was attended by Professor Jeremy Bradshaw, Pro-Vice-Chancellor (International & Doctoral) and Dr Tina Schilbach from the International Relations Office.

Professor David Galbreath, Dean of the Faculty of Humanities and Social Sciences, commented:

> I am very excited about the launch of the USDP programme. Building on our successful partnership with Stellenbosch University, this innovative consortium will see Bath contribute to staff doctoral training in South Africa and join forces to revitalise and strengthen the links between academia and policy-making in the country. As a partner to this programme, we will benefit from new, interdisciplinary links in international development studies while building new policy research networks for our students and staff.

The USDP programme is refreshing in terms of its collaborative approach. Shin, Postiglione, and Ho (2018) observe that discourses on world-class higher education often emphasise global competitiveness at the risk of neglecting local relevance, particularly in relation to doctoral training but also with respect to the knowledge economy. In some parts of the world like India, for example, we note an 'exploding market' with a lack of business school maturity. This holds implications for the nature of global competition and the ability of local market demand to be satisfied through local supply.

Producing Business School Doctoral Graduates for the Knowledge Economy

We are aware that 'knowledge economy' is essentially terminology used in Western discourse. Powell and Snellman (2004, p. 199) define the knowledge economy as 'production and services based on knowledge-intensive activities that contribute to an accelerated pace of technical and scientific advance, as well as rapid obsolescence'.

Doctoral education is in a knowledge creation arena with a shifting agenda. Globally, universities are expected to contribute to the advancement of knowledge and innovation. The idea of knowledge production, specifically in the context of business schools, has received attention (see, e.g., Chia & Holt, 2008; Huff & Huff, 2001; Van Aken, 2005; Wilson & Thomas, 2012). Linked to this, Bartunek and Rynes (2014) have noted the paradoxes inherent in academic–practitioner relationships, a theme further explored by MacIntosh et al. (2017) (relational impact) and Boyer (1996) (engaged scholarship).

Building on these ideas together with the seminal works of Gibbons, Limoges, and Nowotny (1997) (different modes of knowledge production) and Barnett (1999) (applications of knowledge – knowledge in use), the doctorate *per se* can be linked to macro-level national growth policies and knowledge economy strategies (OECD, 2022).

In relation to business schools, Anderson and Gold (2019) recognised the value of the doctorate as part of the broader field (or portfolio) of management education. Debates continue about the shape of this education, namely the extent to which business schools exist as schools for business and the purpose of business education – advancing scientific research knowledge, providing professional training or a combination of both (Bennis & O'Toole, 2005 –) and the legitimacy of the business school in a situation where 'production of management knowledge straddles the precarious divide between academic rigour and practical relevance' (Thomas & Wilson, 2011, p. 443). Linked to this, the nature of business and management doctorates can be associated with the ethos of business schools, wherein 'Far from being the Cinderella of business schools … doctoral researchers are key to knowledge production and advancing the business and management education field' (Davies, Palmer, Braccia, Clegg, & Smith, 2021, p. 1).

Among more than 13,000 business schools worldwide (AACSB as cited in Parker, 2018) there exists a combination of state-funded (e.g., dominant in the UK), privately-owned (e.g., dominant in the USA) public–private partnerships (e.g., dominant in France and largely financed by Chambers of Commerce), for-profit and non-profit institutions. The value of the business school to private investors lies in reputation, quality and excellence linked explicitly to European, US and UK accreditation (Conboye, 2019). From the perspective of 'end users', business schools may be 'the "nurseries" of the corporate world' (van Baardewijk & de Graaf, 2021, p. 188). Afterall, business schools contribute to the ethical education of business leaders (Sigurjonsson, Vaiman, & Arnardottir, 2014). Within higher education institutions, however, the business school often plays a principal role as the 'cash cow' (Starkey & Tiratsoo, 2007). This is based on the popularity of, enduring demand for, and resilience of higher level business education courses in hard times (Moules, 2018; Willetts as cited in Morgan, 2013). Business schools, however, tend not to be regarded as a 'golden goose' for scientific knowledge capabilities (Arora, Belenzon, & Patacconi, 2015).

University leaders often seek to enhance their reputations by expanding postgraduate research (PGR) candidate numbers. Business schools typically offer the most popular subjects and attract the highest numbers of postgraduate and overseas students. Yet academic labour markets may not be able to absorb the number of doctoral graduates produced and businesses may be wary of the benefits of doctoral study and qualifications (Malloy, Young, & Berdahl, 2021; Smith, 2021; The Economist, 2010). Indeed, growth in the provision of PhDs alongside intensified international competition for permanent academic positions has been explored in Calmand, Nohara, and Kobayashi's (2018) study of Japanese PhD graduates and French PhD graduates. The authors found that although Japanese PhD graduates have fewer difficulties in finding a job, both groups of graduates are concerned about their ability to secure contracts in private, commercial organisations.

There are paradoxes in the business school system:

> While there is, if anything, a glut of PhD graduates on the labour market, many cannot find academic jobs. Top business schools want to hire PhDs only from the best programmes, but this talent pool has not grown in line with the rising demand for business education in recent decades. (Murray, 2022, p. 1)

At the same time, there are demands for business schools to serve society more widely and to address real-world challenges with academics developing public and corporate engagement and communications skills for impact beyond the academy (Haley, Cooper, Hoffman, Pitsis, & Greenberg, 2022) and calls to respond to the United Nations' Sustainable Development Goals (SDGs) (Weybrecht, 2022).

Anderson and Gold's (2019) study of the value of the doctorate within the broader field of management education takes multiple UK stakeholder views into account. It notes how applied, personal, and organisational outcomes are expected to be attended to by management educators if expectations of doctoral candidates (and external sponsors) are to be met. Within many business schools, a skewed emphasis towards preparing candidates for careers in academia is noted and 'academic focus limits business schools' contribution to society' (Jack, 2020, p. 1). Linked to this, attention has been drawn to apparent mismatches in descriptions of value attributed to the management doctorate by different stakeholder groups contending that 'current norms in doctoral education privilege the assumptions of the academic community at the expense of the practice community' (Anderson & Gold, 2019, p. 100305).

Back in 1967, Wheeler (1967, p. 35) drew attention to 'hiring practices in business schools and … the career choices of persons who have received doctorates in business' as important factors in the supply and demand of US management doctoral education. Historically, in the 1970s, early 1980s, late 1990s and early 2000s large numbers of applicants, coupled with excess capacity, resulted in a declared shortage of PhD candidates in North American business schools (AACSB, 2003; Bryant & Ebrahimpour, 2009). This was due to increased accreditation standard requirements and higher targets for PhD-qualified faculty. Linked to this, there has been a US business school professor shortage (AACSB, 2007; Alsop, 2007; Owen, 2009). Relatively low numbers of domestic PhD graduates in the USA has generated concerns over future stability and growth of the research base (Baker, 2019). No doubt, this has been exacerbated by the cost-of-living crisis and the COVID-19 pandemic crisis.

There are also differences in business school doctorate numbers across subject areas. This has been particularly discussed in relation to the field of accountancy in the US context. Noland Francisco, and Sinclair (2007) have highlighted a shortage of accounting professors that impacts on what Cardwell, Cardwell,

Norris, and Forrest (2019) have identified as a lack of faculty demand to support programme growth in this area. Similar concerns about a dearth of accounting and finance PhD students in the UK and Australia have also been expressed (Beattie & Smith, 2012; Gebreiter, 2021; O'Connell et al., 2015). The impact of low numbers of accountancy PhD holders has implications for the development, dissemination and validation of knowledge claims and affects the production of accountancy knowledge (Williams & Rodgers, 1995).

Attendees of EFMD doctoral conferences over the years will have noted a recurrent focus on the doctorate as a response to national knowledge economy agendas. This is more overt in some nations than others. Assimakopoulos, Li, and Mouzughi (in Palmer, 2018), for example, have observed an explicit direct relationship between the PhD and national development growth in European, Middle Eastern and Chinese contexts. This theme is not unique to the business and management doctorate. More broadly, Halse and Mowbray (2011, p. 513) have stated how:

> Doctoral research plays a 'crucial role in driving innovation and growth' of nation states, and is a significant contributor to national and international knowledge generation and research outputs. (Smith, 2010, p. 4)

Furthermore, the production of PhD graduates is vital for new and distributed knowledge economies (Harman, 2002; Thune, 2009). Tzanakou (2014, p. 1) has argued that:

> Doctoral education has become of paramount significance in a world where knowledge becomes the new 'fuel', the ultimate economic renewable to economic growth leading to a knowledge-based economy (Brinkley, 2006; Leadbeater, 1999).

Shifts in emphasis on modes of knowledge and new models of economic production have increased the demands on our university systems to create innovative and flexible doctoral programmes. Some countries have responded to this challenge by developing professional doctorates (Park, 2005).

The DBA as a Practice-Based and Work-Based Learning Approach to Doctoral Education

In comparison with the PhD, the DBA has been repeatedly acknowledged for its innovation capacity (Erwee, 2004; Fink, 2006; Pearson, 1999; Robinson, Morgan, & Reed, 2016). It is an award cognisant as a 'product' aligned to business relevance and macro-level economic development and industrial strategy. Indeed, Banerjee and Morley (2013, p. 173) note how:

> professional doctorates were developed by some universities in the face of rising criticism about the relevance of PhD research

to practice and the changing context and content of knowledge in the new economy.

Yet despite an average annual 10% growth in DBA conferrals between 2010 and 2018 in the USA (IPEDS cited in Wiley University Services, 2020), there exists remarkable market concentration: half of the market is owned by 10 programmes, mainly located in for-profit business schools (Wiley University Services, 2020). The PhD remains the first choice for business and management candidates who are seeking academic careers in business schools (Stoten, 2016). The DBA market is still emerging globally but there exists intense competition among rivals. There is less familiarity with this type of doctorate despite its potential for supporting the tightrope walk between the academic and practitioner sides of business (Clinebell & Clinebell, 2008) and the development of scholar-practitioners (Tucker, Wilson, Hannibal, Lawless, & Qu, 2021). The importance of distinctiveness and differentiation in the DBA offer has been highlighted (Wiley University Services, 2020) alongside untapped potential for the DBA to be positioned as a continuation terminal degree route on the back of the MBA.

Kalika (2021) acknowledges latent demand for the DBA from senior managers in continental Europe. He argues that existing prejudices about the quality of the award need to be overcome. It is important to note that the DBA award is not viewed as inferior to the PhD across the globe. Notably, AMBA's direct accreditation of the DBA award (AMBA, 2016) sits alongside MBA accreditation with the aim of assuring and enhancing the highest levels of quality, currency and innovation of qualifications worldwide. It has been termed 'gold standard' (AMBA, n.d.). The DBA programme at Henley Business School is among 11 programmes globally which have gained AMBA accreditation (dependent on retention of AMBA accreditation for the MBA). Other institutions where a DBA is differentiated in the marketplace with AMBA accreditation include: Grenoble Ecole de Management; CENTRUM PUCP Business School, Pontificia Universidad Católica del Perú; and Gordon Institute of Business Science, University of Pretoria. At the time of writing this, we note that four of the AMBA accredited programmes are located in the UK (at Henley Business School, Aston Business School, Cranfield School of Management, and Kingston Business School). The extent to which the accreditation is successfully exploited in terms of competitive positioning of these DBA programmes is questionable. 'The public needs to understand the value and the requirements of accreditation' (Zhao & Ferran, 2016, p. 52).

Differences and Similarities Between the PhD and DBA – Horses for Courses?

Understanding the differences and similarities between the business school PhD and the DBA also merits consideration. Through examination of DBA programme documentation at 16 UK universities, Bareham, Bourner, and Ruggeri Stevens (2000) identified different rationale and intended learning outcomes of the DBA versus PhD. Meeting of growth in demand for practitioner-oriented doctoral education (Lockhart & Stablein, 2002) and the professional development of researching professionals has necessitated the development of broader learning outcomes than what is often referred to as the 'traditional PhD' (monograph-based, studied as a full-time award). Interpretations of the differences between PhD and DBA awards in business and management programmes appear to vary between country contexts. We are familiar with the challenges of validating DBA awards in parts of Europe, such as Germany and Croatia where vocational education and training *vis-à-vis* academic education have different histories and statuses that impact on national ministry approvals.

In the USA, Pina, Maclennan, Moran, and Hafford (2016, p. 6), comparing the curricula of over 100 doctoral business programmes have concluded that 'D.B.A. and Ph.D. students receive very similar preparation and have similar program requirements. Accrediting agencies tend to treat both degrees identically; however, inconsistent doctoral degree classifications within the U.S. Department of Education send a mixed message'. A need to differentiate between DBA and PhD programme offerings has prompted the Australian and New Zealand Academy of Management (ANZAM) to encourage collaborative discussions on the sharing of best practice between DBA programme managers in the USA and Australian universities (Erwee, 2004). Yet, we note the lack of a clearly developed DBA programme management cross-national community of practice. The need to share expertise on developing and operating DBA programmes stems from a belief that 'the specialised nature of professional doctorates requires significant specialisation on the part of those who teach into or administer such programs (Kemp, 2002)' (Erwee, 2004, p. 397). We cannot overlook similarities between some business school PhD and DBA programmes. MacLennan et al. (2018), for example, have observed the American 'Executive PhD' to be closer to the Australian DBA than the Australian business and management PhD. There are some blurred boundaries between Executive PhDs (offered in many parts of Europe and the USA) and the professional doctorate. One obvious area of similarity is the target market – researching professionals located in practice.

Huisman and Naidoo's (2006) consideration of the DBA in the debate on the third cycle of European higher education draws attention to a need for more formal recognition and acceptance of alternatives to the PhD as a 'traditional doctorate'. Kehm (2007, 2009) characterised the professional doctorate as a means of embedding the application of knowledge in the workplace and professional practice. They observe how the DBA advances the delivery of systematic research training in Europe and North America.

However, although management is an applied discipline, it would appear that even professional doctorates in management are decoupled from growing research impact and interdisciplinary agendas (Davies, McGregor, & Horan, 2019; Miller, 2010). Furthermore, in relation to the doctorate as an award within broader business school education portfolios, we note the assertion that 'doctoral education must find its place in *university* strategic planning to ensure quality provision and a healthy research environment' (EHEA, 2009, p. 1). This is particularly apt for the professional doctorate. Indeed, Lundgren-Resenterra and Kahn (2019) have drawn attention to studies that locate the university as 'the central pivot for knowledge production and dissemination' (Malfroy, 2004 as cited in Lundgren-Resenterra & Kahn, 2019, p. 408). McWilliam et al. (2002, cited in

Lundgren-Resenterra & Kahn, 2019, p. 408) pointed out that 'the conflation of profession, workplace and industry [see] little value for knowledge production relevant to the advancement of professional practice'.

There have been systematic attempts to increase dialogue and knowledge creation and dissemination between academics and practitioners outside of the DBA. In France and Germany, the development of business schools can be charted to technical education to develop and sustain both private companies and the regional economy (De Montmorillon, 2011). Academic business and management education has faced opposition from proponents who are convinced that management can only be learned in practice (Kaplan in Porter, Kaplan, Kahneman, & Martin, 2017). The development of industrial PhDs is notably built on foundations where knowledge of business management was socially accepted to belong primarily to practitioners and consultants up until the 1960s (Carton, Dameron, & Durand, 2018).

There is a need, therefore, for more formal recognition and acceptance of professional doctorate awards as alternatives to the academically-focused PhD. For some commentators on business and management, it may be surprising that we have not experienced a discernible growth in industry-funded doctorates akin to the trends that are visible in other areas such as engineering. One factor here relates to the extent to which academic research underpins industrial innovations. Another factor relates to the involvement of industry in the development, design and delivery of professional doctorates and a perception that the benefit is greater for the individual than the funder/employer – perhaps linked to our observations of low numbers of commercial intellectual property (IP) contracts used in business and management doctorates. There have been notable inconsistencies in terms of employer involvement in professional doctorates. This sits alongside a lack of integration of professional doctorate candidates within the higher education research environment (Mellors-Bourne, Robinson, & Metcalfe, 2016, p. 7).

Inside universities, business and management studies have been viewed uncomfortably with a marginalised identity outside conventionally accepted professions (such as law) and social science disciplines (Thomas &Wilson, 2011). Many business schools have traditionally been perceived to focus on the teaching of scientific management theory, delivering highly substitutable 'cookie-cutter' programmes (Doria, Rozanski, & Cohen, 2003). Some organisations have struggled to form meaningful relationships with businesses beyond student internships, placements and hiring graduates (Doria et al., 2003). The political position of business and management education in higher education, business and society requires acknowledgement of the difficulties in what Simon (1967) called the 'challenge of mixing the oil and water of management scholarship and management practice'.

Institutional Strategic Aims of Business and Management Doctorates

There have been attempts to situate the strategic aims of business and management doctorates in the context of the strategic aims of business schools. The idea of doctoral programmes being 'fit for purpose' was explored at the 2018 EFMD

Doctoral Programmes Conference hosted by Frankfurt School of Management. Taking an economics perspective, Michael Grote (in Palmer, 2018) argued the case for cost-benefit analysis of our doctoral programmes, reflecting on what our doctoral programmes are aiming to achieve within host institutions. Diverse reflections by conference participants highlighted commonalities with respect to contributions to research performance metrics and funding, the reproduction of knowledge in the academy, and maintenance of internal research ecosystems. Yet, in relation to this theme, there is a dearth of discussion in the literature that critically considers the strategic aims of business and management doctorates both within and outside university contexts.

The idea of return-on-investment has been recognised in relation to overproduction of doctoral degree holders and the impact on employment, the labour market and career opportunities, particularly for postdoctorates (Kehm, 2006) where we witness tension in the system with early stage researchers and their access to permanent faculty positions. There are macro-level doctoral education strategies that impact on limits to growth and expansion of business school doctorates worldwide. In their analysis of forces in doctoral education worldwide, Nerad and Heggelund (2011, p. 5) argued that:

> the increasingly important role of knowledge production for economic success makes doctoral education vital for nations wishing to remain or become important players in the global knowledge economy.

When we start to examine differences in doctoral education growth patterns by geographical region, we can see some common trends relating to strategic investment in research and higher education, business school accreditation aspirations, and diffusion of Western doctoral education and training.

Centralisation of higher education governance and funding are key factors affecting the development of doctoral education *per se* and, thus, business school doctorate development. This is linked to doctoral programme quality assurance systems (Andres et al., 2015 as cited in Shin et al., 2018) and national research and development (R&D) capacity-building efforts. Indirect state regulation of doctoral programmes has been noted in the UK, the Netherlands, and Nordic countries which differs from direct control in Central and Eastern European countries.

Similarly, we can note marked contrasts in the regulation of doctoral education in the Americas. In Brazil, a National Graduate School Plan directs numbers and locations for doctorates and guides levels of outbound mobility for Brazilian doctoral candidates (Ribiero, 2011). In contrast, in Mexico, changes in government and a subsequent lack of continuity in higher education and doctoral education planning have contributed to the production of few doctoral graduates (Alcantara, Malo, & Fortes, 2011).

Doctoral education in the USA is less centrally controlled in terms of the setting and monitoring of overall doctoral places which are available. In the USA, there is an increasingly competitive job market for new PhD degree holders. PhD graduates are finding it increasingly difficult to secure permanent tenure-track academic positions. Doctoral graduates in business are increasingly expected to have published several articles in leading journals. This intensifies pressure on candidates. In response, we are starting to see some business schools extending time to complete to upskill their doctoral candidates and enhance the employability and high-ranking placement of doctoral graduates. Some doctoral candidates are taking longer to graduate so that they have more time to publish. This strategy may be seen to risk the creation of blockages in the system that will inevitably impact on doctoral education throughput and supervision capacity. Indeed, speaking of doctoral education in Europe and North America, Kehm (2006, p. 72) has noted how 'overproduction' of doctoral degree holders can result in the creation of postdoctoral fellowships and in-between positions that may be:

> characterized as 'holding positions' where post-doctoral researchers stay in a waiting loop until full employment is found. This does not only prolong the time until the beginning of a proper career, it also adds an additional layer of uncertainty to the life-planning of young academics. Seen from a perspective of return on investment and productivity this situation is not very viable.

This observation is supported by research published by Vitae (2022).

In Australia, there has been a traditional reliance on British models of doctoral education (although vivas are less common in Australia). Doctoral education in business and management is long-established with some PhD production modelling visibly linked to workforce demand planning commissioned by the Australian Department of Innovation, Industry, Science and Research. This is seen as an attempt to provide a policy response to facilitate sustainable growth of Australia's knowledge economy (Bexley, James, & Arkoudis, 2011; Edwards, 2010; Harman, 2002) linked to human resource planning. Expansion of doctoral education has happened alongside recognition of a greater need to attract people with PhD qualifications in universities. However, a 'PhD crisis discourse' (Cuthbert & Molla, 2015) has emerged, located within a wider review of higher education provision. It has been observed that excessive numbers of PhD graduates have been produced for too few academic job vacancies and that doctoral graduates are lacking in skills to secure employment in other sectors. Notably, in this context, there has been a shift from an efficiency-based labour market planning focus to a concentration on graduate skills and employability that meet the needs of business and society. Lightbody (2010, p. 3) has argued that the divide between academia and practice has not been helped by the development of an 'increasingly inflexible [and less attractive] work environment driven by AACSB accreditation'.

The provision of business school doctoral education in the UK cannot be divorced from the status of business and management as a discipline and the legitimacy challenge for business schools (Thomas & Wilson, 2011). There has been a fractious history relating to the recognition and status of business and management as an academic discipline, a difficult relationship between management education and research council funders, and a culture of measurement and benchmarking of business school research outputs (Bogle, personal communication with Julie Davies, July 15, 2019; Thomas & Wilson, 2011; Wilson & Thomas, 2012). This predicament has placed pressure on UK-based business school academics. The situation has created a system that has been described as 'often aggressive and harmful' (Coriat, 2021, p. 102) in terms of UK research funding and doctoral awards. This has culminated in fewer research assistants and postdoctoral researchers in circulation in business schools: 'Despite being the second largest community of researchers across the 34 units of assessment, business and management research ranks 30th in terms of research income per FTE per annum, and 28th in terms of doctoral awards' (MacIntosh, 2022, p. 1). Coriat's (2021) work, based on Wellcome's 2017 review of doctoral training, facilitates consideration of the interplay between UK doctoral education policy and funding. It draws attention to funder interests where responsibilities for capacity-building lie and, ultimately, questions 'whether the success of a nation's economy can explicitly be linked to research capability' (Coriat, 2021, p. 101). The latter point appears to be an underlying, and often unquestioned, premise in many countries.

In Estonia, there is explicit recognition that PhD holders provide a crucial input for educational and R&D activities increasingly in public and private sectors as well as through employment in academia (Masso, Eamets, Meriküll, & Kanep, 2014). Inward flows of doctoral graduates are recognised as a potential solution to redress a shortage of talent to meet scientific workforce demands. However, this is frustrated by a lack of internationally competitive salaries. Additionally, societal appreciation of the potential contribution of PhD graduates beyond academia has been observed to be lacking (Masso et al., 2014).

In Finland, the inability of small, geographically scattered Finnish business schools to compete globally and attract international students, faculty members and global corporations (Alajoutsijärvi, Kettunen, & Tikkanen, 2012) has been identified as a challenge to move beyond Finnish national policies for PhD production that are more about economic growth and welfare of the nation than diverse and varied candidate needs, wants and motivations (Vuolanto, Pasanen, & Aittola, 2006). Similarly, in the contexts of Norway and Poland discord is apparent between the utility value of the doctorate for individual candidates *vis-à-vis* national labour market planning (Siemieńska, Matysiak, Domaradzka, & Vabø, 2017). More recently, the Norwegian government has proposed the withdrawal of funding for students from outside the EU (ICEF, 2022) which will have consequences for candidates for doctoral study in business schools. As of December 2022, we noted that this proposal was rejected by the majority of Norway's universities and criticised for being at odds with the country's principle of free higher education (Myklebust, 2022). However, a parliamentary vote in June, 2023 supported the abolition of free tuition for international students outside of the European Economic Area (EEA) and Switzerland (Myklebust, 2023). The implications of this remain to be seen.

Higher education funding models affect the ability of business schools to detach themselves from national priorities. We can see this in the case of France where non-profit business schools like INSEAD have been able to establish themselves as sector leaders. This freedom from regulation appears offer potential for increased innovation in doctoral programme design and delivery. It also represents a possible threat to the *status quo* of USA business school dominance when we consider international business stakeholders. Yet, freedom from state funding is not the sole determinant of the ability of business schools to innovate as non-US institutions such as Peking University's Guanghua School of Management (China) and Rotterdam School of Management (Netherlands) illustrate. These are institutions where thought leaders and trailblazers in sustainable business development may be found. This potential challenge to established US business schools and their dominance has been overlooked or under-estimated by several important business commentators.

One key trend that is hidden by reports of global growth in business school doctoral education is the emergence of joint PhD programmes in high-ranking business schools across continents that enable increased market penetration. The example of the INSEAD-Wharton Center for Global Research and Education demonstrates how innovative programmes can be offered to the international marketplace that neither partner could have undertaken on its own. We have started to witness the introduction of more collaborative business and management doctoral programmes between institutional partners across the globe as part of transnational education strategies over the past decade. The extent to which these alliances reinforce and reproduce the dominance of business schools in the 'super league' may be questioned, not least in terms of degree awarding powers, financial contributions, and market reach that continue to benefit partners in more developed economies. Alongside these programme delivery alliances, we also note the establishment of management education associations that have been set up in an attempt to improve regional competitiveness in the face of US university dominance in management education. These include the French Foundation for Management Education (FNEGE), British Academy of Management (BAM), and the Australian Business Deans Council (ABDC). One recent innovation in collaborative doctoral programmes delivery is the establishment of a quadripartite PhD programme whereby a common course catalogue is offered to the whole Montréal-based PhD student body co-located in business schools at Concordia University, HEC Montréal, McGill University, and Université du Québec à Montréal (UQAM) (Joannidès de Lautour, 2023). We return to this example in Chapter 2.

In many developing countries, there is a lack of co-ordination or collaboration among business schools to ensure competitiveness and quality assurance of programmes (Davies, Thomas, Cornuel, & Cremer, 2023). Doctorates are required for teaching in post-secondary settings in India and this requirement has led to increased production of PhDs in the Indian education system with the risk of declining standards (Jayaram, 2011). Lack of adequate research training and very low government support for research funding as well as low inflows of quality research students affect business schools (Sheel & Vohra, 2014). Increased numbers of business schools (Sahana & Vijila, 2017) have, in turn, contributed to a shortage of management faculty. Indian business schools have sought to replicate US models of business and management doctorates. However, an un-coordinated production line approach, as a result of liberalisation of the business education market during the 1990s, challenges attempts at enhancing quality (Gupta, Gollakota, & Sreekumar, 2014) and aspirations for global competitiveness.

In Italy, a more cautious approach to the development of business school doctoral education may be observed. 'The number of doctoral students accepted into universities is limited to the number of available positions in this [the academic] field' (Kehm, 2006, p. 72). Similarly, Yamamoto (2011) has reported how Japan introduced Western-style doctoral education alongside high levels of government forecasting and monitoring of doctoral numbers. This resulted in the country's standing as a leading producer of high-quality PhDs who are highly regarded in the university system. More academic opportunities exist for business PhD holders *vis-à-vis* other disciplines because of the number of business schools. Limited demand for business and management education, however, has been noted in relation to the employment habits of Japanese firms where in-house training remains valued over advanced education (Shimada & Shimamoto, 2018).

Delivery of Business School Terminal Degrees as Executive Education

We have already highlighted that doctoral programmes in business and management extend beyond the monograph PhD route. Business school portfolios encompass professional doctorates (the DBA/executive PhDs), industry-based collaborations, as well as publication-based awards. In comparison with some other disciplines, business and management doctorates have low barriers to entry for delivery except for the need to hire suitably qualified supervisors. Hence, the relatively low cost of provision has contributed to the proliferation of the award internationally in business schools, with high levels of competition and substitutability between doctoral education providers. However, in terms of fees, the positioning of some business and management doctoral awards such as the DBA as 'executive education' for 'senior level' managers may result in premium pricing. This can place pressure on programme managers of business school doctorates and particularly raises questions about the offer and its value and how completions can be achieved when candidates may be time-strapped executives being supervised by someone who may be perceived as less qualified and experienced.

A focus on executive education may be linked to a trend towards business school redefinitions of organisational identity in an entrepreneurial sense (Passant, 2022). This may be seen as part of repositioning the business school to meet industry needs more explicitly, to become closer to economic practice (Hall, 2008), and to leverage corporate investment, knowledge and innovation (Carayannis, Alexander, & Ioannidis, 2000; Clarke & Rollo, 2001; Mascarenhas, Ferreira, & Marques, 2018; Warhurst, 2001).

For prospective candidates, Columbia Southern University (2018, p. 1) outlined four benefits of DBA study: 'bolstered credibility', 'expanded career opportunities', 'greater opportunities for promotion', and 'better potential for higher salaries'. With respect to the latter point, it has been claimed that the difference in average earnings between employees with doctoral degrees compared with those who possess master's degrees was approximately an annual increase of $20,332 (U.S. Bureau of Labor Statistics cited in Columbia Southern University, 2018). Similarly, outside the USA, the value of the doctorate to candidates who already enjoy executive employment is often promoted in terms of career advancement. However, as Breese, Issa, and Tresidder (2021) pointed out, little is known about the impact of DBA completion on management practice. Indeed, Davies et al. (2019) suggest that well-established and experienced end-of-career individuals may embark on a DBA in order to exit a full-time career path and to follow a portfolio career path (including consultancy, advisory, voluntary work), to step off a career treadmill rather than rise within the ranks. More understanding of professional candidates in business schools is needed in terms of graduate outcomes. In a global context we recognise a 'lack of systematic data collection on these degree awards' (Kot & Hendel, 2012 cited in Kortt et al., 2016, p. 391) but charting the rise and fall of the DBA in Australia, Kortt et al. (2016, p. 406) have estimated the award to have average domestic and overseas attrition rates per year of 17% and 13%, respectively.

The Idea of a 'Modern Doctorate'

Bao, Kehm, and Ma (2018) have identified nine different doctorate formats on offer in Europe and China. In business and management, as in many social science-based disciplines that are not dependent on lab-based facilities and technical equipment, we observe evolution of the doctoral award and the emergence of 'the modern doctorate' (Lee, 2018). This is a qualification that extends beyond the narrowness of a full-time monograph PhD route (often deemed 'a traditional doctorate') to focus on process as well as product, knowledge transfer alongside knowledge creation (Muller, 2009 cited in Lee, 2018), employability beyond academia (Fillery-Travis et al. cited in Lee, 2018), and the use of alternative research methods and tools such as action research (Armsby, Costley, & Cranfield, 2018 cited in Lee, 2018), autoethnography, appreciative inquiry, reflexivity, and reflection.

However, the introduction of new routes is not always accompanied with necessary shifts in cultures and mindsets. Speaking of the increasingly popular PhD by Publication, Jackson's review of policy in an Australian context 'suggests institutional guidelines in universities nationwide are inadequate for producing theses of comparable quality to conventional dissertations and capitalising on the pathway's significant benefits' (Jackson, 2013, p. 355). Moreover, a lack of deep understanding of the demands of the PhD by Publication and institutional responsiveness to the needs of candidates selecting this route has been observed (Mason & Merga, 2018; Mason, Merga, & Morris, 2020).

We acknowledge that the introduction of 'new' and 'modern' doctorates in business and management may face resistance and may be challenged by academic concerns over quality, rigour and what ultimately equates to fear of the alien or unknown. The effectiveness of different doctoral models requires careful evaluation (Dominguez-Whitehead & Maringe, 2020). We support the views of Armsby et al. (2018, p. 2226) that there is scope for 'wider understanding of the values and purpose of doctoral education within and beyond the academy'.

The introduction of new routes to doctorate appears to have generated tensions and resulted in some pitting of new routes against old, with little regard for existing quality issues with the (historically accepted monograph) PhD and the types of change to the doctorate that candidates would like to see (Johnston & Murray, 2004). Doloriert and Sambrook (2011) draw attention to the impact of research traditions on final judgement of thesis quality and, in the context of a traditional business school, the extent to which accommodation of new approaches to the doctoral thesis may be dependent on the bounded discretion of supervisors and examiners.

We have seen a shift in delivery mechanisms for business and management doctorates that appear on the surface to be market-driven. For example, fast-track PhD and DBA programmes provide opportunities for candidates to enjoy shorter times to completion (and often lower tuition fees where doctoral education is not free). Creighton University's DBA has been acknowledged to be 'the best accelerated online DBA programme' (Great Business Schools, 2021, p. 1). The programme can be completed part-time in three years through a hybrid delivery model. Trevecca Nazarene University's online DBA, with a programme duration of 32 months, fees charged at cost/credit hour $699 for 60 hours in total and no GMAT® requirements, is advertised as equipping students 'to teach, consult or advance in a corporate or academic setting' (Trevecca Nazarene University, 2023, p. 1). Thus, a shift in delivery modes appears to also present a shift in positioning and reinforces our questioning of the extent to which business school DBA programmes may be differentiated from (part-time) PhD programmes in terms of target market. How this may affect diversity and inclusion remains to be seen.

While scholars such as Mertkan, Arsan, Inal Cavlan, and Onurkan Aliusta (2017, p. 46) are advocating a need for business schools to focus on enriching a knowledge base 'with leadership and management practices from different socio-cultural contexts and system structures with a multiplicity of voices to portray a more nuanced and balanced picture of leadership and management practices', innovations in the business and management doctorate appear to be more concentrated on routes to new markets in a crowded globally competitive marketplace. The extent to which fast-track doctorates will thrive and be sustainable remains to be seen. There are 'hidden costs' to these delivery models. We heed Mason Goulden, and Frasch's (2009, p. 11) comments on the rejection of fast-track PhDs in the USA: 'In the eyes of many doctoral students, the academic fast-track has a bad reputation—one of unrelenting work hours that allow little or no room for a satisfying family life'. Furthermore, as Van Ours and Ridder (2003, p. 157) have found in the context of the Netherlands, 'Universities succeed in making students who are unlikely to graduate or will need a long time to graduate quit the program'. Through the work of Stoten (2022, p. 8), we also note that some UK business schools are viewing fast-track part-time doctoral programmes as a way to target faculty doctoral completions 'in a little over two years', with little consideration for the subjective well-being of candidates.

Changes During the COVID-19 Pandemic and Reflections on the Future

We have largely witnessed growth in the provision of the business school doctorate based on traditionally established models to date. However, since 2020, the COVID-19 global pandemic has forced a shift in the delivery patterns of higher education across the globe, not least in terms of what has been termed a 'digital revolution' (Strielkowski, 2020). Doctoral education has not been immune from disruptive forces and the increased use of educational technology. Even in countries where national measures have been less stringent, such as in Sweden, adjustments to supervision and time-to-completion rates have been noted to support candidates (Börgeson et al., 2021).

To some extent, the pandemic accelerated the development trajectory of doctoral education. There had already been calls for innovative disruption in the provision of business school doctorates (Diaz in Palmer, 2018) and proactive responses had been slow to emerge. Growth patterns of business and management doctorates had largely been based on traditional, conservative models and new pioneering approaches to embracing the future were lacking.

During the COVID-19 pandemic, assumptions about the international mobility of doctoral candidates were severely challenged by national lockdowns, especially in Australia and China. Concerns over the delivery of doctoral programmes to existing candidates occupied the minds of many providers. This prompted a variety of responses, not least a shift to online delivery of training and supervision. In some cases, certainly in the UK where a higher education state funding bailout was offered, there were decisions to reduce numbers but provide scholarships for all (e.g., Warwick Business School). We observe that UKRI did lead the way with extensions to scholarship funding for candidates already in-programme but the way these funding extensions were applied was not consistent by institutions and the provision for self-funded candidates was in many cases negligible.

In Australia, reliance on international business education students heightened the impact of COVID-19 on demand levels and public university budgets (Hogan, Charles, & Kortt, 2021). The extent to which contraction of the market in many countries is temporary remains to be seen. In the UK, lockdown practices like online vivas are still common in many universities and there have been reconfigurations of physical campus space that have impacted the co-location of doctoral candidates.

Reflections on lessons learned are beginning to be shared as we move forwards post-pandemic. Hogan et al. (2021) contended that 'business as usual' may not be an option. From their experiences of continuing to deliver an international DBA throughout the pandemic, Tucker et al. (2021) advocated proactively designing professional doctorate programmes that are resilient to disruption. This is in terms of delivery method but also in terms of practices that enable engaged scholarship and promote the development of scholarly practitioners.

Cornuel, Thomas, and Wood (2022) called for strategic reflection on business school missions and values in terms of the relevance and impact of programmes. This chimes with our sentiments early in this chapter when we argue that 'shifts in emphasis on modes of knowledge and new models of economic production have increased the demands on our university systems to create innovative and flexible doctoral programmes'.

However, to date, in many countries around the world, we have seen a disproportionate emphasis on the reproduction of business school academic resource rather than demonstrations of more localised responses in line with local economic needs.

In the USA, where we have noted particular emphasis on producing business school doctoral graduates to feed the academic pipeline, research findings are beginning to emerge that suggest a shift towards increased PhD candidate interest in non-academic careers (Haas, Gureghian, Díaz, & Williams, 2022). In the UK, the government's publication of its response to the *Augur Post-18 Education and Funding Review* (Lewis & Bolton, 2022) sits in a climate where routes to careers through higher education (and through alternative pathways) are poorly mapped generally. Renewed interested in lifelong learning, a concept previously pushed by the UK government in the 1990s (Blunkett, 1998), has been more recently positioned alongside disadvantage and levelling up agendas. This situation may suggest that expansion and growth in diverse pathways or routes to doctorates are the way forward.

Shin et al. (2018, p. 150) have reported how in Singapore:

> the Committee on University Pathways beyond 2015 has looked to Finland and Germanys' Applied Sciences Model to advocate an industry-focused practice-oriented education. (Singapore Ministry of Education, 2017)

They noted that while this is an undergraduate-based model, there may be an accompanying doctoral education emphasis. So too might other business school providers turn to undergraduate and postgraduate models for inspiration which are based increasingly on an industry focus and on positioning the doctorate as a terminal degree.

As we have declared previously (Davies et al., 2021, p. 21), 'doctoral researchers are key to knowledge production and advancing the business and management education field'. The strategic value of the doctorate to any business school requires continued consideration through a multi-stakeholder approach that not only recognises that the doctorate can be valuable as 'an essential bridge between academia and industry' (Lange, Smith, Spradley, & Johnston, 2018, p. 3) but seeks to leverage and realise value. How this happens in a context of value pluralism is far from simple.

Anderson and Gold (2019, p. 2) have observed that:

> policy-driven descriptions of value assume that the purpose of the doctorate is to prepare candidates for a career in academia, something that is at variance with Organization for Economic Cooperation and Development (OECD) data about the career trajectories of doctoral graduates in a knowledge economy context. (Neumann & Tan, 2011)

We return to the idea that the (recognised) value of the doctorate is situated in a broader field (or portfolio) of management education (Anderson & Gold, 2019). How might the doctorate be differentiated from other business school courses with its potential to bridge the industry-academia divide?

Some of the most innovative and industry-facing developments in business school curricula are being driven by the commercial sector. Indeed, McDonald's Hamburger University with campuses worldwide, grew out of a small training seminar in a branch of McDonalds in the 1960s into a 'gold standard' corporate training facility that focuses on teaching business acumen (Furdyk, 2021). It provides an example of industry-driven business education that takes direct control and influence of the shaping of workforce talent. Similarly, in the postgraduate management education marketplace, we note the introduction of Pepsico's MBA programme, developed by the Pepsico CEO, Ramon Laguarta, as a former MBA graduate of ESADE business school in Spain. Through business-to-business connections, the Pepsico MBA programme can offer an internship programme that provides 'opportunities to make a real-world impact on some of the world's biggest brands' (Pepsico, n.d., p. 1). The need for the traditional business school model to evolve in mature markets has been acknowledged for many years (Hawawini, 2005). As we write, Pfeffer and Fong's (2004, p. 1516) comments about vanilla business school offerings still resonate:

> As others have noted, the problem now is that business schools are basically (a) all doing about the same thing and (b) all doing about the same thing as many of their competitors – attempting, although sometimes failing, to provide relevant education and research.

Summary

Our key observations on growth patterns of business and management doctorates are:

- An overall increase in doctoral qualifications worldwide masks contextual differences and nuances. This is not least because of the reliance on international flows of students and faculty in some countries such as Australia and in business schools in particular.
- Elite reproduction and academic excellence are more complex than West to East diffusion. Mangematin and Baden-Fuller (2008, p. 117) note the 'greatest challenges to the existing [global business school] order [are] … coming from European and Asian institutions'. The extent to which this might prompt disruptive innovation remains to be seen.
- Training for research excellence and quality assurance is heavily driven by Western conceptions of 'world-class higher education'. But has any business school generated a model of graduate skills and competencies desired by businesses?
- A heavy focus on the reproduction of the academy in business and management frustrates the acknowledgement of where knowledge sits in knowledge economies. It fails to exploit the potential role of the doctorate within management education portfolios and wider impact on society for economic development and innovation in a volatile, uncertain, complex and ambiguous (VUCA) world as we grapple with the United Nations' Sustainable Development Goals.
- There is scope to extend exploration of practice-based and work-based learning approaches beyond business and management PhD and DBA scholarship in academic outputs. This is important to demonstrate impact on organisations and society more widely. It also matters to enhance the legitimacy of business schools and business school doctorates in multiple domains and different types

of organisations and sectors beyond academia and is dependent on the 'openness' of business schools and business.

- Regulation of doctoral education appears to potentially have a positive impact on the health of business school doctorates. It raises standards, self-evaluation and benchmarking. Peer review teams from accreditation bodies such as AMBA provide valuable opportunities for external feedback and quality assurance and enhancements. However, disciplinary benefits of this might be secured more effectively through a mentality of sector-wide sharing rather than individually competing.

Questions you might like to consider:

- What are the aims of business school doctoral programmes?
- How are these aligned to higher education doctoral programme aims?
- How do our programmes fit institutional/provider national and regional strategies and priorities?
- What are the requirements of different types of employers in our localities and further afield?
- Are we clear about our end-user, doctoral candidates' needs, wants and motivations?
- Is our doctoral provision changing in light of shifting knowledge production agendas?
- How should business school portfolios be evolving to accommodate changing needs in society as well as employer/business needs?

References

AACSB. (2003). *Sustaining Scholarship in Business Schools: Report of the Doctoral Faculty Commission to AACSB International's Board of Directors*. Tampa, FL: AACSB.

AACSB. (2007, June). *Becoming a Business Professor*. Tampa, FL: AACSB International – The Association to Advance Collegiate Schools of Business.

Alajoutsijärvi, K., Kettunen, K., & Tikkanen, H. (2012). The evolution of business schools as an institution in Finland 1909–2009. *Management & Organizational History*, 7(4), 337–367.

Alcantara, A., Malo, S., & Fortes, M. (2011). Mexico. In M. Nerad & M. Heggelund (Eds.), (2011). *Toward a global PhD?: Forces and forms in doctoral education worldwide* (pp. 146–170). Washington, DC: University of Washington Press.

Alsop, R. (2007, January 9). Ph.D. Shortage: Business schools seek professors. *The Wall Street Journal*. Retrieved from https://www.wsj.com/articles/SB116830887516070925. Accessed on February 22, 2023.

AMBA. (2016). DBA accreditation criteria. Association of MBAs. Retrieved from https://www.associationofmbas.com/app/uploads/2021/11/dba-accreditation-criteria.pdf. Accessed on January 10, 2023.

AMBA. (n.d.). Why is AMBA accreditation important for students and graduates? Retrieved from https://www.associationofmbas.com/why-is-amba-accreditation-important-for-students-and-graduates/. Accessed on December 11, 2022.

Anderson, V., & Gold, J. (2019). The value of the research doctorate: A conceptual examination. *The International Journal of Management Education, 17*(3), 100305.

Armsby, P., Costley, C., & Cranfield, S. (2018). The design of doctorate curricula for practising professionals. *Studies in Higher Education, 43*(12), 2226–2237.

Arora, A., Belenzon, S., & Patacconi, A. (2015). Killing the golden goose? The decline of science in corporate R&D. No. w20902. National Bureau of Economic Research, Cambridge, MA.

Baker, S. (2019). Reliance on foreign PhD students 'could harm US research. *Times Higher Education*, September 26. Retrieved from https://www.timeshighereducation.com/news/reliance-foreign-phd-students-could-harm-us-research. Accessed on December 11, 2022.

Banerjee, S., & Morley, C. (2013). Professional doctorates in management: Toward a practice-based approach to doctoral education. *Academy of Management Learning & Education, 12*(2), 173–193.

Bao, Y., Kehm, B. M., & Ma, Y. (2018). From product to process. The reform of doctoral education in Europe and China. *Studies in Higher Education, 43*(3), 524–541.

Bareham, J., Bourner, T., & Ruggeri Stevens, G. (2000). The DBA: what is it for? *Career Development International, 5*(7), 394–403.

Barnett, R. (1999). *Realizing the university in an age of supercomplexity.* Buckingham: Open University.

Bartunek, J. M., & Rynes, S. L. (2014). Academics and practitioners are alike and unlike: The paradoxes of academic–practitioner relationships. *Journal of Management, 40*(5), 1181–1201.

Beattie, V., & Smith, S. J. (2012). *Today's PhD students–Is there a future generation of accounting academics or are they a dying breed? A UK perspective.* The Institute of Chartered Accountants of Scotland (ICAS).

Bennis, W. G. & O'Toole, J. (2005). How business schools have lost their way. *Harvard Business Review, 83*(5), 96–104.

Bexley, E., James, R., & Arkoudis, S. (2011). *The Australian academic profession in transition. Canberra: Department of Education*, Employment and Workplace Relations, Commonwealth of Australia.

Blunkett, D. (1998). *Preface to the learning age: A renaissance for a New Britain.* London: HMSO.

Börgeson, E., Sotak, M., Kraft, J., Bagunu, G., Biörserud, C., & Lange, S. (2021). Challenges in PhD education due to COVID-19-disrupted supervision or business as usual: A cross-sectional survey of Swedish biomedical sciences graduate students. *BMC Medical Education, 21*(1), 1–11.

Boyer, E. L. (1996). The scholarship of engagement. *Bulletin of the American Academy of Arts and Sciences, 49*(7), 18–33.

Breese, R., Issa, S., & Tresidder, R. (2021, October). Impact on management practice after completing the DBA. *Proceedings of the Eleventh International Conference on Engaged Management Scholarship-EMS.*

Brinkley, I. (2006). *Defining the knowledge economy. Knowledge economy programme report.* Lancashire: The Work Foundation, Lancaster University.

Bruner, R. F., & Iannarelli, J. (2011). Globalization of management education. *Journal of Teaching in International Business, 22*(4), 232–242.

Bryant, S. K., & Ebrahimpour, M. (2009). *A survey of the PhD. candidate shortage in business schools Academy of Business Disciplines Journal, 1*, 96–106.

Calmand, J., Nohara, H., & Kobayashi, Y. (2018). The transition from doctoral dissertation to labor market in France and Japan: A comparative exploration. NISTEP Discussion Paper, No. 156. National Institute of Science and Technology Policy, Tokyo. http://doi.org/10.15108/dp156

Carayannis, E. G., Alexander, J., & Ioannidis, A. (2000). Leveraging knowledge, learning, and innovation in forming strategic government–university–industry (GUI) R&D partnerships in the US, Germany, and France. *Technovation, 20*(9), 477–488.

Cardwell, R. L., Cardwell, R. O., Norris, J. T., & Forrest, M. P. (2019). The accounting doctoral shortage: Accounting faculty opinions on hiring JD-CPAs as accounting educators. *Administrative Issues Journal*, *9*(1), 3.

Carter, S., Fazey, J., Gonzalez Geraldo, J. L., & Trevitt, C. (2010). The doctorate of the bologna process third cycle: Mapping the dimensions and impact of the European higher education area. *Journal of Research in International Education*, *9*(3), 245–258.

Carton, G., Dameron, S., & Durand, T. (2018). Higher education in management: The case of France. In S. Dameron & T. Durand (Eds.), *The future of management education* (pp. 261–296). London:Palgrave Macmillan.

Cheit, E. F. (1985). Business schools and their critics. *California Management Review*, *27*(3), 43–62.

Chia, R., & Holt, R. (2008). The nature of knowledge in business schools. *Academy of Management Learning & Education*, *7*(4), 471–486.

China Admissions. (2022). China Scholarships – The 2023 Guide for International Students. Retrieved from https://www.china-admissions.com/blog/china-scholarship/. Accessed oin March 29, 2023.

China Admissions. (2023). Study PhD Program in China in English in 2023. Retrieved from china-admissions.com. Accessed on March 29, 2023.

Clarke, T., & Rollo, C. (2001). Corporate initiatives in knowledge management. *Education+Training*, *43*(4/5), 206–214.

Clinebell, S. K., & Clinebell, J. M. (2008). The tension in business education between academic rigor and real-world relevance: The role of executive professors. *Academy of Management Learning & Education*, *7*(1), 99–107.

Collet, F., & Vives, L. (2013). From preeminence to prominence: The fall of US business schools and the rise of European and Asian business schools in the Financial Times Global MBA Rankings. *Academy of Management Learning & Education*, *12*(4), 540–563.

Columbia Southern University. (2018). 4 Reasons why earning a DBA is worth it. *Columbia Southern University The Link*, January 18. Retrieved from https://www.columbia-southern.edu/blog/blog-articles/2018/january/is-a-dba-degree-worth-it/. Accessed on 10 November, 2022.

Conboye, J. (2019). French business schools' funding conundrum. *Financial Times*, December 2. Retrieved from https://www.ft.com/content/cdaf2ba0-0c7d-11ea-8fb7-8fcec0c3b0f9. Accessed on February 27, 2023.

Coriat, A. M. (2021). The interplay between policy and funding. In A. Lee & R. Bongaardt (Eds.), *The future of doctoral research: Challenges and opportunities* (pp. 101–109).Abingdon: Routledge.

Cornuel, E., Thomas, H., & Wood, M. (Eds.). (2022). *The value & purpose of management education: Looking back and thinking forward in global focus*. Abingdon: Routledge.

Cuthbert, D., & Molla, T. (2015). PhD crisis discourse: A critical approach to the framing of the problem and some Australian 'solutions'. *Higher Education*, *69*, 33–53.

Davies, J., McGregor, F., & Horan, M. (2019). Autoethnography and the doctorate in business administration: Personal, practical and scholarly impacts. *The International Journal of Management Education*, *17*(2), 201–213.

Davies, J., Palmer, N., Braccia, E., Clegg, K., & Smith, M. (2021). Supporting doctoral programmes during a global pandemic: Crisis as opportunity. *EFMD Global Focus*, *1*(15), 20–24.

Davies, J., Thomas, H., Cornuel, E., & Cremer, R. D. (2023). *Leading a business school*. Abingdon: Routledge.

Davies, J., Yarrow, E., & Syed, J. (2020). The curious under-representation of women impact case leaders: Can we disengender inequality regimes? *Gender, Work & Organization*, *27*(2), 129–148. doi:10.1111/gwao.12409

De Meyer, A. (2013). The future of doctoral education in business administration. *Journal of Management Development, 32*(5), 477–486.

De Montmorillon, B. (2011). Redesigning business management education: Functional silos versus cross-functional views–A historical and social perspective. In S. Dameron & T. Durand (Eds.), *Redesigning management education and research* (pp. 93–118). Cheltenham: Edward Elgar Publishing.

Deem, R. (2022). On doctoral (in) visibility and reframing the doctorate for the twenty-first century. *European Journal of Higher Education, 12*(4), 373–392.

Doloriert, C., & Sambrook, S. (2011). Accommodating an autoethnographic PhD: The tale of the thesis, the viva voce, and the traditional business school. *Journal of contemporary ethnography, 40*(5), 582–615.

Dominguez-Whitehead, Y., & Maringe, F. (2020). A cross-national analysis of PhD models. *International Journal of Comparative Education and Development, 22*(3), 233–245.

Doria, J., Rozanski, H., & Cohen, E. (2003). What business needs from business schools. *Strategy and Business, Fall* (32), 38–45.

Edwards, D. (2010). The future of the research workforce: Estimating demand for PhDs in Australia. *Journal of Higher Education Policy and Management, 32*(2), 199–210.

EHEA. (2009). Third cycle: doctoral education. Retrieved from http://www.ehea.info/cid102847/third-cycle-doctoral-education-2009.html. Accessed on November 11, 2023.

EIASM & EDAMBA. (2020). Code of practice for doctoral studies in management. Retrieved from https://www.eiasm.net/eden/code-of-practice. Accessed on 23 March, 2023.

El Hassan, K. (2013). Quality assurance in higher education in 20 MENA economies. *Higher Education Management and Policy, 24*(2), 73–84.

Erwee, R. (2004). Professional doctorates and DBAs in Australia: Dilemmas and opportunities to innovate. *International Journal of Organisational Behaviour, 7*(3), 394–400.

Fink, D. (2006). The professional doctorate: Its relativity to the PhD and relevance for the knowledge economy. *International Journal of Doctoral Studies, 1*(1), 35–44.

Forster, N. (2018). Why are there so few world-class universities in the Middle East and North Africa? *Journal of Further and Higher Education, 42*(8), 1025–1039.

Friga, P. N., Bettis, R. A., & Sullivan, R. S. (2003). Changes in graduate management education and new business school strategies for the 21st century. *Academy of Management Learning & Education, 2*(3), 233–249.

Furdyk, B. (2021). The Untold Truth of McDonald's Hamburger University. *Mashed,* March 8. Retrieved from https://www.mashed.com/320192/the-untold-truth-of-mcdonalds-hamburger-university/. Accessed on November 3, 2022.

Gebreiter, F. (2021). A profession in peril? University corporatization, performance measurement and the sustainability of accounting academia. *Critical Perspectives on Accounting,* 87, 102292.

Gibbons, M., Limoges, C., & Nowotny, H. (1997). *The new production of knowledge: The dynamics of science and research in contemporary societies.* Thousand Oaks, CA: Sage.

Glen, R., Suciu, C., & Baughn, C. (2014). The need for design thinking in business schools. *Academy of Management Learning & Education, 13*(4), 653–667.

Graf, T. (2014). DBA Acceptance in Germany - how to find the right program, Doctorate of Business Administration. *COMPASS,* March 18. Retrieved from https://www.dba-compass.com/ask-an-expert-forum-for-doctor-of-business-administration-dba-programs/program-selection/dba-acceptance-in-germany-how-to-find-the-right-program/. Accessed on March 23, 2023.

Great Business Schools. (2021). 10 Fastest online business doctorates for 2021, May 18. Retrieved from https://www.greatbusinessschools.org/accelerated-online-dba-programs/. Accessed on February 12, 2023.

Gupta, V., Gollakota, K., & Sreekumar, A. (2014). Quality in business education: A study of the Indian context. In J. R. McIntyre & I. Alon (Eds.), *Business and management education in transitioning and developing countries: A handbook* (pp. 31–49). Abingdon:Routledge.

Haas, N., Gureghian, A., Díaz, C. J., & Williams, A. (2022). Through their own eyes: The implications of COVID-19 for PhD students. *Journal of Experimental Political Science, 9*(1) 1–21.

Haley, U. C., Cooper, C. L., Hoffman, A. J., Pitsis, T. S., & Greenberg, D. (2022). In search of scholarly impact. *Academy of Management Learning & Education, 21*(3), 343–349.

Hall, S. (2008). Geographies of business education: MBA programmes, reflexive business schools and the cultural circuit of capital. *Transactions of the Institute of British Geographers, 33*(1), 27–41.

Halse, C., & Mowbray, S. (2011). The impact of the doctorate. *Studies in Higher Education, 36*(5), 513–525.

Harman, G. (2002). Producing PhD graduates in Australia for the knowledge economy. *Higher Education Research & Development, 21*(2), 179–190.

Hawawini, G. (2005). The future of business schools. *Journal of Management Development, 24*(9), 770–782.

Hill, C., & Thabet, R. (2021). Publication challenges facing doctoral students: perspective and analysis from the UAE. *Quality in Higher Education, 27*(3), 324–337.

Hogan, O., Charles, M. B., & Kortt, M. A. (2021). Business education in Australia: COVID-19 and beyond. *Journal of Higher Education Policy and Management, 43*(6), 559–575.

Huff, A. S., & Huff, J. O. (2001). Re-focusing the business school agenda. *British Journal of Management, 12,* S49–S54.

Huisman, J., & Naidoo, R. (2006). The professional doctorate: From Anglo-Saxon to European challenges. *Higher Education Management and Policy, 18*(2), 1–13.

ICEF. (2022). Norway moving towards tuition fees for non-EU students in 2023. *ICEF Monitor,* November 16. Retrieved from https://monitor.icef.com/2022/11/norway-moving-towards-tuition-fees-for-non-eu-students-in-2023/. Accessed on 29 December, 2022.

Ingeborgrud, L., Korseberg, L., & Lyby, L. (2021). Mellom kall og karriere: Om forskeres karrierer, arbeidsbetingelser og forståelser av forskerrollen. Rapport 2021:21. Nordisk Institutt for Studier av Innovasjon, Forskning og Utdanning (NIFU), Oslo.

Jack, A. (2020). Academic focus limits business schools' contribution to society, *Financial Times.* Retrieved from https://www.ft.com/content/5953739c-3b94-11ea-b84f-a62c46f39bc2. Accessed on February 9, 2022.

Jack, A. (2022). Business school rankings: The financial times' experience and evolutions. *Business & Society, 61*(4), 795–800. https://doi.org/10.1177/00076503211016783

Jackson, D. (2013). Completing a PhD by publication: A review of Australian policy and implications for practice. *Higher Education Research & Development, 32*(3), 355–368.

Jayaram. (2011). India. In M. Nerad & M. Heggelund (Eds.), *Toward a global PhD?: Forces and forms in doctoral education worldwide* (pp. 221–248). Washington, DC: University of Washington Press.

Jin, J. C. (2019). Research productivity in business and economics: South Korea, 1990–2016. *East Asian Economic Review, 23*(1), 89–107.

Joannidès de Lautour, V. (2023). Academic partners in a city-wide doctoral ecosystem. *EFMD Global Focus 17*(2, special suppl.), 10–15.

Johnston, B., & Murray, R. (2004). New routes to the PhD: Cause for concern?*Higher Education Quarterly, 58*(1), 31–42.

Jowi, J. O. (2021). Doctoral training in African universities: Recent trends, developments and issues. *Journal of the British Academy, 9*(s1), 159–181.

Juusola, K., Kettunen, K., & Alajoutsijärvi, K. (2015). Accelerating the Americanization of management education: Five responses from business schools. *Journal of Management Inquiry*, 24(4), 347–369.

Kalika, M. (2021). The PhD is losing its currency for business leaders. *Times Higher Education*, December 29. Retrieved from https://www.timeshighereducation.com/blog/phd-losing-its-currency-business-leaders. Accessed on December 18, 2022.

Kehm, B. M. (2006). Doctoral education in Europe and North America: A comparative analysis. *Wenner Gren International Series, 83*, 67.

Kehm, B. M. (2007). Quo vadis doctoral education? New European approaches in the context of global changes. *European Journal of Education*, 42(3), 307–319.

Kehm, B. M. (2009). New forms of doctoral education and training in the European higher education area. In B. M. Kehm, B. Stensaker, & J. Huisman (Eds.), *The European higher education area* (pp. 223–241). London: Brill.

Kim, S. (2007, November). Employment and career pattern of US-trained PhDs in Korea. Unpublished manuscript presented at the NBER conference. Career Patterns of Foreign-Born Scientists and Engineers. Cambridge, MA.

Kortt, M. A., Pervan, S. J., & Hogan, O. (2016). The rise and fall of the Australian DBA. *Education + Training*, 58(4), 390–408.

Krishnamurthy, S. (2020). The future of business education: A commentary in the shadow of the Covid-19 pandemic. *Journal of Business Research, 117*, 1–5.

Lages, C. R., Pfajfar, G., & Shoham, A. (2015). Challenges in conducting and publishing research on the Middle East and Africa in leading journals. *International Marketing Review* 32(1): 52–77.

Lange, G., Smith, K., Spradley, K., & Johnston, W. J. (2018, August). Executive business doctorate: A journey of motivations, risks, and real-world outcomes. In *2018 Engaged management scholarship conference,* Philadelphia, PA.

Lean, J., Wilkins, S., Moizer, J., & Heffernan, T. (2022). Doctoral education in business and management. *International Journal of Management Education*, 20(1), 100580.

Leadbeater, C. (1999). *Living on thin air*. London: Viking, Penguin.

Lee, A. (2018). How can we develop supervisors for the modern doctorate? *Studies in Higher Education*, 43(5), 878–890.

Lem, P. (2022a). Chinese student flows tipped to peak within five years. *Times Higher Education,* May 18. Retrieved from https://www.timeshighereducation.com/news/chinese-student-flows-tipped-peak-within-five-years/. Accessed on January 4, 2023.

Lewis, J., & Bolton, P., (2022). The post-18 education and funding review: Government conclusion. *House of Commons Library*, April 29. Retrieved from https://researchbriefings.files.parliament.uk/documents/CBP-9348/CBP-9348.pdf. Accessed on 10 December, 2022.

Lightbody, M. (2010). Exacerbating staff shortages and student dissatisfaction? The impact of AACSB accreditation on faculty recruitment in Australia. *Australasian Accounting, Business and Finance Journal*, 4(2), 3–18.

Lockhart, J. C., & Stablein, R. E. (2002). Spanning the academy-practice divide with doctoral education in business. *Higher Education Research & Development, 21*(2), 191–202.

Lundgren-Resenterra, M., & Kahn, P. E. (2019). The organisational impact of undertaking a professional doctorate: Forming critical leaders. *British Educational Research Journal*, 45(2), 407–424.

MacIntosh, R. (2022). Does business research in the UK need levelling up? *CABS*. Retrieved from https://charteredabs.org/does-business-research-in-the-uk-need-levelling-up/. Accessed on March 23, 2023.

MacIntosh, R., Beech, N., Bartunek, J., Mason, K., Cooke, B., & Denyer, D. (2017). Impact and management research: Exploring relationships between temporality, dialogue, reflexivity and praxis. *British Journal of Management*, 28(1), 3–13.

MacLennan, H., Piña, A., & Gibbons, S. (2018). Content analysis of DBA and PhD dissertations in business. *Journal of Education for Business*, 93(4), 149–154.

Malloy, J., Young, L., & Berdahl, L. (2021). Ph.D. oversupply: The system is the problem. *Insidehighered*, June 22. Retrieved from https://www.insidehighered.com/advice/2021/06/22/how-phd-job-crisis-built-system-and-what-can-be-done-about-it-opinion. Accessed on February 12, 2022.

Mangematin, V., & Baden-Fuller, C. (2008). Global contests in the production of business knowledge: Regional centres and individual business schools. *Long Range Planning*, *41*(1), 117–139.

Marakas, G. M. (n.d.). The DBA versus the PhD – What's the difference? Retrieved from https://business.fiu.edu/graduate/insights/the-dba-versus-the-phd-what-is-the-difference.cfm. Accessed on February 15, 2022.

Marini, G., & Yang, L. (2021). *The research productivity of Chinese academic returnees from the Global West: An evaluation of young 1000 talents recipients' productivity*. DoQSS Working Paper 21-02. Social Research Institute, UCL Institute of Education, London.

Mascarenhas, C., Ferreira, J. J., & Marques, C. (2018). University–industry cooperation: A systematic literature review and research agenda. *Science and Public Policy*, *45*(5), 708–718.

Mason, M. A., Goulden, M., & Frasch, K. (2009). Why graduate students reject the fast track. *Academe*, *95*(1), 11–16.

Mason, S., & Merga, M. (2018). Integrating publications in the social science doctoral thesis by publication. *Higher Education Research & Development*, *37*(7), 1454–1471.

Mason, S., Merga, M. K., & Morris, J. E. (2020). Typical scope of time commitment and research outputs of thesis by publication in Australia. *Higher Education Research & Development*, *39*(2), 244–258.

Masso, J., Eamets, R., Meriküll, J., & Kanep, H. (2014). *Estimating the need for PhDs in the academic, public and private sectors of Estonia*. Tartu: Tartu University Press.

McWilliam, E., Taylor, P. G., Thomson, P., Green, B., Maxwell, T., Wildy, H., & Simons, D. (2002). Research training in doctoral programs: What can be learned from professional doctorates? Canberra: Department of Communications, Information Technology and the Arts.

Mellors-Bourne, R., Robinson, C., & Metcalfe, J. (2016). Provision of professional doctorates in English HE institutions: report for HEFCE by the Careers Research and Advisory Centre (CRAC), supported by the University of Brighton. January 2016.

Mertkan, S., Arsan, N., Inal Cavlan, G., & Onurkan Aliusta, G. (2017). Diversity and equality in academic publishing: The case of educational leadership. *Compare: A Journal of Comparative and International Education*, *47*(1), 46–61.

Miller, P. (2010). Global discipline confusion in management and business related doctorate programmes. *Revista de Management Comparat Internaţional*, *11*(4), 623–639.

Morgan, J. (2013). Business schools were 'used as a cash cow', says Willetts. *Times Higher Education*, October 1. Retrieved from https://www.timeshighereducation.com/news/business-schools-were-used-as-a-cash-cow-says-willetts/2007850.article. Accessed on February 23, 2023.

Moules, J. (2018). UK universities use business schools as cash cows. *Financial Times*, April 25. Retrieved from https://www.ft.com/content/05a18eac-47bf-11e8-8ee8-cae73aab-7ccb. Accessed on February 20, 2023.

Murray, S. (2022). MBA professors under pressure to show business relevance. *Financial Times*, February 13.

Myklebust, J. P. (2022). Public hearing shows poor support for non-EU tuition fees. University World News, December 14. Retrieved from https://www.universityworldnews.com/post.php?story=20221214133207402. Accessed on February 12, 2023.

Myklebust, J. P. (2023). Parliament votes to end free tuition for non-EU students. *University World News*, 9 June 2023. Retrieved July 22, 2023 from: https://www.universityworldnews.com/post.php?story=20230609171347481#:~:text=Ending%20years%20of%20intense%20political,the%20principle%20of%20free%20education.

Navarro, P. (2008). The MBA core curricula of top-ranked US business schools: a study in failure? *Academy of management learning & education, 7*(1), 108–123.

Nerad, M., & Heggelund, M. (Eds.). (2011). *Toward a global PhD?: Forces and forms in doctoral education worldwide*. University of Washington Press.

Neumann, R., & Tan, K. K. (2011). From PhD to initial employment: The doctorate in a knowledge economy. *Studies in Higher Education, 36*(5), 601–614.

Noland, T. G., Francisco, B., & Sinclair, D. (2007). Pursuing a PhD in accounting: What to expect. *CPA Journal, 77*(3), 66.

O'Connell, B., Carnegie, G. D., Carter, A. J., De Lange, P., Hancock, P., Helliar, C., & Watty, K. (2015). *Shaping the future of accounting in business education in Australia.* Melbourne: CPA.

OECD. (2017). *Science, technology and industry scoreboard 2017: The digital transformation.* Paris: OECD Publishing. Retrieved from https://doi.org/10.1787/9789264268821-en. Accessed on March 19, 2018.

OECD. (2019). OECD Education at a glance 2019. Retrieved from https://www.oecd-ilibrary.org/education/education-at-a-glance-2019_f8d7880d-en. Accessed on February 10, 2020.

OECD. (2022). *Education at a glance*. Paris: OECD.

Orozco, L. A., & Villaveces, J. L. (2015). Heterogeneous research networks in Latin American schools of business management. *Academia Revista Latinoamericana de Administración, 28*(1), 115–134.

Owen, R. S. (2009). Managing a US business school professor shortage. *Research in Higher Education Journal, 2*, 1.

Palmer, N. (2018). Are our doctoral programmes fit for purpose and the future? *EFMD Global,* May 16. Retrieved from https://blog.efmdglobal.org/2018/05/16/are-our-doctoral-programmes-fit-for-purpose-and-the-future/. Accessed on February 2, 2023.

Park, C. (2005). New variant PhD: The changing nature of the doctorate in the UK. *Journal of Higher Education Policy and Management, 27*(2), 189–207.

Parker, M. (2018). Why we should bulldoze the business school, *The Guardian*, April 27. Retrieved from https://www.theguardian.com/news/2018/apr/27/bulldoze-the-business-school. Accessed on March 23, 2022.

Passant, A. J. G. (2016). Issues in European business education in the mid-nineteenth century: A comparative perspective. *Business History, 58*(7), 1118–1145.

Passant, A. J. G. (2022). Making European managers in business schools: A longitudinal case study on evolution, processes, and actors from the late 1960s onward. *Enterprise & Society, 23*(2), 478–511.

Pearson, M. (1999). The changing environment for doctoral education in Australia: Implications for quality management, improvement and innovation. *Higher Education Research & Development, 18*(3), 269–287.

Pepsico. (n.d.). Dare for brands that do good. *Pepsico Careers*. Retrieved from https://www.pepsicojobs.com/main/student. Accessed on August 12, 2022.

Pfeffer, J., & Fong, C. T. (2002). The end of business schools? Less success than meets the eye. *Academy of Management Learning & Education, 1*(1), 78–95.

Pfeffer, J., & Fong, C. T. (2004). The business school 'business': Some lessons from the US experience. *Journal of Management Studies, 41*(8), 1501–1520.

Pina, A. A., Maclennan, H. L., Moran, K. A., & Hafford, P. F. (2016). The DBA vs. Ph. D. in US business and management programs: Different by degrees? *Journal for Excellence in Business & Education, 4*(1), 6–19.

Pitt-Watson, D., & Quigley, E. (2019). Business school rankings for the 21st century. Retrieved from https://www.unglobalcompact.org/library/5654. Accessed on 23 March, 2023.

Porter, M. E., Kaplan, R. S., Kahneman, D., & Martin, R. L. (2017). *HBR's 10 Must Reads 2018: The definitive management ideas of the year from Harvard Business Review (with bonus article "Customer Loyalty Is Overrated") (HBR's 10 Must Reads)*. New York, NY: Harvard Business Press.

Powell, W. W., & Snellman, K. (2004). The knowledge economy. *Annual Review of Sociology.*, *30*, 199–220.

Reddy, Y. M. (2008). Global accreditation systems in management education: A critical analysis. *South Asian Journal of Management*, *15*(2), 61.

Ribiero, R. J. (2011). Brazil. In M. Nerad & M. Heggelund (Eds.), *Toward a global PhD?: Forces and forms in doctoral education worldwide* (pp.131–145). Washington, DC: University of Washington Press.

Robinson, G., Morgan, J., & Reed, W. (2016). Disruptive innovation in higher education: The professional doctorate. *International Journal of Information and Education Technology*, *6*(1), 85.

Sahana, A., & Vijila, K. (2017). Director, K. C. T. Need for developing the competencies of business school faculty – a review. *Asia Pacific Journal of Research ISSN (Print)*, *2320*, 5504.

Saunders, J., Wong, V., & Saunders, C. (2011). The research evaluation and globalization of business research. *British Journal of Management*, *22*(3), 401–419.

Sheel, R., & Vohra, N. (2014). Fostering academic research among management scholars in India: An introduction to the special issue. *Vikalpa*, *39*(2), v–xi.

Shimada, S., & Shimamoto, M. (2018). *Higher education in management: The case of Japan*. The Future of Management Education: Volume 2 (pp. 155–170). London: Differentiation Strategies for Business Schools, Palgrave Macmillan.

Shin, J. C., Postiglione, G. A., & Ho, K. C. (2018). Challenges for doctoral education in East Asia: A global and comparative perspective. *Asia Pacific Education Review*, *19*(2), 141–155.

Siemieńska, R., Matysiak, I., Domaradzka, A., & Vabø, A. (2017). *Expectations and satisfaction levels of Polish and Norwegian PhD graduates regarding the utility of their doctoral programmes in the labour market*. NIFU Working Paper 2016:20. Nordic Institute for Studies in Innovation, Research and Education, NIFU, Oslo.

Sigurjonsson, T. O., Vaiman, V., & Arnardottir, A. A. (2014). The role of business schools in ethics education in Iceland: The managers' perspective. *Journal of Business Ethics*, *122*, 25–38.

Simon, H. A. (1967). The business school a problem in organizational design. *Journal of management Studies*, *4*(1), 1–16.

Smith McGloin, R. (2021). A new mobilities approach to re-examining the doctoral journey: Mobility and fixity in the borderlands space. *Teaching in Higher Education*, *26*(3), 370–386.

Starkey, K., & Tiratsoo, N. (2007). *The business school and the bottom line*. Cambridge: Cambridge University Press.

Stoten, D. W. (2022). "I've been in a box too long and I didn't even realise that I was." How can we conceptualise the subjective well-being of students undertaking a part-time DBA? The IICC model. *The Journal of Continuing Higher Education*, 1–18.

Strielkowski, W. (2020). COVID-19 pandemic and the digital revolution in academia and higher education. *Preprints*, *1*, 1–6.

Suh, N. P. (2008). Globalization of research universities in Korea. *Part III Global Strategies for Emerging Universities*, *141*.

Sun, D.-T. (2010). Gaige woguo boshisheng peiyang moshi de ruogan sikao [Some thoughts on reforming doctoral programmes in China]. *Gaojiao Yanjiu Yu shijian*《高教研究与实践》*Research and Practice on Higher Education*, *29*(3), 3–7.

Suomi, K., Kuoppakangas, P., Kivistö, J., Stenvall, J., & Pekkola, E. (2020). Exploring doctorate holders' perceptions of the non-academic labour market and reputational problems they relate to their employment. *Tertiary Education and Management, 26*(4), 397–414.

The Economist. (2010). The disposable academic. *The Economist.* Retrieved from https://www.economist.com/christmas-specials/2010/12/16/the-disposable-academic. Accessed on February 10, 2022.

Thomas, H., Thomas, L., & Wilson, A. (2013). The unfulfilled promise of management education (ME): The role, value and purposes of ME. *Journal of Management Development, 32*(5), 460–476.

Thomas, H., & Wilson, A. D. (2011). 'Physics envy', cognitive legitimacy or practical relevance: Dilemmas in the evolution of management research in the UK. *British Journal of Management, 22*(3), 443–456.

Thune, T. (2009). Doctoral students on the university–industry interface: A review of the literature. *Higher Education, 58*, 637–651.

Trevecca Nazarene University. (2023). Doctorate in Business Administration (DBA). Retrieved from https://www.trevecca.edu/academics/program/doctor-of-business-administration. Accessed on March 28, 2023.

Tshabangu-Soko, T. S., & Caron, R. M. (2012). The Western model of higher education: Applications and implications for African development. In R. Caron (Ed.), *Educational policy in the twenty-first century* (pp. 37–47), Hauppauge, NY: Nova Science Publishers, Inc..

Tucker, M. P., Wilson, H., Hannibal, C., Lawless, A., & Qu, Z. (2021, March). Delivering professional doctorate education: Challenges and experiences during the COVID-19 pandemic. In *SHS Web of conferences* (Vol. 99). EDP Sciences.

Tzanakou, C. (2014). The value of the PhD in a knowledge-based economy: Beyond financial and career gains. *Europe of Knowledge*, March 11. Retrieved from https://era.ideasoneurope.eu/2014/03/11/the-value-of-the-phd-in-a-knowledge-based-economy-beyond-financial-and-career-gains/. Accessed on November 10, 2023.

University of Bath. (2021, February 22). New doctoral training consortium launched with South African partners. Retrieved from https://www.bath.ac.uk/announcements/new-doctoral-training-consortium-launched-with-south-african-partners/. Accessed on March 29, 2023.

Van Aken, J. E. (2005). Management research as a design science: Articulating the research products of mode 2 knowledge production in management. *British Journal of Management, 16*(1), 19–36.

van Baardewijk, J., & de Graaf, G. (2021). The ethos of business students. *Business Ethics, the Environment & Responsibility, 30*(2), 188–201.

Van Ours, J. C., & Ridder, G. (2003). Fast track or failure: A study of the graduation and dropout rates of Ph D students in economics. *Economics of Education Review, 22*(2), 157–166.

Vidaver-Cohen, D. (2007). Reputation beyond the rankings: A conceptual framework for business school research. *Corporate reputation review, 10*, 278–304.

Vitae. (2022). What do researchers do? Retrieved from https://www.Vitae.ac.uk/events/Vitae-international-researcher-development-conference-2022/Vitae-zone-2022/wdrd-2022-report.pdf. Accessed on March 24, 2023.

Vitae. (n.d.). About the Vitae Researcher Development Framework. Retrieved from https://www.Vitae.ac.uk/researchers-professional-development/about-the-Vitae-researcher-development-framework/. Accessed on March 24, 2023.

Vuolanto, P., Pasanen, H. M., & Aittola, H. (2006). Employment of PhDs in Finland. Prospects and expectations of doctoral students. *VEST: Journal of Science & Technology Studies, 19*, 31–56

Wang, L., & Byram, M. (2019). International doctoral students' experience of supervision: A case study in a Chinese university. *Cambridge Journal of Education, 49*(3), 255–274.

Warhurst, C. (2001). Knowing in firms: understanding, managing and measuring knowledge. *Management Learning, 32*(1), 148.

Wedlin, L. (2006). *Ranking business schools: Forming fields, identities and boundaries in international management education.* Edward Elgar Publishing.

Weybrecht, G. (2022). Business schools are embracing the SDGs–But is it enough?–How business schools are reporting on their engagement in the SDGs. *The International Journal of Management Education, 20*(1), 100589.

Wheeler, J. T. (1967). Doctorates in Business Administration: A demand and supply analysis. *California Management Review, 10*(1), 35–50.

Wiley University Services. (2020). Doctorate in business administration: Growth, trends, online program design, and recruitment. Retrieved from https://universityservices.wiley.com/doctor-business-administration/. Accessed on 10 December, 2022.

Williams, P. F., & Rodgers, J. L. (1995). The accounting review and the production of accounting knowledge. *Critical Perspectives on Accounting, 6*(3), 263–287.

Wilson, D. C., & Thomas, H. (2012). The legitimacy of the business of business schools: What's the future? *Journal of Management Development, 31*(4), 368–376.

Woetzl, J., & Seong, J. (2019). We've entered the Asian Century and there is no turning back. *World Economic Forum*, October 11. Retrieved from https://www.weforum.org/agenda/2019/10/has-world-entered-asian-century-what-does-it-mean/. Accessed on March 28, 2023.

Xu, D. (2009). Opportunities and challenges for academic returnees in China. *Asia Pacific Journal of Management, 26*(1), 27–35.

Yamamoto. (2011). Japan. In M. Nerad & M. Heggelund (Eds.), *Toward a global PhD?: Forces and forms in doctoral education worldwide* (pp. 204–220). Washington, DC: University of Washington Press.

Yarrow, E., & Davies, E. (2023a). Delegitimizing the underrepresentation of women management scholars in the research impact agenda. In A. Ortenblad & R. Koris (Eds.), *Anthology on debating business school legitimacy* (pp. 147–166). Basingstoke: Palgrave Macmillan.

Yarrow, E., & Davies, E. (2023b). A typology of sexism in contemporary business schools: Belligerent, benevolent, ambivalent, and oblivious sexism. *Gender, Work & Organization.* https://doi.org/10.1111/gwao.12914

Zhao, J., & Ferran, C. (2016). Business school accreditation in the changing global marketplace: A comparative study of the agencies and their competitive strategies. *Journal of International Education in Business, 9*(1), 52–69.

Zweig, D., & Yang, F. (2014). Overseas students, returnees, and the diffusion of international norms into post-Mao China. *International Studies Review, 16*(2), 252–263.

Chapter 2

Recruitment, Selection and Retention in Business and Management Doctorates Around the World

Overview

In this chapter, we explore issues relating to programme choice, recruitment, selection and retention. Additionally, we acknowledge how institutional infrastructure and support, intrinsic motivation and the financial and employment/student status of doctoral candidates can impact retention and attrition rates. Differences in organisational contingencies and stakeholders and between expectations and realities such as immigration law and post-study work options can significantly impact candidate mobility and experiences in management doctorates.

Who is Being Targeted for Business Doctorate Recruitment?

In Chapter 1, we acknowledged the increasing globalisation of business school doctorates. Demand and supply-side patterns were noted in the overall expansion of business and management doctorates internationally. In particular, we drew attention to contextual differences and nuances in business school doctorate provision. Similarly, we note variations between business schools when we begin to explore fee structures and market positioning that impact on recruitment practices.

An influx of doctoral students from overseas can be viewed as a threat to internal doctoral training systems in candidate-generating countries. However, the activity offers 'brain gain' to countries developing doctoral programmes through dispersed knowledge diaspora. Doctoral returnees from studying in countries with established reputations for delivering high-quality doctoral education such as the USA often gain prestige (Akay, 2008; Hu, 2021). The soft power benefits of internationalised higher education systems (CRAC, 2013) to countries that have transitioned from command to market economies like Russia and China have been noted. The potential to achieve foreign policy goals (not least in terms of country image) is recognised through 'embracing the international norm on

Business and Management Doctorates World-Wide: Developing the Next Generation, 35–68
Copyright © 2024 by Nicola J. Palmer, Julie Davies and Clare Viney
Published under exclusive licence by Emerald Publishing Limited
doi:10.1108/978-1-78973-499-720231002

world-class universities' (Crowley-Vigneau, Baykov, & Kalyuzhnova, 2022, p. 120). International expansion of business schools is associated with attempts to compete for influence across global markets. As Iliev (cited in De Novellis, 2018, p. 1) observed:

> Russia is now increasingly concentrated on China and the post-Soviet space ... I see growing collaboration between schools there and schools in Moscow and Saint Petersburg. Now, pretty much every school has some sort of partnership in China – in Hong Kong, Beijing, or Shanghai – and that's to the detriment of the US.

Geopolitical analysis of the growth in collaborative business doctorate partnerships is lacking. Nevertheless, as acknowledged in Chapter 1, international partnerships have become valuable for capacity-building, market entry and expansion. These alliances often provide opportunities for business schools to improve their status by association with higher ranked institutions. The partnerships provide strategic opportunities to enable faculty and student mobility across regions (De Onzoño & Carmona, 2007).

The influence of a global ranking systems game (Shastry, 2017) is apparent. Furthermore, global rankings are of relevance to applicants to doctorates, particularly potential international candidates (Archer, 2016; Cabrera, Mariel, & Abadía, 2022; Sirkeci & O'Leary, 2022).

However, in relation to business school status as perceived by business, academic and student stakeholders, D'Aveni (1996, p. 166) has suggested that:

> In Ph.D. markets, status hierarchies tend to make groups of [business] schools a closed system, leading to homosocial reproduction of senior faculties and social isolation and immobility for certain Ph.D. graduates.

The extent to which status hierarchies negatively impact on doctoral programme choice is under-explored. Bar, Wanat, and Gonzalez' (2017, p. 23) research on racial and ethnic differences in candidates' selection of biomedical science doctoral programmes in the USA found that the criteria used in selecting graduate schools for application were highly similar. But there were 'clear differences in the factors affecting the choice of [graduate] school to attend' across racial and ethnic groups. Here, we note that a sense of belonging and inclusion are important factors.

Recruiting to a Diverse and Inclusive Research Environment?

Diversity across multiple characteristics is worthy of consideration and review. Some publicly-shared data relate to business school doctorate demographics in terms of applications and admissions. The Graduate Management Admission Council (GMAC), a global non-profit education organisation of leading graduate business schools and the owner of the Graduate Management Admission Test® (GMAT®), reported that only 36% of specialised master's and PhD/DBA degree applicants were female in 2011, although this figure had increased slightly from previous years (Estrada, 2011). The latest GMAC reports do not include data on research degree applicant trends.

While women represent a majority of postgraduate students across all disciplines (Mattocks & Briscoe-Palmer, 2016), gender remains an issue in business school recruitment. EFMD's Gender Gap Report (Roseberry, Remke, Klæsson, & Holgersson, 2016) noted that on average only 33% of full-time faculty employed by the top 85 business schools on the *Financial Times* 2015 European Business School Rankings were female. For the top 10 business schools on the list, that figure fell to 23.3%. We note that this imbalance persists. A lack of diverse faculty presents challenges for role modelling, belonging and sense of inclusion amongst minoritised doctoral candidates (Stewart, Williamson, & King, 2008). Additionally, as Kantola's (2008) work in a Finnish context reveals:

> PhD supervision by men is a particularly strong structural barrier for women because of the gendered nature of interaction in supervision and the difficulties that female PhD students have in a male-dominated environment. (Kantola, 2008, p. 202)

The attractiveness of the research environment to which doctoral candidates are applying is important. Mattocks and Briscoe-Palmer (2016) explored barriers and challenges faced by women, black minority ethnic groups, and candidates living with a disability in relation to UK political science PhD programmes. Their work emphasises a need to acknowledge common structural and operational biases that impact on particular social groupings throughout the lifecycle of the doctorate.

Hannam-Swain (2018) has provided valuable insights into life as a disabled PhD candidate. She highlights an absence of representation and lack of appreciation about the additional time-consuming events that occur as part of living with a disability. Additionally, Butler-Rees and Robinson (2020) have drawn attention to everyday anxiety as part of the doctoral experience. They have argued that the impact of this on candidates with disabilities needs to be acknowledged. However, there remains a notable dearth of discussion about candidates who '[interpret] their own position as marginal or as outsiders' (Kantola, 2008, p. 202) in the context of doctoral programme recruitment *per se* and especially in relation to business schools.

We know that age diversity is present in many business school doctoral programmes where there are high levels of part-time candidature and DBA provision inevitably skews this due to entry requirements that include management experience measured in number of years. In the sense that doctoral candidates bring with them diverse personal and professional backgrounds, we also recognise that there is diversity amongst all business and management doctoral candidates. Although institutional doctoral recruitment data have generally improved over the past decade, less is known about (or spoken about) issues of merit, diversity, power and influence in doctoral admissions decision-making from an internal faculty perspective as Posselt (2016) has acknowledged.

We have, however, started to see increased recognition of a need to consider issues of fairness and equity of opportunity in relation to doctoral programme recruitment across all disciplines. This reflects more interest in the lived experiences of diverse candidate groups and minoritised communities. Ecton, Bennett, Nienhusser, Castillo-Montoya, and Dougherty (2021, p. 1), for example, have noted that 'racially/ethnically minoritized students, in particular, face persistent challenges during the graduate application and enrollment process'. In line with this, Research England and the Office for Students (UK) funded 13 projects to increase access and participation for Black, Asian and minority ethnic groups in postgraduate research (PGR) study (UKRI, 2022). Race equity initiatives are visible also in US graduate schools such as the University of Washington Graduate School where specific scholarships are offered to improve recruitment of under-represented minority candidates and race discussion and dialogue spaces are provided to increase access, success and postgraduate professional opportunities. However, Forray and Goodnight's (2014) observation that US minority candidate enrolments require mentorship by business faculty is challenged by a lack of faculty diversity in business schools (Grier & Poole, 2020). In this regard, Minefee, Rabelo, Stewart, and Young (2015, p. 79) identify AACSB as 'an institution that can facilitate change and reduce social closure within business schools' through its power as an accreditation body.

With respect to doctoral recruitment, a failure to acknowledge the potential exclusion of minoritised groups limits the prospective doctoral talent pool of recruitment in the battle in which Smith (2018) has identified as a quest to find 'the best doctoral students'.

Pricing and Fees

International recruitment practices in business and management doctorates are varied. We might expect an unequivocal relationship between funding and recruitment. Indeed, Powell and Green's (2007) focus on the doctorate world-wide draws attention to how sources of doctoral funding affect out of country and international recruitment practices. We can observe this in doctoral provision in public research universities in Germany, Finland, Norway and Sweden where no PhD fees are charged to students of any nationality and in Saudi Arabia where scholarships are used to cover all PhD candidate fees (Bennett, 2021). The latter approach produces finite limits on how many doctoral candidates may be recruited each year in line with higher education financial resources. Charging no fees also inevitably impacts on doctoral education capacity and growth. In public universities in Sweden decisions on how many doctoral candidates are recruited per discipline are deferred to public universities who distribute PGR funding for research and dissertation-based programmes across departments, depending on institutional academic research priorities. In contrast, very low levels of doctoral funding in Russia result in a high proportion of self-funding candidates, many of whom have to work full time to afford fee levels (Bekova, 2019). This reliance on self-funding candidates impacts on recruitment, admissions decisions and completion rates. Bekova and Terentev (2020, p. 51) report that 'universities in Russia pay no or little attention to the previous academic achievements of candidates'.

Pricing of the doctorate is inevitably associated with certain expectations about the attractiveness and quality of the experience on offer. In the UK differential fee levels between home and international candidates at publicly funded universities coupled with unequal access to UK government doctoral loans and other funding streams have been noted to place international self-funding candidates at a disadvantage (Mogaji, Adamu, & Nguyen, 2021). Business schools that are not publicly funded have more leeway to adjust doctoral fee profiles. Ecton et al. (2021, drawing on the work of Belasco, Trivette, & Webber, 2014, and Denecke, Feaster, Okahana, Allum, & Stone, 2016) have noted that we have witnessed a trend across graduate schools to increase the financial appeal of programmes to prospective candidates in recognition of the influence of financial considerations on application and enrolment decisions.

Differences in fee levels are not only observable between countries but also between business and management doctorate awards. One of the most expensive DBA programmes in the world in 2021–2022 in terms of fee level was offered by Pepperdine Graziadio private business school in the USA, priced at $161,205 (including fees, all meals for the six residential sessions, access to online course content and research resources and software licenses). As Mellors-Bourne, Metcalfe, Pearce, and Hooley (2014) have noted, the costs associated with doctoral programme provision are often viewed as part of broader institutional investments in research activity, not least the generation of research publications and outputs that count to research assessment exercises. Yet, in the context of the business school cost, value and viability considerations are observed to be relevant:

> Despite an often overwhelming sense of intrinsic value, doctoral education is widely viewed as being a cost center to schools, especially in comparison to other degree programs. The resources required to deliver a quality doctoral program are substantial and the outcomes, it is argued, are often not immediately realized and are difficult to quantify. (AACSB International, 2013, p. 27)

The resource-intensive nature of doctoral programmes activities and unlikeliness of them becoming a revenue source for business schools is a theme highlighted by Smith (2018). Furthermore, he has argued that they require high levels of investment and commitment but should be recognised as contributing to the development and sustainability of reputation and rankings.

Questions have been raised as to the profitability of the business doctorate and there have been calls for broader cost-benefit analyses not only in private business schools but also in state-funded institutions (Grote in Palmer, 2018). The positioning of the business doctorate in wider institutional doctoral education provision and the extent to which there exists autonomy will be affected by business school funding and governance arrangements. The importance of internally generated resources through tuition fees and executive education revenue to Instituts d'Administration des Entreprises (IAEs), aligned to larger public universities but benefitting from some administrative freedom, in France has been observed (Thietart, 2009). Furthermore, Pon and Duncan (2019) have identified the value of alliances and networks for medium-sized French business schools to internationalise and gain global education market reach.

Amongst the most visible examples of collaboration in business school doctorates is the Montréal model (mentioned in Chapter 1) where, for example, PhD programmes are offered by the triple-accredited HEC Montréal jointly with Concordia and McGill universities and the Université du Québec à Montréal (UQAM). This arrangement has enabled the offering of PhD programmes across 12 specialisations in French or English to 440 joint programme PhD candidates, supported by 'world class research and faculty' under a standardised model whereby tuition fees are waived, and four years of competitive funding is offered (HEC Montréal, 2022). Financial support is also advertised at Harvard, where the DBA is no longer offered, and, regardless of need and background, all PhD candidates are guaranteed funding for up to five years through a fellowship that covers tuition costs, single-person health fees, and a living stipend ($43,860 for 2021–2022). This shift to 'all inclusive' style doctoral education offers appears to be gaining traction in a crowded and more readily substitutable marketplace. However, for many PhD programmes, it is often unclear what differentiates the offer for the tuition fee but we can note a trend in shifts in doctoral education 'towards a programme model with increased institutional responsibility' (Kehm, Shin, & Jones, 2018, p. 237) in terms of quality assurance. Increased attention on accountability and quality enhancement has been particularly noted in doctoral education provided by European universities (Byrne, Jørgensen, & Loukkola, 2013), with a rising emphasis on supervision as an activity that is often seen as central to the quality of doctoral education (Friedrich-Nel & MacKinnon, 2019).

Fee structures and the doctoral programmes offer inevitably impact on targeting and recruitment. The complex and dynamic nature of doctoral candidate recruitment in a fight for the most highly qualified applicants has received little academic attention (Kim & Spencer-Oatey, 2021; Wall Bortz et al., 2020). Strong levels of competition between doctoral programmes in business and management are visible, reflecting the globalisation of doctoral education that was acknowledged in Chapter 1. Competitive forces often result in recruitment mechanisms that are predominantly based on financial investment and funding availability for doctorate places, particularly in Western doctoral education systems (Grote et al., 2021), and all too often neglect values-based considerations. As Wall Bortz et al. (2020, p. 927) note:

> competitive forces may lead programs to adopt non-evidence-based recruitment strategies that may not align with either program leaders' stated values or students' priorities.

In our *Global Focus* article based on an EFMD webinar on business school doctorates (Davies, Palmer, Braccia, Clegg, & Smith, 2021), we noted, as Mark Saunders at Birmingham Business School observed, that there is a risk of doctorates in business schools being treated as a Cinderella project in a portfolio of offerings. Crucially, however, doctorates develop the next generation of research leaders. The pandemic may have exacerbated this as lost overseas students and executive tuition fees concentrated deans' minds on the bottom line and on recruiting higher numbers of undergraduates and taught postgraduates for tuition fee income. Nevertheless, within this Cinderella scenario, heads of universities may be aware of premium-priced DBAs as a ready source of income. For example, following the observation by Morgan (2016) noted in Chapter 1, at Cambridge Judge Business School, the 2021 entry fee for the Business Doctorate (BusD) was £80,000 for the first year and £50,000 for each of years 2–4, that is, £230,000 (€268,548 or almost US$300,000) in total. Curiously, in the 2021/2022 academic year, the Cambridge University website listed only three current doctoral researchers on the BusD – three male candidates supervised by three male professors. Clearly, this niche is highly exclusive where there is a strong brand!

Differential pricing between the PhD and the professional doctorate in business and management has been explained as reflecting perceived professional doctorate candidate affordability (Allen et al., 2002 as cited in Kot & Hendel, 2012). The potential economic return from professional doctorate fees has not been overlooked (Jones, 2018). The extent to which DBA candidates are employer-funded or self-funding has received some acknowledgement but is open to further exploration. Davies et al. (2019, p. 204) observed that:

> Currently, UK research council funding does not support the Doctorate in Business Administration, possibly on the assumption that employers and working practitioners will be self-funded.

However, individual business schools have offered DBA scholarships. The School of Management at the University of Bradford (UK), for example, has previously advertised that successful applicants for self-funded DBAs, originating from countries designated by the World Bank as low- or middle-income may apply for 'scholarships valued at 50% of overall DBA fee for first and second year, up to 12,500 GBP' and a 50% DBA fee discount for the first and second year of study, up to 12,500 GBP, is offered to successful self-funding applicants from the UK or Europe (European Funding Guide, n.d). Although it is unclear if these scholarships are still offered to successful applicants, the initiative appears to recognise and respond to potential disadvantage faced by international self-funding doctoral candidates which Mogaji et al. (2021) have highlighted.

A desire to internationalise the doctoral candidate market fits with some of the globalisation issues acknowledged in Chapter 1, not least in terms of training of future faculty. There has been some research attention paid to candidate responses to opportunities to study abroad for a doctorate (Ndofirepi, Farinloye, & Mogaji, 2020) and Noble (1994 as cited in Park, 2005, p. 190) has highlighted how the doctorate can offer an 'academic passport with international reciprocity'. We have seen that doctoral education capacity-building strategies employed by some countries involve the encouragement of PhD candidates to complete their training overseas. However, there has been little consideration of intercultural competences to prepare international candidates for doctoral studies that endure over several years and the re-adjustment of returnees to home cultures at the end of their international doctoral candidatures. These issues are beginning to attract research interest. Xu (2020) has considered the lived experiences of Chinese doctoral candidates in Australia in the context of cross-cultural adaptation. Alkubaidi and Alzhrani (2020) warned about the potential for 'culture shock' for Saudi postdoctoral returnees resulting from their exposure to cultural diversity in Western universities and from having to shift back to a more conservative regime.

Doctoral Admissions to Reproduce the Academy

The effectiveness of undergraduate student recruitment activities is a perpetual concern for many universities whereas far less attention has been placed on the efficacy of doctoral candidate recruitment. This is partly explained by the way in which doctoral places are advertised and how candidates apply for doctoral studies. Although PGR is generally referenced in institutional research strategies, the extent to which strategic recruitment happens at doctoral level is questionable (Mellors-Bourne et al., 2014).

Recruitment strategies for attractive doctoral talent merit attention (Smith, 2018). The strategic importance of doctoral researchers to institutional research capacity and outputs (Mellors-Bourne et al., 2014) does not always translate to equity of opportunity in terms of who is targeted through the doctoral pipeline.

Doctoral-level study grants and scholarships are often accompanied by expectations that successful candidates will carry out teaching and/or administrative duties. This opportunity for socialisation into the academic department and the discipline can be a valuable part of the doctoral candidate's experience (Sverdlik, Hall, McAlpine, & Hubbard, 2018). However, it needs to be clearly managed, reviewed and, ideally, accompanied by formal and informal mentoring support (Chiu & Corrigan, 2019; Jepsen, Varhegyi, & Edwards, 2012; Soomere & Karm, 2021). Furthermore, the extent to which there is equity of opportunity in terms of teaching opportunities for international doctoral candidates has been questioned (Zheng, 2019). A lack of meaningful intercultural faculty interactions for international doctoral candidates can contribute to isolation, loneliness and alienation. Li and Collins (2014) challenge the extent to which doctoral candidate socialisation is fully realised in many business schools. The idea of graduate school as preparation for academic careers is pertinent to the perceived efficacy of doctoral recruitment strategies employed by many business schools.

Despite a relatively high proportion of international doctoral candidates in business and management, it is only relatively recently that concerted attempts to support international graduate teaching assistants have begun to emerge (McLaughlan, 2021). This is often driven by institutional concerns about managing the quality of teaching delivered to undergraduate students by doctoral candidates (Nasser-Abu Alhija & Fresko, 2018) and visa restrictions (Mogaji et al., 2021). Placing the focus on the doctoral candidate, we observe that programme design and communications at recruitment stage shape applicants' expectations and impact on the construction of doctoral identity

(Sun & Trent, 2020). In the USA and the UK, in many university departments, including business and management, teaching positions for doctoral candidates sit alongside adjunct positions. Opportunities to teach are often characterised as limited and competitive, involving assessments of aptitude and competence (based on criteria decided by existing faculty). Teaching assistantships may be regarded as an honour or privilege (Schwieger, Gros, & Barberan, 2010) or, in some situations, these opportunities may not be clearly communicated to candidates (Kantola, 2008). There is little open discussion in many business schools about doctoral candidate's attitudes towards their development needs and experiences of teaching (although in the UK students may complete a postgraduate teaching qualification and apply for Advance HE Associate Fellowship status). Lack of open discussion is in spite of high-profile debates over academic casualisation and precarity (see, e.g., the University and College Union in the UK – UCU, 2021; Columbia University, New York – Sainato, 2022).

The reported popularity of community of practice activities such as the University of Warwick's Journal of PGR Pedagogic Practice and Survey of PGR Teachers aimed at ascertaining what support may be valuable to doctoral candidates who teach (Patel, 2021) suggests that there is an appetite for increased dialogue and more open conversations about PGR teaching. Despite the employment of doctoral candidates to deliver teaching across university departments, however, the accreditation body AACSB still speaks about a *doctoral* degree as 'qualifying candidates to *teach* in a university setting' (AACSB, 2022, p. 1) post-completion. This is in contrast to acknowledging that teaching is a developmental activity in-doctorate. It is in line with the Humboldtian higher education model whereby the PhD is seen as a licence to teach (Park, 2005). In business and management doctoral education in Africa, in particular, 'the PhD is slowly becoming the basic entry requirement to teach at the university level' (Darley, 2021, p. 1). Thus, we might acknowledge the academic teaching pool to be restricted by who is given a place on a PhD programme.

Journeying Across Boundaries

As we have noted in Chapter 1, the number of doctoral programmes in business and management has grown internationally. Furthermore, strong application volumes in Canada and Europe have been reported to be driven primarily by international demand (Schoenfeld, 2017). Many prospective doctoral candidates have a choice to make in terms of where to apply. Location is one of the fundamental decisions facing doctoral programme applicants (Cuschieri, 2021). The notion of international mobility across business school doctorates depends on the wherewithal for candidates to study across geographical boundaries. Mobility can be restricted by the personal and professional circumstances of applicants. This is particularly the case for those who are applying for part-time doctoral study. Typically, part-timers are juggling doctoral studies with paid work and caring responsibilities. Similar challenges have been flagged for full-time self-funding candidates (Mogaji et al., 2021).

The idea that self-funded international students are a 'migratory elite' in terms of the perceived privilege associated with being able to afford to study abroad has been challenged by Pásztor (2015). Attention is drawn to the potential of international doctoral study to facilitate capital accumulation. For international business school doctoral applicants, decisions over which university to apply to for completion of graduate studies have been linked to activities related to the internationalisation of education, such as faculty exchanges and collaborations (Chen, 2008).

The value of these signals of intercultural competence may lie in an applicant's assessments of scope for belonging and acceptance. In general, there is a lack of shared intelligence about the application, admissions and pre-arrival experiences of international doctoral applicants. Where this has been considered, emphasis has been placed on interactive online and social media sources for potential doctoral candidates interested in studying overseas, especially applicants in Asia (Archer, 2016; Kim & Spencer-Oatley, 2021).

How doctoral candidates are targeted varies by type of institution and country. In M7 business schools in the USA (the University of Chicago's Booth School of Business, Columbia, Harvard, Kellogg School of Management, MIT Sloan School of Management, Stanford Graduate School of Business, and Wharton) prestige often negates the need to advertise to PhD applicants. The ability of these institutions to attract high-performing candidates in terms of previous grade point average (GPA) perpetuates 'the preservation of dominant group identities' (Minefee et al., 2014, p. 79). However, in contrast, in many UK institutions, there is a tendency to target existing students on master's programmes within an institution. Some lower ranked business schools may even offer free places for doctoral candidates to ensure a steady supply. Universities offer loyalty discounts on fees to self-funding applicants, or market PhD places externally through generic channels such as *FindAPhD* rather than exploiting opportunities for 'targeted promotion or more direct contact through other UK universities' (Mellors-Bourne et al., 2014, p. 33).

Funding does however impact on mobility in relation to sourcing doctoral candidates from different parts of the world. In some cases, there may be too many doctoral candidates from Saudi Arabia or China in one business school. In Canada, we are aware of one business school that attracted many candidates from Iran because of attractive visa opportunities and while the students were very good, the programme director felt that the lack of diversity in the cohort was unhelpful. Funding is linked to important developmental activities such as placements, conferences, workshops and travel, which enable doctoral candidates to publish and enhance their social capital and networks and to gain further funding and jobs. This is the 'Matthew effect' (Merton, 1968) which has implications for equity, diversity, inclusion and belonging. It is important to consider who is receiving scholarships for doctoral study in the business school and to seek opportunities to improve funding for first-generation and under-represented groups to access doctoral studies and be supported during and after their doctoral training.

Variations in the Recruitment of Business School Doctorate Candidates

Most DBA programmes that bring candidates together in cohort-based study blocks on campus require professional experience as mandatory, in line with the contribution to practice expectations of the award. Professional experience is common as an enhanced or additional doctoral programmes' entry requirement to the DBA (Kot & Hendel, 2012; Neumann, 2005) and at some business schools, such as ESCE International Business School (France) where a three-year DBA programme is offered jointly with the University of Valencia (Spain), there are expectations of sustained senior level, international management experience. This provides a clear differentiation in terms of market orientation.

For the business doctorate, one key motivation to apply relates to professional development and career management. In its 2022, online promotion of the Executive DBA, Cranfield School of Management advises how employer sponsorship 'not only boosts the overall learning experience, but also enhances future career development' (Cranfield School of Management, 2022, p. 1). Publicly shared 'hard evidence' of this is lacking. Similar messaging about the value of employer buy-in is evident in relation to the University of London's distance and flexible learning programmes (Alexander, 2020) and underpinned the promotion of employer-sponsored apprenticeship degrees in the UK (Phoenix, 2016).

As Costley and Abukari (2015) highlighted, employer–employee–university involvement in work-based projects at masters and professional doctorate level vary in terms of relationship proximity between stakeholders. This is because different factors affect employee and employer motivations and the decision to undertake doctoral study is most often employee-initiated. The extent to which the 'values and purposes' of professional doctorates are appreciated by employers beyond the development of candidates' personal and professional knowledge remains open to question (Armsby, Costley, & Cranfield, 2018). Lack of employer support to enable candidates to 'earn while they learn' may restrict the recruitment, progression and completion of part-time, mature doctoral learners. Indeed, we note how some programmes require employer support at application stage. For example, we are familiar with the practices of the online DBA offered by Birmingham City Business School (UK). Here, the 'formal agreement and active co-operation of the organisation where the DBA studies are to take place' is an entry requirement (BCU, 2022, p. 1). This reflects the positioning of the DBA between research degree and 'executive education' by some business schools. Amdam (2020), charting the development of executive education in business schools in the USA, has noted that, historically, learner nomination was subject to senior executive selection of male participants. This is based on hierarchical positions within companies and has emphasised the relevance of symbolic capital linked to the status and prestige associated with advanced education opportunities.

In a similar vein, we might acknowledge potential bias located in relation to requests for research proposals, references and previous experience details in many business doctorate applications. We have already discussed the significance of business school rankings as symbols of status and prestige. We also cannot over-emphasise the influence of cultural capital on the doctorate applications process. Quite simply, completing the doctoral application form to achieve the best chance of succeeding in the selection process requires some degree of specialised or insider knowledge.

The use of agents as intermediaries for business school international doctoral candidate recruitment in linking markets to programmes, for example, in Asia-Australia and South America-the USA, has raised ethical concerns (Denisova-Schmidt, de Wit, & Wan, 2020). There is a case for more attention to be paid to the provision of accessible support and guidance pre-application. Where resources sit for this is open to further exploration and discussion. We are aware that 'research summer schools' have been offered by some UK universities for almost two decades as a means of providing research 'tasters' to undergraduate and master-level students, alongside open days and other community outreach activities (Mellors-Bourne et al., 2014). However, these types of activities are often dependent on the effort and commitment provided by doctoral programme staff and research supervisors and, for many academics, are not often work-planned or recognised at institutional level unless clear conversion rates can be demonstrated.

The Language of Application

A high proportion of business and management programmes require English language proficiency. In the joint Montréal PhD model mentioned earlier in this chapter, where the programmes are offered in French or English, applicants may select to meet French or English language entry requirements (HEC Montréal, 2022). However, for most doctoral applications worldwide, English language requirements are stipulated. This is notable in the case of business school doctorates. We observe that the language of instruction of DBAs at business schools across Asia is advertised as English. Furthermore, even at institutions such as Africa Business School, where online course information is provided in English and French, English language proficiency is still required as a DBA programme entry requirement.

Published work on issues of social justice linked to hegemonic structures and processes at doctoral applications stage is emergent but the subaltern academic status of enrolled international doctoral candidates, particularly those originating from what has been referred to as the global South has received more attention (see, e.g., Gopaul, 2011; Kidman, Manathunga, & Cornforth, 2017; Pifer & Baker, 2014). It is apparent that the USA has been proactive in establishing graduate school preparation programmes and research internships that seek to contribute to redressing the under-representation of specific social groups through the development of dispositions (habitus) relevant to being a doctoral candidate (Greer, Johnson, & Delk, 2021; Ishiyama & Hopkins, 2003; McCoy & Winkle-Wagner, 2015; Nnadozie, Ishiyama, & Chon, 2000; Winkle-Wagner & McCoy, 2016). We note an established body of research in psychology that explores the idea of graduate school preparation activities from the perspective of prospective applicants in particular (see, e.g., Huss, Randall, Patry, Davis, & Hansen, 2002;

Landrum, 2010; Niemczyk, 2015; Nordstrom & Segrist, 2009; Sanders & Landrum, 2012; Strapp, Bredimus, Wright, Cochrane, & Fields, 2021). However, there has been a lack of acknowledgement of the value of preparation programmes for the business school doctorate. We note that such programmes are particularly germane given Western dominance in the development of the award that may necessitate cultural adjustments beyond the development of critical thinking skills and exposure to threshold concepts. Yet, many business schools tend to rely on previous masters' level programme skills and highlight in-programme doctoral training benefits in terms of academic research skills acquired through the process of studying for a doctorate.

Business and management doctoral applications tend to require written research proposals but there is a lack of systematic support available to applicants to develop these components. Expert assistance, advice and formative feedback are often dependent on potential supervisor willingness and ability to help voluntarily; aspects of social capital can be recognised to be relevant. Greener (2021) has acknowledged the pivotal role that current doctoral candidates can play in educating future candidates as critical friends. In relation to support in place for doctoral applicants in business and management in the UK, it is observed that:

> Institutions vary in how easy or difficult it may be for a prospective doctoral student to track down relevant supervision for their proposed study, with many Schools offering a front end application which is generic. This gives little guidance, given the diversity of discipline and methodology within Business Schools, on how to build a research proposal which can attract attention and gain interview. Students may put many hours of detailed research into building a proposal, only to find there are no suitable supervision opportunities in that School. (Greener, 2021, p. 100463)

Chiu's (2015) argument that the personal statement element, often a mandatory part of many business school doctoral applications in the USA and the UK, may also be seen as a form of 'academic' writing at admission stage is interesting and important. The influence of academic communities and 'conceptual understanding of the culture of doctoral level study' (Chiu, 2015, p. 63) draws attention to power and gatekeeping in the evaluation of personal statements (Chiu, 2019). This means that there are admissions stage expectations held by evaluators of applications that are often unfamiliar to many applicants who are located outside of academia in particular and / or within different cultural systems or environments. As Chiu (2015, p. 63) explains 'the situated knowledge of institutional settings where these academics are based will affect the ways in which they act and think in relation to particular forms of discourse'.

We acknowledge that the nature of the assessment of doctoral studies internationally means that English language proficiency is an essential part of 'improving the quality of outcomes for all PhD students' (Bernstein et al., 2014, p. 6). Thus, it is perhaps unsurprising that English language scores are included as an entry requirement for applicants for whom English is not their first language.

However, mixed practice exists in terms of other attempts to predict academic performance and success. Business Schools vary in their use of open admissions and selected admissions processes. As Chowfla (2019, p. 1) observes, 'business school admissions has always been about selection' in an environment where there exists a surplus of applicants to places. In theory, this presents an opportunity for the recruitment of talent. The nature of the potential talent pool is particularly interesting given the multidisciplinarity of business and management and a shifting of disciplines for some scholars towards management (Aguinis, Bradley, & Brodersen, 2014).

Recruitment, Selection and Admissions

A study by Mellors-Bourne et al. (2014) which aimed to provide greater understanding of the recruitment and selection of PGRs by English higher education institutions found that prior to making selection decisions a certain level of interaction with potential shortlisted applicants is desired (Mellors-Bourne et al., 2014). However, the authors draw attention to the issue of fairness particularly in relation to propensity for internal candidates to receive more feedback and support throughout the doctoral application process in comparison to external candidates. This reflects decentralisation of doctoral recruitment whereby in universities in countries such as the USA and the UK 'much of the recruitment, selection and management of doctoral researchers takes place at the departmental and not the institutional level' and 'there is little direction in recruitment of postgraduate students from the executive of the university' (Mellors-Bourne et al., 2014, p. 8).

Linked to the issue of recruitment and selection, Gardner and Holley (2011) have drawn attention to gatekeeping as a means of restricting 'who has a place in the academy and who does not' (Kosut, 2006, p. 249). This may negatively impact on post-experience applicants lacking an accumulation of academic knowledge and contacts that comes through a linear, continuous progression through the education system (Clark & Corcoran, 1986). Pre-application guidance and workshops have been highlighted as one potential way of addressing this problem. We are aware of the latter being used successfully by at least one private German business school collaborative DBA partner but these practices are not routinely implemented.

The Graduate Management Admission Test® (GMAT®) is an established MBA admissions tool, despite question marks over its efficacy as a predictor of academic success and performance *vis-à-vis* other measures such as work experience (Gropper, 2007). The use of selected admissions tends to follow a trend established by four Ivy League universities as part of attempts to encourage the most talented applicants as defined by standardised general academic abilities that act as 'qualifying evidence'. Gender, cultural, and other biases have been noted to exist in GMAT® and scores have been reported to serve as gatekeepers for business leadership (Aggarwal, Goodell, & Goodell, 2014). In North American business schools, with the proviso that scores cannot be more than five years old, Graduate Record Examinations (GRE) and GMAT® scores tend to be accepted as part of PhD programme applications, although GMAT®

has often traditionally been preferred (Quist, 2011). In their study of PhD programmes in business-to-business marketing, Danneels and Lilien (1998) observed that GMAT® scores were important when making admissions decisions for a high percentage of their research participants; however, they noted that of outside North America GMAT® scores were rarely used in business school PhD admissions and a heavier emphasis was placed on previous academic grades and research interests.

In Europe, the shape of doctoral programmes has evolved in line with the Bologna Declaration and the strengthening of doctoral education across the European Higher Education and Research Areas (EUA, n.d.; Kehm, 2007). This has contributed to a shift away from the requirement of successful completion of a master's degree before embarking on PhD study in Germany. In Finland, a low-entry threshold to doctoral studies has been noted and potential candidate competence is assessed via open applications. There is a lack of data on how this affects graduate schools' ability to meet university targets across different fields of study (Creech, Cooper, Aplin-Kalisz, Maynard, & Baker, 2018). Furthermore, there has been a history of collaboration in student selection for business students between universities that has been threatened by intensified competition for talent (Ahola & Kokko, 2001).

Although candidate-supervisor expectations of intellectual capacity in business and management PhDs have been expressed (Bui, 2014), there is a need to not lose sight of other important considerations at the admissions stage. Chowfla (2019) has argued that graduate schools in business and management need to pay attention to readiness, cohort fit, likelihood of completion and employability in terms of selecting the most suitable applicants. Perhaps surprisingly, until recently, there has been relatively little attention paid to MBA graduates as a potential market for DBA programmes.

The importance of the admissions system on candidate retention should not be overlooked. Kraft, Lamina, Kluckner, Wild, and Prodinger (2013), for example, have reported how a change to the admissions system for Austrian state medical universities, involving the implementation of aptitude tests to guide the selection process, resulted in a significant reduction in the dropout rates for male and female students.

More recently, new approaches to doctoral admissions systems are being explored including the concept of narrative CVs linked to the development of inclusive research cultures (Royal Society, n.d.; UKRI, 2021). This approach is recognised to offer a fairer assessment of candidate strengths and aptitudes, potentially. Holistic file review that considers 'a broad range of characteristics, including both cognitive and non-cognitive qualities, when reviewing applicants' files' has also gained the attention of universities in the USA seeking to diversify graduate programmes admissions procedures (Michel, Belur, Naemi, & Kell, 2019, p. 1). Across Europe, there is increased recognition that recruitment of researchers should take the whole range of experience of the candidates into consideration (Euraxess, n.d.).

Applying to study for a terminal degree is a highly competitive process. In the UK, for example, there has been a rise in the number of doctoral applicants over the last decade (Universities UK, 2017 in Hales, Burns, & Partridge, 2017) at a faster rate than an increase in the number of doctoral programme places. More recently, as a result of COVID-19, we witnessed a contraction or consolidation of supply in recognition of a need to focus on the progress of existing enrolled candidates. We are now beginning to see a return to focusing on doctoral programme growth. Indeed, as Kim and Spencer-Oatley (2021, p. 917) write:

> In the UK there is a national strategic imperative to recruit more PGRs. The UK Council for Graduate Education (UKCGE, 2020) reports that there needs to be a 10.16% rise in postgraduate research enrolments, if the 2027 target of the government's R&D Industrial Strategy is to be met.

It is not unusual to find that programme expansion is accompanied by a strain on resources. In Italy, for example, a restricted number of tenured postdoctoral academic staff positions presents an argument for limiting numbers of doctoral programme places and the use of entrance examinations (Kehm, 2007). In many parts of Europe and former Soviet republics a postdoctoral qualification - Habilitation à diriger des recherches (HDR) - has been required to supervise research. This has linked to the idea of academic research tenure. It has been reported that at Victoria Business School (New Zealand), a dramatic 500% increase in the overall number of PhD applications annually has given rise to concerns about time pressures on academic supervisors (Cooper, 2019). These types of reports indicate that doctoral expansion is not always effectively assisting universities to achieve their strategic goals. Furthermore, findings from 3,435 research supervisors who completed The UK Research Supervision Survey (UKRSS) in 2021 indicate that formal workload allocations for research supervision are not always present, a lack of time is a stressor and impacts on well-being and work/life balance are negative (Clegg & Gower, 2021). Additionally, Kortt et al.'s (2016) examination of the rise and fall of the DBA in Australia drew attention to the importance of DBA supervision quality and governance, particularly in view of a reliance on overseas adjunct doctoral supervisory capacity in collaborative awards.

Research focusing on the doctoral candidate selection process from the perspective of higher education institutions is lacking. The work of Mellors-Bourne et al. (2014, p. 3) remains notable, highlighting the variety and complexity of doctoral programme recruitment and selection processes in terms of:

> the decision-making process and the individuals involved, including the roles played by the potential supervisor, departmental academic panel, senior research academic, research degrees committee, and central admissions.

Variation in the exact roles, power and influence of individuals is noted although the existence of a 'hierarchical chain of approval following a departmental recommendation' is identified with 'the final decision ... rarely with the potential supervisor' (Mellors-Bourne et al., 2014, p. 41).

The idea of gatekeepers in the doctoral candidate recruitment and selection process across disciplines (Chiu, 2015; Gardner & Holley, 2011; Mellors-Bourne et al., 2014; Posselt, 2014; Potvin, Chari, & Hodapp, 2017) is a recurrent theme that potentially impacts upon wider issues of merit and diversity in the academy. As Posselt (2018, p. 497) argues 'Privileging elite academic pedigrees in graduate admissions preserves racial and socioeconomic inequities that many institutions say they wish to reduce'. For business schools, where lack of diversity of faculty has been highlighted as a persistent challenge in many countries, there is a danger that faculty relies on 'a conventional notion of merit that undermines diversity's realization' (Posselt, 2013, p. xii) as a result of entrenched situated judgements. The extent to which faculty should hold power in terms of candidate selection is open to question. In the Turkish context, for example, Alrawadieh and Yazit (2021) have found that the right of PhD candidates to choose their advisors was supported by most faculty members.

In many countries, it is possible to apply to study for a doctorate to more than one university simultaneously. This is often used as a strategy by applicants to secure funding and means that it is difficult to predict conversion between offers and acceptances. Aithal, Kumar, and Revathi (2018) have explained how this can present a specific challenge to private universities, heavily dependent on student fees for revenue, in India. We can also recognise this to be an issue for business schools that operate in a highly competitive marketplace.

From the perspective of applicants, Li, Qi, and Guo (2021) have highlighted the significance of *mian zi*, 'a claimed sense of favourable social self-worth that a person wants others to have of her or him [that] can be enhanced or threatened in any uncertain social situation' (Ting-toomey & Kurogi, 1998, p. 187), on Chinese candidates' selection of overseas PhD programmes. Notably 'university ranking, subject ranking, and supervisor's reputation are regarded as attributes which played an important role in gaining mian zi in the students and their parents' eyes' (Li et al., 2021, p. 9). Based on this, we can envisage how business schools will be mentally compartmentalised into choice sets in the candidate decision-making process. Admissions yield, the percentage of enrolments to unconditional offers, has been noted to be negatively impacted by highly substitutable programmes. Alongside scholarship offers, ranking and prestige appear to be key determinants of potential candidate choice of institution when multiple offers of a doctoral programme place are made. In the context of business schools, ranking systems can present a key challenge to any attempts at repositioning to be an institution of choice.

Retention of Business School Doctorate Candidates

Once doctoral candidates have been recruited, a heavy emphasis is placed on progression and retention. Where doctoral programme places are sponsored, there is understandable funder interest in award completion rates, linked to return-on-investment. Aldoukalee (2013) has reported how a stronger joint approach to monitoring barriers to progression is important when examining Libyan government funding of PhD candidates for studying in Britain and the USA. There is a lack of visible information on the extent to which clawback clauses are written into conditions of PhD scholarships. However, for university faculty on doctorates as part of their continuous professional development (CPD), we acknowledge that PhD fee waivers are sometimes subject to contractual penalties even if the recipient completes the award. For example, the University of Aberystwyth (UK) has stated that:

> Employees who leave the University within 2 years of completing the degree or higher degree/Doctorate agreed under this scheme must pay back 50% of the total course fee within 6 months of leaving the employment of the University.

In some post-1992 universities in the UK, it is not unusual to find business school faculty enrolled in internal doctorate programmes, reflecting a 're-professionalisation' of education and external accreditation (Stoten & Kirkham, 2021) and some of the 'unique circumstances currently being faced in the UK business school sector' (De Vita & Case, 2016, p. 348). As noted by Stoten (2020, p. 13) has stated conscription of faculty to doctoral programmes often results in some degree of 'othering'; 'although research allowances are provided, staff do perceive themselves as very different to PhD students' and as a separate community. However, some commonalities may be found in the experiences of faculty on doctorates *vis-à-vis* part-time doctoral candidates in employment, not least in terms of the range of pressures and stressors that impact on wellbeing and paths to completion. Stoten (2022, p. 17), reflecting on the enrolment of candidates in Dutch and British business school professional doctorates draws attention to 'the frailty of learning and support systems within Higher Education for part-time students enrolled on professional doctorates'. A need to acknowledge the diversity of needs and expectations across different doctoral candidates is highlighted.

In contrast, the idea of reducing the length of the doctorate 'to prevent or reduce drop-out and to provide a more targeted research training' (Kehm, 2007, p. 135) has been mooted in the context of Europe for all doctoral candidates. International concerns over time to PhD completion have been well-documented (Bourke, Holbrook, Lovat, & Farley, 2004; Tamrat & Fetene, 2021; Torka, 2021; Wiley, 2015). In contrast, as acknowledged in Chapter 1, more recently, we have witnessed a lengthening of the registration period of the doctorate in business schools in the USA. This is intended to enhance the employability of candidates, providing a longer time-period to accumulate publications in support of tenured recruitment to academic positions postdoctorate. In short, it represents an action intended to support candidates to compete in (academic) employment. The move also supports the placement of candidates in higher ranking institutions as measured by schemes such as the FT Business School Rankings, a common measure of concern for business schools and potential applicants alongside other ranking systems (Sirkeci & O'Leary, 2022).

Benefits of providing an extension to the DBA have been recognised. In Europe, a one-year post-award programme has been offered as an additional course for DBA completers by the French Foundation for Management Education (FNEGE), Business Science Institute (BSI) Luxembourg, and Bordeaux (IAE). This 'added extra' has been aimed at practitioners qualified with a DBA aspiring to develop further academic skills postdoctorate. Speaking of the motivations behind the programme Emeritus Professor Michel Kalika (BSI

Luxembourg, 2021) argues that it is in response to latent demand and recognition that the main purpose of the DBA is to create impact (although the Post-DBA programme is also offered to graduates of PhDs in business and management). It attracted a €150 application fee and €4,900 tuition fee in the 2021–2022 academic year. Notably, there will also be accrued benefits from ranked journal publications to affiliated universities (and individual professors). Nevertheless, the course may be acknowledged as an innovative offer.

However, the idea of extended training sits alongside challenges in supporting doctoral candidates to completion of their in-programme doctoral training, especially in countries where there are two phases of the doctorate (e.g. the MRes plus PhD model often referred to as the 1+3 model or structured assessments followed by the thesis). The term 'all but thesis' or 'all but dissertation' (ABD) has been used as a 'pseudo degree classification' in reference to the partial completion of the doctorate by a high number of candidates in the USA (Kehm, 2007; Wilson, 1965 as cited in Mah, 1986). Similar exit awards are notable for professional doctorates like the DBA in the UK, although they tend to map to existing validated qualifications, for example, the MProf. In Sweden, Spain and Russia, intermediary degrees such as the licentiate and Diploma of Advanced Studies are also used to signal completion of some parts of doctoral training. Perhaps most significantly the introduction of 'doctorandus' as an honorary title in the Netherlands to denote being part of a doctoral programme at some stage but not completing the award has been highlighted (Kehm, 2007). Yet, around the world, many doctoral candidates leave their programmes of study without any formal acknowledgement of accumulated training.

The decision by doctoral candidates to leave their programmes of study is complex, multifaceted and complicated by virtue of the length of the doctorate and life stages of candidates *vis-à-vis* other university degrees. Despite, the presence of progression points in PhDs and professional doctorate programmes at most universities, Greener (2021, p. 2) relates how '[i]n 2019, in a survey of 50,600 PGR students [in the UK], more than a quarter said they had considered leaving their course (Williams, 2019)'. In Estonia, it has been reported that fewer than one in three PhD candidates complete their doctorates (Vassil & Solvak, 2012) and as Greener (2021, p. 3) notes:

> Spronken-Smith et al. (2018) in a recent study cite US completion rates, i.e., the proportion of registered candidates who submit and are awarded their doctoral degrees, of around 50%, while Canadian completion rates varied within a range of 40 and 83%, Australian rates between 62 and 72% and UK rates between 70 and 87%. Bekova (2019) mentions dropout or attrition rates of 87% in Russia in 2017 and a 36% completion rate in 2018.

Skakni (2018) draws attention to the insufficiency of intellectual capabilities to predict or determine progression which brings into question the efficacy of admissions testing and Herman (2011) stresses a lack of shared understanding of reasons for doctoral attrition between candidates and PhD programme leaders.

The extent to which doctoral candidate withdrawal receives scrutiny is questionable and often reflects a lack of knowledge of or intelligence on institutional PGR populations (Ribau & Alves, 2018).

However, as Greener (2021) notes in the context of business schools, non-completion and withdrawal may be linked to social isolation and the support of formalised initiatives to provide peer mentoring and critical friends can have positive impacts. Indeed, highlighting the influence of internal institutional factors on doctoral-level attrition, Rigler, Bowlin, Sweat, Watts, and Throne (2017) have drawn attention to three constructs affecting candidate persistence to completion alongside commonly cited financial considerations: chair agency and chair–candidate relationship; candidate socialisation and support systems; candidate preparedness. Social integration has been particularly flagged as an issue facing part-time and online doctoral candidates in relation to attrition in the USA (Fraenza & Rye, 2021; Turner, 2021). This is a pertinent issue in terms of a notable increase in online business and management doctorate programmes globally and a recent need for many doctoral programmes to rely more heavily on private online candidate workspaces during COVID-19, which bring challenges around engagement, communication and isolation (Ames, Berman, & Casteel, 2018).

Kis et al.'s (2022, p. 2) exploration of PhD attrition in the context of a Dutch university highlights the impact of 'a less healthy research environment (including experiences with unethical supervision, questionable practices and barriers to responsible research)' on candidate considerations to leave PhD positions and academia as a whole. The idea of 'performativity pressures' has been put forward by Raineri (2013) and attention has been drawn to a one-way 'socialization process leading to membership in the business academic community' (Raineri, 2015, p. 99) reinforcing a set of dominant scholarly values and practices. The retention of candidates on doctoral programmes may be seen to relate negatively with institutionalised cultural norms and expectations of candidate-supervisor relations based on the notion of a 'traditional doctoral learner' that perhaps hinder the raising of concerns from candidates, particularly those from high power-distance cultures (Greener, 2021).

In spite of attempts to predict candidate aptitude at recruitment and selection stages withdrawal from the doctorate can also occur at the request of the university, typically based on 'poor candidate performance'. Where doctoral candidates are contracted to the university or where little or no selectivity exists at recruitment stage (such as in Austria or at Swiss State Universities), it is extremely difficult to remove candidates from programmes. Little has been documented about the removal of candidates from doctoral programmes pre-examination stage. Bebba and Al-Hawary (2017) have provided a refreshingly open discussion of the realities of doctoral programmes management in Algeria where, although the Ministry of Higher Education determines the number of candidates admitted to the country's doctoral schools each year, supervisory capacity influences individual doctoral school candidate numbers. Late submission of the PhD sometimes results in removal of the PhD research programme from the candidate on the grounds of freeing up a supervisor to take on new candidates (who may choose to study with a specific supervisor) and avoiding the burdening of supervisors with excessive workloads. Here, it appears that the onus of completing on time is placed very much on the candidate. However, in many universities, we note that doctoral completions are used as a measure of supervisor capability and success and, ultimately, as a marker of quality of provision. Speaking of the progression experiences of PhD candidates in industrial engineering and management in the context of Finland, Martinsuo and Turkulainen (2011, p. 117) note:

> time committed matters and this needs to be made very clear for new doctoral students: no matter what support the student gets, to progress in research students need to be willing and able to devote significant time.

The importance of the development of realistic applicant expectations throughout the recruitment process cannot be over-emphasised. Additionally, the linking of completion with 'persistence' by many researchers reveals a need to acknowledge assumed candidate ability to possess and maintain mental strength throughout the doctorate. This is an area that business school doctoral programmes are advised to pay more attention to give the importance of a combination of candidate commitment and institutional support to achieve doctoral completion. As McCray and Joseph-Richard (2021, p. 1) remark:

> individual business schools should review their training curriculum for doctoral students to prevent over-reliance on the supervisory team and offer more formal training on managing mental well-being.

More generally, there is scope to recognise that career and professional development support is important to empower the researcher at all stages of the doctorate, including during recruitment.

Changes During the COVID-19 Pandemic and Future Prospects

Prior to the COVID-19 global pandemic, international student mobility gained attention as a key determinant for business school programmes in terms of application volumes at graduate school level. Removal of barriers to international mobility in countries such as China and the former Soviet Union resulted in 'a number of excellent students [going] abroad to study for foreign doctoral degrees' (Shen et al., 2016, p. 333). However, COVID-19 lockdowns and tense geopolitical relations changed study abroad options and student flows. The flow of Chinese students is expected to peak by 2027 (Lem, 2022a), with students from India and Vietnam gaining momentum. There are also concerns about antagonistic US policies which are deterring Chinese students from applying to study in the USA (Nietzel, 2022) with issues over sanctions and intellectual property. Clearly, Russia's war on Ukraine and the cost-of-living crisis caused by geopolitical disruptions have altered recruitment patterns. We note, for example, that 2022–2023

PhD applications to Kyiv-Mohyla Business School (Ukraine) notably increased in line with a surge in PhD applications nationally, mainly from men (Lem, 2022b).

Post-COVID-19, we are witnessing an increase in online doctorate programmes and this trend is visible in business and management, where potential to pass cost savings in delivery on to candidates, and potentially make doctoral education more accessible, has been celebrated. The Swiss School of Business Management, Geneva has taken advantage of demand for remote delivery, advertising 'Doctorate at half campus cost' and encouraging referral feedback for its Global DBA through financial incentives: 'Refer someone you know and receive Amazon.com vouchers worth 49 USD!' (upGrad Europe, n.d., p. 1). The remote model enables the institution to draw on faculty from across Europe and the USA. For this award, minimum entry requirements are set at 'Master's Degree (or equivalent) **or** 5+ years work experience'.

A pedagogic shift to distance education across all sectors of higher education has generated debates over quality and effectiveness of remote programmes (Irawan, 2021). This shift has stimulated interest in assuring excellence in online programme design and delivery (Myers, Singletary, Rogers, Ellor, & Barham, 2019). Speaking of an unprecedented pivot to distance education during the COVID-19 pandemic, Fast, Semenog, Vovk, Buhaichuk, and Golya (2022, p. 73) emphasised the importance of institutional readiness to support PhD learners, requiring 'a system approach to the development of the online environment of educational institutions, development of skills and abilities to use educational content'.

Less-focused attention, however, has been paid to some of the associated challenges that may arise linked to the applications process for online doctoral learning and the readiness of learners (Cigdem, 2014; Hashim & Tasir, 2014; McVay Lynch, 2001) in a PGR context. In their study of Thai PhD candidates, Wattakiecharoen and Nilsook (2013) found motivation to be the least promising aspect of e-learning readiness. There has been a tendency for discussions of online learning to be linked to the concept of lifelong learning. These bring with them challenges for those who are returning to academic study post-experience when the decision to apply is often flanked by multiple stakeholder interests.

Summary

Key points that we highlight in relation to recruitment, selection and retention in business and management doctorates are:

- The extent to which recruitment to business school doctorates is targeted strategically is open to question. Exogenous forces affect who applies to which programmes and why. A competitive international environment in which the programmes sit adds complications.
- Lack of systematic diversity and inclusion practices threatens the ability of business school doctoral programmes to attract a broader, optimal talent pool.
- Despite an appetite for internationalising business school doctorate programmes, fees and funding structures do not always support the mobility of self-funded international candidates in particular.

- PGR recruitment is often seen as an academic capacity-building activity which may reproduce inequalities in the academy and society more broadly.
- The business doctorate may be positioned as a professional development and career management opportunity but access depends on applicants' existing cultural capital.
- There appears to be little acknowledgement of potential barriers to doctoral application that relate to lack of equity of opportunity across a full spectrum of personal characteristics
- There is value in exploring further the idea that 'students do not want to be retained but to persist' (Lekhetho, 2022, p. 25). This is especially the case in view of the need to recognise the demand-side forces that contribute to business school doctorate completion.

Questions you might like to consider:

- Is there an opportunity for strategic developments such as the EU's Research Competency Framework to inform recruitment and selection practices for the doctorate beyond a European context?
- Where is career and professional development support available to assist potential applicants in decisions to apply for a business school doctorate?
- How does the work of professional bodies and chartered status in business and management align with the doctorate as career development?
- To what extent are doctoral admissions processes sympathetic to emerging trends including an increase of neurodiversity and mental health disclosures amongst researchers who are at an early career stage?

References

AACSB. (2022). Doctoral business programs. Retrieved from https://www.aacsb.edu/learners/journey/doctorate. Accessed on March 29, 2023.

AACSB International. (2013). *The promise of business doctoral education – Setting the pace for innovation, sustainability, relevance, and quality*. Tampa, FL: AACSB.

Aggarwal, R., Goodell, J. E., & Goodell, J. W. (2014). Culture, gender, and GMAT scores: Implications for corporate ethics. *Journal of Business Ethics*, *123*, 125–143.

Aguinis, H., Bradley, K. J., & Brodersen, A. (2014). Industrial–organizational psychologists in business schools: Brain drain or eye opener? *Industrial and Organizational Psychology: Perspectives on Science and Practice*, *7*(3), 284–303.

Ahola, S., & Kokko, A. (2001). Finding the best possible students: Student selection and its problems in the field of business. *Journal of Higher Education Policy and Management*, *23*(2), 191–203.

Aithal, P. S., Kumar, A., & Revathi, R. (2018). Investigation of business strategies in higher education service model of selected private universities in India. *International Journal of Computational Research and Development (IJCRD)*, *3*(1), 77–100.

Akay, A. (2008). A renaissance in engineering PhD education. *European Journal of Engineering Education*, *33*(4), 403–413.

Aldoukalee, S. A. (2014). *An investigation into the challenges faced By Libyan PhD students in Britain: [A study of the three universities in Manchester and Salford].* Salford: University of Salford.

Alexander, L. (2020, March 9). Employer sponsorship – *Why your employer should invest in you.* University of London. Retrieved from https://london.ac.uk/news-opinion/london-connection/top-tip/why-your-employer-should-invest-you. Accessed on December 10, 2022.

Alkubaidi, M., & Alzhrani, N. (2020). "We are back": Reverse culture shock among Saudi scholars after doctoral study abroad. *SAGE Open, 10*(4), 2158244020970555.

Allen, C. M., Smyth, E. M., & Wahlstrom, M. (2002). Responding to the field and to the academy: Ontario's evolving PhD. *Higher Education Research & Development, 21*(2), 203–214.

Alrawadieh, D. D., & Yazit, H. (2021) Doktora deneyiminin öğrenciler ve akademisyenler açısından değerlendirilmesi. *Balıkesir Üniversitesi Sosyal Bilimler Enstitüsü Dergisi, 24*(46), 1229–1245.

Amdam, R. P. (2020). Creating the new executive: Postwar executive education and socialization into the managerial elite. *Management & Organizational History, 15*(2), 106–122.

Ames, C., Berman, R., & Casteel, A. (2018). A preliminary examination of doctoral student retention factors in private online workspaces. *International Journal of Doctoral Studies, 13*(1), 79–107.

Anastasia, C. M., & Burrington, D. D. (2022). Scholar to practitioner: A new paradigm for research chairs. In Information Resources Management Association (IRMA) (Ed.), *Research anthology on doctoral student professional development* (pp. 210–231). Hershey, PA: IGI Global.

Archer, W. (2016). *International postgraduate research students: The UK's competitive advantage.* London: The UK HE International Unit. Retrieved from https://www.universitiesuk.ac.uk/International/news/Pages/uk-competitive-advantage.aspx. Accessed on March 2, 2022.

Armsby, P. M., Costley, C., & Cranfield, S. (2018). The design of doctorate curricula for practising professionals. *Studies in Higher Education, 43*(12), 2226–2237.

Bahtilla, M. (2022). Supervisory feedback: Supervisors' reasons for not giving timely feedback. *Innovations in Education and Teaching International,* 1–12.

Bar, D. A., Wanat, S., & Gonzalez, M. (2007). Racial and ethnic differences in students' selection of a doctoral program to attend from those offering admission: The case of biomedical sciences. *Journal of Women and Minorities in Science and Engineering, 13*(1), 23–36.

Bekova, S., & Dzhafarova, Z. (2019). Who is happy in doctoral programs: The connection between employment and learning outcomes of PhD students. *Вопросы образования, 1*(eng), 87–108.

BCU. (2022). Doctor of Business Administration (part time) – DBA. Retrieved from https://www.bcu.ac.uk/courses/doctorate-in-business-administration-dba-2022-23. Accessed on April 19, 2022.

Bebba, I., & Al-Hawary, S. I. S. (2017). The reality of Algerian universities doctoral students configuration. *Global Journal of Management and Business Research, 17*(G3), 21–33.

Bekova, S. (2021). Does employment during doctoral training reduce the PhD completion rate? *Studies in Higher Education, 46*(6), 1068–1080.

Bekova, S. K., & Terentev, E. A. (2020). Doctoral education: international experience and opportunities for its implementation in Russia. *Vysshee obrazovanie v Rossii [Higher Education in Russia], 29*(6), 51–64.

Belasco, A. S., Trivette, M. J., & Webber, K. L. (2014). Advanced degrees of debt: Analyzing the patterns and determinants of graduate student borrowing. *The Review of Higher Education, 37*(4), 469–497.

Bennett, M. (2021). PhD study, for free? – 14 Countries that charge very little (or nothing!) for doctoral degrees. *Find-a-PhD*. Retrieved from https://www.findaphd.com/advice/blog/5164/phd-study-for-free-14-countries-that-charge-very-little-or-nothing-for-doctoral-degrees. Accessed on April 19, 2022.

Bernstein, B. L., Evans, B., Fyffe, J., Halai, N., Hall, F. L., Jensen, H. S., & Ortega, S. (2014). The continuing evolution of the research doctorate. In M. Nerad & B. Evans (Eds.), *Globalization and its impacts on the quality of PhD education* (pp. 5–30). Amsterdam: Brill Sense.

Billot, J., King, V., Smith, J., & Clouder, L. (2021). Borderlanders: Academic staff being and becoming doctoral students. *Teaching in Higher Education*, *26*(3), 438–453.

Bourke, S., Holbrook, A., Lovat, T., & Farley, P. (2004, November). Attrition, completion and completion times of PhD candidates. In *AARE annual conference,* Melbourne (Vol. 28, pp. 2–14).

Breese, R., Issa, S., & Tresidder, R. (2021, October). Impact on management practice after completing the DBA. In *Proceedings of the eleventh international conference on engaged management scholarship-EMS*, Miami, FL.

Breier, M., Herman, C., & Towers, L. (2020). Doctoral rites and liminal spaces: Academics without PhDs in South Africa and Australia. *Studies in Higher Education*, *45*(4), 834–846.

BSI Luxembourg. (2021). Post-DBA Program. Retrieved from https://en.business-science-institute.com/post-dba-program/. Accessed on August 8, 2022.

Bui, H. T. (2014). Student–supervisor expectations in the doctoral supervision process for business and management students. *Business and Management Education in HE*, *1*(1), 12–27.

Burkholder, G. J. (2022). Mentoring doctoral students in a distance learning environment. In D. Stein, H. R. Glazer, & C. Wanstreet (Eds.), *Driving innovation with for-profit adult higher education online institutions* (pp. 142–172). Hershey, PA: IGI Global.

Butler-Rees, A., & Robinson, N. (2020). Encountering precarity, uncertainty and everyday anxiety as part of the postgraduate research journey. *Emotion, Space and Society*, *37*, 100743.

Byrne, J., Jørgensen, T., & Loukkola, T. (2013). *Quality assurance in doctoral education: Results of the ARDE Project*. Brussels: European University Association.

Cabrera, G. M., Mariel, P., & Abadía, L. K. (2022). Postgraduate study preferences of business administration and economics students from Colombia, Ecuador, and Spain. *International Journal of Educational Research*, *112*, 101935.

Chen, L. H. (2008). Internationalization or international marketing? Two frameworks for understanding international students' choice of Canadian universities. *Journal of Marketing for Higher Education*, *18*(1), 1–33.

Chiu, P. H. P., & Corrigan, P. (2019). A study of graduate teaching assistants' self-efficacy in teaching: Fits and starts in the first triennium of teaching. *Cogent Education*, *6*(1), 1579964.

Chiu, Y. L. T. (2015). Personal statement in PhD applications: Gatekeepers' evaluative perspectives. *Journal of English for Academic Purposes*, *17*, 63–73.

Chiu, Y. L. T. (2019). 'It's a match, but is it a good fit?': Admissions tutors' evaluation of personal statements for PhD study. *Oxford Review of Education*, *45*(1), 136–150.

Chowfla, S. (2019). The changing nature of 'selection' in graduate management education. *AACSB*, July 2. Retrieved from https://www.aacsb.edu/insights/articles/2019/07/changing-nature-selection-graduate-management-education. Accessed on March 24, 2023.

Cigdem, H. (2014). Effects of students' characteristics on online learning readiness: A vocational college example. *Turkish Online Journal of Distance Education*, *15*(3), 80–93.

Clark, S. M., & Corcoran, M. (1986). Perspectives on the professional socialization of women faculty: A case of accumulative disadvantage? *The Journal of Higher Education*, *57*(1), 20–43.

Clegg, K., & Gower, O. (2021) PhD supervisors need better support, recognition and reward. *WONKHE*, October 8. Retrieved from https://wonkhe.com/blogs/phd-supervisors-need-better-support-recognition-and-reward/. Accessed on March 23, 2023.

Cooper, P. (2019). *A multi-framing approach to analysing the effectiveness of the PhD application process at the victoria business school.* Master's thesis. Te Herenga Waka – Victoria University of Wellington.

Costley, C., & Abukari, A. (2015). The impact of work-based research projects at post-graduate level. *Journal of Work-Applied Management, 7*(1), 3–14.

CRAC. (2013, September). *The wider benefits of international higher education in the UK.* BIS Research Paper Number 128. Department for Business, Innovation & Skills.

Cranfield School of Management. (2022). Executive DBA. Retrieved from https://www.cranfield.ac.uk/som/research-degrees/executive-dba. Accessed on March 24, 2023.

Creech, C., Cooper, D., Aplin-Kalisz, C., Maynard, G., & Baker, S. (2018). Examining admission factors predicting success in a doctor of nursing practice program. *Journal of Nursing Education, 57*(1), 49–52.

Crowley-Vigneau, A., Baykov, A. A., & Kalyuzhnova, E. (2022). "That'll teach them": Investigating the soft power conversion model through the case of Russian higher education. *Vysshee obrazovanie v Rossii [Higher Education in Russia], 31*(1), 120–140.

Cuschieri, S. (2021). The initial steps towards a PhD. *To Do or Not to Do a PhD? Insight and Guidance from a Public Health PhD Graduate* (pp. 9–14).

D'Aveni, R. A. (1996). A multiple-constituency, status-based approach to interorganizational mobility of faculty and input–output competition among top business schools. *Organization Science, 7*(2), 166–189.

Danneels, E., & Lilien, G. L. (1998). Doctoral programs in business-to-business marketing: Status and prospects. *Journal of Business-to-Business Marketing, 5*(1–2), 7–34.

Darley, W. K. (2021). Doctoral education in business and management in Africa: Challenges and imperatives in policies and strategies .*International Journal of Management Education, 19*(2), 100504.

Davies, J., McGregor, F., & Horan, M. (2019). Autoethnography and the doctorate in business administration: Personal, practical and scholarly impacts. *International Journal of Management Education, 17*(2), 201–213.

Davies, J., Palmer, N., Braccia, E., Clegg, K., & Smith, M. (2021). Supporting doctoral programmes during a global pandemic: Crisis as opportunity. *EFMD Global Focus, 1*(15), 20–24.

De Novellis, M. (2018). Russia and China are building a business school empire in the East. *Business Because*, July 31. Retrieved from https://www.businessbecause.com/news/in-the-news/5409/russia-china-building-business-school-empire-in-the-east. Accessed on November 10, 2022.

De Onzoño, S. I., & Carmona, S. (2007). The changing business model of B-schools. *Journal of Management Development, 26*(1), 22–32.

Deleuze, G., & Guattari, F. (1987). *A thousand plateaus: Capitalism and schizophrenia.* London: Continuum.

Denecke, D., Feaster, K., Okahana, H., Allum, J., & Stone, K. (2016). *Financial education: Developing high impact programs for graduate and undergraduate students.* Washington, DC: Council of Graduate Schools.

Denisova-Schmidt, E., de Wit, H., & Wan, X. (2020). Ethical concerns on the use of agents in international student recruitment. In E. Denisova-Schmidt (Ed.), *Corruption in higher education* (pp. 82–87). Amsterdam: Brill.

Douglas, A. S. (2021). Dimensions of fit for doctoral candidates: Supporting an academic identity. *Research Papers in Education, 37*(6) 1–21.

Ecton, W. G., Bennett, C. T., Nienhusser, H. K., Castillo-Montoya, M., & Dougherty, S. M. (2021). If you fund them, will they come? Implications from a PhD fellowship program on racial/ethnic student diversity. *AERA Open, 7*, 23328584211040485.

Engwall, L. (2000). Foreign role models and standardisation in Nordic business education. *Scandinavian Journal of Management, 16*(1), 1–24.

Elliot, D. L., Bengtsen, S. S., Guccione, K., & Kobayashi, S. (2020). A 'Doctoral Learning Ecology Model'. In D. L. Elliot, S. S. Bengsten, K. Guccione, & S. Kobayashi (Eds.), *The hidden curriculum in doctoral education* (pp. 97–111). Springer.

ESCE – INSEEC: IFG Executive (2020) DBA (Doctorate of Business Administration) Management. Retrieved from https://www.ifgexecutive.com/product/management-general-international-executive-dba/. Accessed on July 23, 2023.

Erwee, R., & Perry, C. (2018). Examination of doctoral theses: Research about the process and proposed procedures. In R. Erwee, M. Harmes, M. Harmes, P. Danaher, & F. Padró (Eds.), *Postgraduate education in higher education* (pp. 359–374). Springer Nature.

Estrada, R. (2011). *Application trends survey, 2011. Survey report*. Reston, VA: Graduate Management Admission Council.

EUA. (n.d.). Doctoral education. Retrieved from https://eua.eu/issues/13:doctoral-education.html. Accessed on March 23, 2023.

Euraxess. (n.d.). The code of conduct for recruitment. Retrieved from https://euraxess.ec.europa.eu/jobs/charter/code. Accessed on March 23, 2023.

European Funding Guide. (n.d.). European funding guide. Retrieved from european-funding-guide.eu. Accessed on March 23, 2023.

Fast, O., Semenog, O., Vovk, M., Buhaichuk, N., & Golya, G. (2022). Examining the practices and challenges of distance education of PhD candidates in the context of COVID-19. *Journal of Learning for Development, 9*(1), 73–88.

Forray, J. M., & Goodnight, J. E. (2014). Recruiting business PhDs: US minority motives and concerns. *Equality, Diversity and Inclusion, 33*(1), 2–41.

Fraenza, C., & Rye, T. (2021). Supporting the social integration of online doctoral students through peer mentoring. *Learning Assistance Review, 26*(1), 133–161

Friedrich-Nel, H., & MacKinnon, J. (2019). The quality culture in doctoral education: Establishing the critical role of the doctoral supervisor. *Innovations in Education and Teaching International, 56*(2), 140–149.

Fry, G., Tress, B., & Tress, G. (2005). PhD students and integrative research. In B. Tress, G. Tres, G. Fry, & P. Opdam (Eds.), *From landscape research to landscape planning; Aspects of integration, education and application* (Vol. 12, pp. 193–205). New York, NY: Springer.

Gardner, S. K., & Holley, K. A. (2011). "Those invisible barriers are real": The progression of first-generation students through doctoral education. *Equity & Excellence in Education, 44*(1), 77–92.

Gatfield, T., & Alpert, F. (2002). The supervisory management styles model. Quality conversations. In *Proceedings of the 25th HERDSA annual conference*, Perth, WA (pp. 263–273).

Gravett, K. (2021). Disrupting the doctoral journey: Re-imagining doctoral pedagogies and temporal practices in higher education. *Teaching in Higher Education, 26*(3), 293–305.

Gopaul, B. (2011). Distinction in doctoral education: Using Bourdieu's tools to assess the socialization of doctoral students. *Equity & Excellence in Education, 44*(1), 10–21.

Gorup, M., & Laufer, M. (2020). More than a case of a few bad apples: When relationships between supervisors and doctoral researchers go wrong. *Elephant in the Lab*, November 30. Retrieved from https://elephantinthelab.org/when-relationships-between-supervisors-and-doctoral-researchers-go-wrong/. Accessed on January 23, 2023.

Greener, S. L. (2021). Non-supervisory support for doctoral students in business and management: A critical friend. *The International Journal of Management Education, 19*(2), 100463.

Greer, T., Johnson, O., & Delk, D. (2021). Graduate enhancement for minority studies (GEMS): Case study of a graduate student recruitment program. *College Student Journal, 55*(4), 371–386.

Grier, S. A., & Poole, S. M. (2020). Reproducing inequity: The role of race in the business school faculty search. *Journal of Marketing Management, 36*(13–14), 1190–1222.

Gropper, D. M. (2007). Does the GMAT matter for executive MBA students? Some empirical evidence. *Academy of Management Learning & Education, 6*(2), 206–216.

Grote, D., Patrick, A., Lyles, C., Knight, D., Borrego, M., & Alsharif, A. (2021). STEM doctoral students' skill development: Does funding mechanism matter? *International Journal of STEM Education, 8*(1), 1–19.

Guccione, K. (2016). *Trust me! Building and breaking professional trust in doctoral student–supervisor relationships.* SRHE annual research conference, December, London.

Hales, S., Burns, D. W., & Partridge, B. (2019). *Getting on to a PhD.* In H. Walton (Ed.), *A guide for psychology postgraduates* (pp. 12–18).

Hannam-Swain, S. (2018). The additional labour of a disabled PhD student. *Disability & Society, 33*(1), 138–142.

Hardwicke, N., Mahlberg, T., & Riemer, K. (2018). The existential doctorate: Liminality in industry-academic doctoral partnerships. *ACIS 2018 Proceedings.* 71. https://aisel.aisnet.org/acis2018/71

Hashim, H., & Tasir, Z. (2014, April). E-learning readiness: A literature review. In *International conference on teaching and learning in computing and engineering* (pp. 267–271). IEEE.

HEC Montréal. (2022). PhD in administration. Retrieved from https://www.hec.ca/en/programs/phd/. Accessed on March 15, 2022.

Herman, C. (2011). Obstacles to success-doctoral student attrition in South Africa. *Perspectives in Education, 29*(1), 40–52.

Horta, H., & Li, H. (2022). Nothing but publishing: The overriding goal of PhD students in mainland China, Hong Kong, and Macau. *Studies in Higher Education*, 1–20. https://doi.org/10.1080/03075079.2022.2131764

Hu, D. (2021). Understanding transnational academic migration: US doctorate recipients' choices of returning to Chinese academe. *International Journal for Educational and Vocational Guidance, 21*(3), 653–669.

Huss, M. T., Randall, B. A., Patry, M., Davis, S. F., & Hansen, D. J. (2002). Factors influencing self-rated preparedness for graduate school: A survey of graduate students. *Teaching of Psychology, 29*(4), 275–281.

Irawan, N. (2021, April). Does online learning work for international students? In *2nd Annual conference on social science and humanities* (pp. 366–370). Amsterdam: Atlantis Press.

Ishiyama, J. T., & Hopkins, V. M. (2003). Assessing the impact of a graduate school preparation program on first-generation, low-income college students at a public liberal arts university. *Journal of College Student Retention: Research, Theory & Practice, 4*(4), 393–405.

Jepsen, D. M., Varhegyi, M. M., & Edwards, D. (2012). Academics' attitudes towards PhD students' teaching: Preparing research higher degree students for an academic career. *Journal of Higher Education Policy and Management, 34*(6), 629–645.

Johnson, R. L., Coleman, R. A., Batten, N. H., Hallsworth, D., & Spencer, E. E. (2020). *The quiet crisis of PhDs and COVID-19: Reaching the financial tipping point.* Durham, NC: Research Square.

Jones, M. (2018). Contemporary trends in professional doctorates. *Studies in Higher Education, 43*(5), 814–825.

Kantola, J. (2008). 'Why do all the women disappear?' Gendering processes in a political science department. *Gender, Work & Organization, 15*(2), 202–225.

Kehm, B. M. (2007). Quo vadis doctoral education? New European approaches in the context of global changes. *European Journal of Education, 42*(3), 307–319.

Kehm, B. M., Shin, J. C., & Jones, G. A. (2018). Conclusion: Doctoral education and training–A global convergence? In J. C. Shin, B. M. Kehm, & G. A. Jones (Eds.), *Doctoral education for the knowledge society* (pp. 237–255). Cham: Springer.

Kidman, J., Manathunga, C., & Cornforth, S. (2017). Intercultural PhD supervision: Exploring the hidden curriculum in a social science faculty doctoral programme. *Higher Education Research & Development, 36*(6), 1208–1221.

Kim, K. H., & Spencer-Oatey, H. (2021). Enhancing the recruitment of postgraduate researchers from diverse countries: Managing the application process. *Higher Education, 82*(5), 917–935.

Kis, A., Tur, E. M., Lakens, D., Vaesen, K., & Houkes, W. (2022). Leaving academia: PhD attrition and unhealthy research environments. *Plos One, 17*(10), e0274976.

Kosut, M. (2006). Professorial capital: Blue-collar reflections on class, culture, and the academy. *Cultural Studies-Critical Methodologies, 6*(2), 245–262.

Kot, F. C., & Hendel, D. D. (2012). Emergence and growth of professional doctorates in the United States, United Kingdom, Canada and Australia: A comparative analysis. *Studies in Higher Education, 37*(3), 345–364.

Kortt, M. A., Pervan, S. J., & Hogan, O. (2016). The rise and fall of the Australian DBA. *Education+ Training, 58*(4), 390–408.

Kraft, H. G., Lamina, C., Kluckner, T., Wild, C., & Prodinger, W. M. (2013). Paradise lost or paradise regained? Changes in admission system affect academic performance and drop-out rates of medical students. *Medical Teacher, 35*(5), e1123–e1129.

Landrum, R. E. (2010). Intent to apply to graduate school: Perceptions of senior year psychology majors. *North American Journal of Psychology, 12*(2), 243.

Lee, A. (2008). How are doctoral students supervised? Concepts of doctoral research supervision. *Studies in Higher Education, 33*(3), 267–281.

Lem, P. (2022a). Chinese student flows tipped to peak within five years. *Times Higher Education*, May 18. Retrieved from https://www.timeshighereducation.com/news/chinese-student-flows-tipped-peak-within-five-years/. Accessed on January 4, 2023.

Lem, P. (2022b). Ukrainian universities see surge in PhD applications. *Times Higher Education*, August 19. Retrieved from https://www.timeshighereducation.com/news/ukrainian-universities-see-surge-phd-applications/. Accessed on February 27, 2023.

Lekhetho, M. (2022). Postgraduate students' perceptions of support services rendered by a distance learning institution. *International Journal of Higher Education, 11*(7), 1–24.

Li, F. S., Qi, H., & Guo, Q. (2021). Factors influencing Chinese tourism students' choice of an overseas PhD program. *Journal of Hospitality, Leisure, Sport & Tourism Education, 29*, 100286.

Li, W., & Collins, C. S. (2014). Chinese doctoral student socialization in the United States: A qualitative study. In *FIRE: forum for international research in education* (Vol. 1, No. 2, pp. 32–57). Bethlehem, PA: Lehigh University Library and Technology Services.

Mah, D. M. (1986). *The process of doctoral candidate attrition: A study of the all but dissertation (ABD) phenomenon.* Ph.D. thesis, University of Washington, Washington, DC.

Mahn, H., & John-Steiner, V. (2008). The gift of confidence: A Vygotskian view of emotions. In G. Wells & G. Claxton (Eds.), *Learning for life in the 21st century: Sociocultural perspectives on the future of education* (pp. 46–58).

Mandalawi, S. M., Henderson, R., Huijser, H., Dr, & Kek, M. Y. C. A. (2022). Issues of belonging, pedagogy and learning in doctoral study at a distance. *Journal of University Teaching & Learning Practice, 19*(4), 15.

Martinsuo, M., & Turkulainen, V. (2011). Personal commitment, support and progress in doctoral studies. *Studies in Higher Education, 36*(1), 103–120.

Mattocks, K., & Briscoe-Palmer, S. (2016). Diversity, inclusion, and doctoral study: Challenges facing minority PhD students in the United Kingdom. *European Political Science, 15*, 476–492.

McCoy, D. L., & Winkle-Wagner, R. (2015). Bridging the divide: Developing a scholarly habitus for aspiring graduate students through summer bridge programs participation. *Journal of College Student Development, 56*(5), 423–439.

McAlpine, L., & Lucas, L. (2011). Different places, different specialisms: Similar questions of doctoral identities under construction. *Teaching in Higher Education, 16*(6), 695–706.

McCray, J., & Joseph-Richard, P. (2021). Doctoral students' well-being in United Kingdom business schools: A survey of personal experience and support mechanisms. *The International Journal of Management Education, 19*(2), 100490.

McLaughlan, T. (2021). Facilitating factors in cultivating diverse online communities of practice: A case of international teaching assistants during the COVID-19 crisis. *The International Journal of Information and Learning Technology, 38*(2), 177–195.

McVay Lynch, M. (2001). *How to be a successful distance education student: Learning on the Internet.* New York, NY: Prentice Hall.

Mellors-Bourne, R., Metcalfe, J., Pearce, E., & Hooley, T. (2014). Understanding the recruitment and selection of postgraduate researchers by English higher education institutions. Report to HEFCE by CRAC/Vitae and iCeGS. Retrieved from http://www.ukcge.ac.uk/Search/Default.aspx?q=Understanding±the±recruitment±and±selection±of±postgraduate±researchers±by±English±higher±education±institutions. Accessed on September 30, 2020.

Mellors-Bourne, R., Robinson, C., & Metcalfe, J. (2016). *Provision of professional doctorates in English HE institutions.* Cambridge: Careers Research and Advisory Centre.

Michel, R. S., Belur, V., Naemi, B., & Kell, H. J. (2019). Graduate admissions practices: A targeted review of the literature. *ETS Research Report Series, 2019*(1), 1–18.

Minefee, I., Rabelo, V. C., Stewart, O. J. C., IV, & Young, N. C. J. (2018). Repairing leaks in the pipeline: A social closure perspective on underrepresented racial/ethnic minority recruitment and retention in business schools. *Academy of Management Learning & Education, 17*(1), 79–95.

Mogaji, E., Adamu, N., & Nguyen, N. P. (2021). Stakeholders shaping experiences of self-funded international PhD students in UK business schools. *International Journal of Management Education, 19*(3), 100543.

Morgan, J. (2016). Cambridge plans to charge £230K fees for business doctorate course for world's 'most senior business leaders' will cost 'gigantic' £80K for first year. *Times Higher Education,* May 6. Retrieved from https://www.timeshighereducation.com/news/cambridge-plans-charge-ps230k-fees-business-doctorate. Accessed on March 3, 2023.

Myers, D., Singletary, J., Rogers, R., Ellor, J., & Barham, S. (2019). A synchronous online social work PhD program: Educational design and student/faculty response. *Journal of Teaching in Social Work, 39*(4–5), 323–343.

Nasser-Abu Alhija, F., & Fresko, B. (2018). Graduate teaching assistants: How well do their students think they do? *Assessment & Evaluation in Higher Education, 43*(6), 943–954.

Ndofirepi, E., Farinloye, T., & Mogaji, E. (2020). Marketing mix in a heterogenous higher education market: A case of Africa. In E. Mogaji, F. Maringe, & R. E. Hinson (Eds.), *Understanding the higher education market in Africa* (pp. 241–262). Oxford: Routledge.

Neumann, R. (2005). Doctoral differences: Professional doctorates and PhDs compared. *Journal of Higher Education Policy and Management, 27*(2), 173–188.

Neumann, R., & Tan, K. K. (2011). From PhD to initial employment: The doctorate in a knowledge economy. *Studies in Higher Education, 36*(5), 601–614.

Niemczyk, E. (2015). A case study of doctoral research assistantships: Access and experiences of full-time and part-time education students. Unpublished doctoral thesis. Brock University, St. Catharines, ON.

Nietzel, M. T. (2022). U.S. universities face headwinds in recruiting international students. *Forbes,* August 13. Retrieved from https://www.forbes.com/sites/michaeltnietzel/2022/08/13/american-universities-facing-several-headwinds-in-recruitment-of-international-students/?sh=12863da055b6. Accessed on March 2, 2023.

Nnadozie, E., Ishiyama, J., & Chon, J. (2000). Undergraduate research internships and graduate school success.

Nordstrom, C. R., & Segrist, D. J. (2009). Predicting the likelihood of going to graduate school: The importance of locus of control. *College Student Journal, 43*(1), 200–207.

Palmer, N. (2018) Are our doctoral programmes fit for purpose and the future? EFMD Global, May 16. Retrieved from https://blog.efmdglobal.org/2018/05/16/are-our-doctoral-programmes-fit-for-purpose-and-the-future/. Accessed on February 2, 2023.

Park, C. (2005). New variant PhD: The changing nature of the doctorate in the UK. *Journal of Higher Education Policy and Management, 27*(2), 189–207.

Pásztor, A. (2015). Careers on the move: International doctoral students at an elite British university. *Population, Space and Place, 21*(8), 832–842.

Patel, J. (2021) Editorial: PGR pandemic pedagogie. *Journal of PGR Pedagogic Practice.* Retrieved from https://journals.warwick.ac.uk/index.php/jppp/article/view/925

Phoenix, D. (2016). *Making a success of employer sponsored education.* Higher Education Policy Institute.

Pifer, M. J., & Baker, V. L. (2014). "It could be just because I'm different": Otherness and its outcomes in doctoral education. *Journal of Diversity in Higher Education, 7*(1), 14.

Pina, A. A., Maclennan, H. L., Moran, K. A., & Hafford, P. F. (2016). The DBA vs. Ph.D. in US Business and Management Programs: Different by degrees? *Journal for Excellence in Business & Education, 4*(1), 6–19.

Pon, K., & Duncan, A. L. (2019). Networks and alliances–business schools' answer to mergers and acquisitions? *Journal of Management Development, 38*(10), 773–795.

Posselt, J. R. (2013). *The merit-diversity paradox in doctoral admissions: Examining situated judgment in faculty decision making.* Unpublished doctoral dissertation. The University of Michigan, Arbor, MI.

Posselt, J. R. (2014). Toward inclusive excellence in graduate education: Constructing merit and diversity in PhD admissions. *American Journal of Education, 120*(4), 481–514.

Posselt, J. R. (2016). *Inside graduate admissions.* Boston, MA: Harvard University Press.

Posselt, J. R. (2018). Trust networks: A new perspective on pedigree and the ambiguities of admissions. *The Review of Higher Education, 41*(4), 497–521.

Potvin, G., Chari, D., & Hodapp, T. (2017). Investigating approaches to diversity in a national survey of physics doctoral degree programs: The graduate admissions landscape. *Physical Review Physics Education Research, 13*(2), 020142.

Powell, S., & Green, H. (Eds.). (2007). *The doctorate worldwide.* Maidenhead: McGraw-Hill Education.

Pyhältö, K., Tikkanen, L., & Anttila, H. (2022). The influence of the COVID-19 pandemic on PhD candidates' study progress and study wellbeing. *Higher Education Research & Development, 42*(2), 1–14.

Pyrzynska, A. (2020). Selected problems regarding the status of PhD student. *Bialstockie Studia Prawnicze, 25*, 111.

Quist, D. M. (2011). Seeking further education: A rubric for evaluating organizational behavior PhD programs. Unpublished doctoral thesis. University of Las Vegas, NV. Retrieved from http://digitalscholarship.unlv.edu/thesesdissertations/1158/

Raineiri, N. (2013). The PhD program: Between conformity and reflexivity. *Journal of Organizational Ethnography, 2*(1), 37–56.

Raineri, N. (2015). Business doctoral education as a liminal period of transition: Comparing theory and practice. *Critical Perspectives on Accounting, 26*, 99–107.

Ribau, I., & Alves, M. G. (2018). Doctoral supervision at NOVA Lisbon University: An overview. *Universal Journal of Educational Research, 6*(11), 2530–2542.

Rigler, K. L., Jr, Anastasia, C. M., El-Amin, A., & Throne, R. (2021). Scholarly voice and academic identity: A systematic review of doctoral student agency. In A. S. Zimmerman (Ed.), *Handbook of research on developing students' scholarly dispositions in higher education* (pp. 63–89).

Rigler, K. L., Jr, Bowlin, L. K., Sweat, K., Watts, S., & Throne, R. (2017). *Agency, socialization, and support: A critical review of doctoral student attrition.* Online Submission.

Robertson, M. J. (2017). Trust: The power that binds in team supervision of doctoral students. *Higher Education Research & Development, 36*(7), 1463–1475.

Roseberry, L., Remke, R., Klæsson, J., & Holgersson, T. (2016). *The gender gap in European business schools: A leadership perspective.* Brussels: EFMD. Retrieved from EFMD_Gender_Gap_Report_2016.pdf (efmdglobal.org)

Rostron, A. (2021). Failing better: Learning from failure and learning to fail in the Doctorate of Business Administration. In K. Black & R. Warhurst (Eds.), *Organisation studies and human resource management* (pp. 191–201). London: Routledge.

Royal Society. (n.d.). Résumé for researchers. Retrieved from https://royalsociety.org/topics-policy/projects/research-culture/tools-for-support/resume-for-researchers/. Accessed on March 26, 2023.

Sanders, C. E., & Landrum, R. E. (2012). The graduate school application process: What our students report they know. *Teaching of Psychology, 39*(2), 128–132.

Sainato, M. (2022). US graduate students protest against low pay while universities profit from their work. *The Guardian*, March 30.

Schoenfeld, G. (2017). *Application trends survey report, 2017.* Reston, VA: Graduate Management Admission Council.

Schwieger, F., Gros, E., & Barberan, L. (2010). Lessons from the culturally diverse classroom: Intellectual challenges and opportunities of teaching in the American university. *College Teaching, 58*(4), 148–155.

Shastry, V. (2017). Inside the global university rankings game. *Mint*, October 12. Retrieved from https://www.livemint.com/Sundayapp/SxzP28yPCeSyNUCDpfSYiJ/Inside-the-global-university-rankings-game.html. Accessed on November 13, 2022.

Shen, W., Wang, C., & Jin, W. (2016). International mobility of PhD students since the 1990s and its effect on China: A cross-national analysis. *Journal of Higher Education Policy and Management, 38*(3), 333–353.

Sirkeci, I., & O'Leary, S. (2022). The role of research reputation in choosing a UK Business School and the contrasting perspectives of students and research leaders. *International Journal of Management Education, 20*(1), 100566.

Skakni, I. (2018). Doctoral studies as an initiatory trial: Expected and taken-for-granted practices that impede PhD students' progress. *Teaching in Higher Education, 23*(8), 927–944.

Smith, M. (2018). The battle for doctoral talent. *EFMD Global Focus, 2*(12). Retrieved from https://www.globalfocusmagazine.com/vol-12-issue-02-18/

Soomere, T., & Karm, M. (2021). PhD students' conversations that lead to learning about teaching: The interplay of formal and informal learning. *International Journal for Academic Development, 26*(3), 252–265.

Spronken-Smith, R., Cameron, C., & Quigg, R. (2018). Factors contributing to high PhD completion rates: A case study in a research-intensive university in New Zealand. *Assessment & Evaluation in Higher Education, 43*(1), 94–109.

Stewart, M. M., Williamson, I. O., & King Jr, J. E. (2008). Who wants to be a business PhD? Exploring minority entry into the faculty "pipeline". *Academy of Management Learning & Education, 7*(1), 42–55.

Stoten, D. W. (2020). How do doctoral students interpret the idea of being part of a doctoral community at an English business school? *Qualitative Research Journal, 20*(1), 1–18.

Stoten, D. W. (2022a). "I've been in a box too long and I didn't even realise that I was." How can we conceptualise the subjective well-being of students undertaking a part-time DBA? The IICC model. *The Journal of Continuing Higher Education*, 1–18. https://doi.org/10.1080/07377363.2022.2037067

Stoten, D. W. (2022b). "I've been in a box too long and I didn't even realise that I was." How can we conceptualise the subjective well-being of students undertaking a part-time

DBA? The IICC Model. *The Journal of Continuing Higher Education*, 1–18. https://doi.org/10.1080/07377363.2022.2037067

Stoten, D. W., & Kirkham, S. J. (2021). The constriction of identity: The impact of accreditation on academics in an English business school. *Research in Post-Compulsory Education*, 26(1), 81–111.

Strapp, C. M., Bredimus, K., Wright, T., Cochrane, R., & Fields, E. (2021). Entering the workforce or going to graduate school: Themes in psychology alumni decision making. *Teaching of Psychology*, 48(2), 144–154.

Sun, X., & Trent, J. (2020). Ongoing doctoral study process to live by: A narrative inquiry into the doctoral identity construction experiences—A Chinese case. *Frontiers of Education in China*, 15(3), 422–452.

Sverdlik, A., Hall, N. C., McAlpine, L., & Hubbard, K. (2018). The PhD experience: A review of the factors influencing doctoral students' completion, achievement, and well-being. *International Journal of Doctoral Studies*, 13, 361–388.

Sweitzer, V. (2009). Towards a theory of doctoral student professional identity development: A developmental networks approach. *The Journal of Higher Education*, 80(1), 1–33.

Szadkowski, K. (2014). The long shadow of doctoral candidate status. Case study-Poland. *Social Work & Society*, 12(2), 1–17.

Tamrat, W., & Fetene, G. T. (2021) Delays in doctoral studies need urgent attention. *University World News*, January 21. Retrieved from https://www.universityworldnews.com/post.php?story=20210119050351208/. Accessed on September 10, 2022.

Tavares, O., Sin, C., & Soares, D. (2020). Building bridges between industry and academia: What is the profile of an industrial doctorate student? In S. Cardoso, O. Tavares, C. Sin, & T. Carvalho (Eds.), *Structural and institutional transformations in doctoral education: Social, political and student expectations* (pp. 347–373). Springer Nature.

Thietart, R. A. (2009). The research challenge of French business schools: The case of the Grandes Ecoles. *Journal of Management Development*, 28(8), 711–717.

Ting-Toomey, S., & Kurogi, A. (1998). Facework competence in intercultural conflict: An updated face-negotiation theory. *International Journal of Intercultural Relations*, 22(2), 187–225.

Torka, M. (2020). Change and continuity in Australian doctoral education: PhD completion rates and times (2005–2018). *The Australian Universities' Review*, 62(2), 69–82.

Turner, H. A. (2021). *I'm still valid: an explanatory sequential mixed-methods study of part-time PhD students' motivation and satisfaction*. PhD dissertation, University of Louisville, Louisville, KY.

UCU. (2021). PGRs as staff. Retrieved from https://www.ucu.org.uk/PGRs-as-staff. Accessed on March 25, 2023.

UKRI. (2021). Funders' statement. Retrieved from https://www.ukri.org/wpcontent/uploads/2021/07/UKRI-230721-4995CommsResumeJointFundersStatementFinal.pdf). Accessed on January 10, 2022.

UKRI. (2022). Widening participation in postgraduate research. Retrieved from https://www.ukri.org/about-us/research-england/research-excellence/widening-participation-in-postgraduate-research/improving-black-asian-and-minority-ethnic-students-access-to-postgraduate-research-projects/. Accessed on March 23, 2023.

upGrad Europe. (n.d.). Global Doctor of Business Administration (DBA) from SSBM. Retrieved from: https://www.upgrad.com/europe/doctor-of-business-administration-ssbm/. Accessed on March 25, 2023.

Vassil, K., & Solvak, M. (2012). When failing is the only option: Explaining failure to finish PhDs in Estonia. *Higher Education*, 64(4), 503–516.

Wall Bortz, W. E., Knight, D. B., Lyles, C. H., Kinoshita, T., Choe, N.H., Denton, M., & Borrego, M. (2020). A competitive system: Graduate student recruitment in STEM and why money may not be the answer. *The Journal of Higher Education*, 91(6), 927–952.

Wattakiecharoen, J., & Nilsook, P. (2013, August). E-learning readiness of PhD students *.International conference on excellent innovation for educational research and IT learning in the 21st century*, 8–9 August, Nakhon Pathom.

Wiley. (2015). Improving PhD completion rates – Where should we start? Retrieved from https://www.wiley.com/network/researchers/writing-and-conducting-research/improving-phd-completion-rates-where-should-we-start/. Accessed on September 11, 2022.

Willison, J., & O'Regan, K. (2006/2015). *Research skill development framework*. Retrieved from www.adelaide.edu.au/rsd

Winkle-Wagner, R., & McCoy, D. L. (2016). Entering the (postgraduate) field: Underrepresented students' acquisition of cultural and social capital in graduate school preparation programs. *The Journal of Higher Education, 87*(2), 178–205.

Xu, X. (2020). *A qualitative investigation into Chinese doctoral students' cross-cultural adaptation in Australian universities*. Ph.D. thesis, Newcastle: University of Newcastle.

Yarrow, E., & Davies, J. (2022). A typology of sexism in contemporary business schools: Belligerent, benevolent, ambivalent, and oblivious sexism. *Gender, Work & Organization*. https://doi.org/10.1111/gwao.12914

Zheng, G. (2019). Deconstructing doctoral students' socialization from an institutional logics perspective: A qualitative study of the socialization of Chinese doctoral students in Finland. *Frontiers of Education in China, 14*(2), 206–233.

Chapter 3

The Business School Doctoral Experience

Overview

In this chapter, our attention turns to the in-programme experiences of the business doctorate. We consider the idea of doctoral training in more depth. Specifically, we look at community-building, supervision, doctoral assessment processes and practices, and quality assurance of the award. In particular, we highlight how the business school doctoral experience may differ from the multiple perspectives of providers, candidates, and funders. We draw attention to issues of agency and structure which invariably impact the quality and vicissitudes of the business school doctoral experience.

Socialisation into Business and Management Doctoral Studies

Easterby-Smith, Jaspersen, Thorpe, and Valizade (2021, p. 2) define management and business research as 'a systematic inquiry that helps to solve business problems and contributes to management knowledge'. Most business school doctorates around the world continue to place a heavy emphasis on the production of a written thesis. Kamler and Thomson (2014) question the formation of 'the doctoral scholar' as often locating the problem in the candidate as a writer but argue that we need to recognise personal, institutional and cultural contexts. Indeed, noted accessibility and engagement gaps between academic journals and business people (Perea & Brady, 2017) can leave many post-experience candidates embarking on doctoral studies with little experience in academic writing (Lee & Murray, 2013; Lindsay, 2015).

The socialisation of part-time working candidates in the academy can be contrasted with those who are registered full-time and may have uninterrupted, continuous higher education study experience. A lack of familiarity with the social practice of academic writing can place some candidates in a state of liminality (Keefer, 2015). In this liminal state, they may face confusion, doubt and disorientation in navigating a new habitus (Bourdieu, 1977). They must adjust to academic norms, values, attitudes and behaviours. The idea of scholar–practitioner dichotomies has generated

Business and Management Doctorates World-Wide: Developing the Next Generation, 69–102
Copyright © 2024 by Nicola J. Palmer, Julie Davies and Clare Viney
Published under exclusive licence by Emerald Publishing Limited
doi:10.1108/978-1-78973-499-720231003

discussion around proximity, distance, self-efficacy and agency. As Wrigley, Wolifson, and Matthews (2021, p. 1177) have noted: 'for experienced practitioners, existing socialisation into the workplace may prove a difficult barrier to academic socialisation and the associated learning of academic research skills'.

Doctoral candidate liminal experiences have been found to play out as 'a sense of isolation, lack of confidence, impostor syndrome, and research misalignment' (Keefer, 2015, p. 17). This holds implications for the support of candidates, particularly from advisors and supervisors. There are additional challenges posed to doctoral programmes management not least in terms of university orientation, study skills, and ultimately, completion.

Extended doctoral induction programmes have been introduced in some business schools, providing intensive introductions to doctoral-level study (see, e.g., Cranfield School of Management, UK). However, given the prevalence of part-time doctoral candidates who may not have studied for a length of time and, in the case of the professional doctorate, may never have attended university, there appears to be a lack of responsive and flexible demand-led approaches to business school doctorate induction; many programmes focus on formal research and methodological training as part of the programme structure rather than paying attention to the establishment of study skills at the outset of the doctoral degree. Mentoring initiatives as a way of supporting new doctoral candidates have gained popularity but this approach is open to criticism in that it risks the inheritance of institutionalised biases, in terms of racism, sexism, and classism, for example, culminating in unequal socialisation (Ramirez, 2017).

In relation to 'first generation' doctoral candidates, Costley (2008) and Cotterall (2013) have highlighted the potential emotional impact of labelling and, from the candidate's perspective, being seen as deficient. The impact of not feeling good enough is commonly linked to the concept of 'imposter syndrome', initially used to describe 'an internal experience of intellectual phoniness' experienced by high-achieving women (Clance & Imes, 1978, p. 241) and open to criticism in that it locates a 'problem' in the individual and places the onus on them to change rather than addressing the cause of the issue which is the environment (Metcalfe, Wilson, & Levecque, 2018). Bothello and Roulet (2019, p. 854) have argued that management academics have certain intrinsic characteristics that progressively intensify a sense of the imposter phenomenon:

> our occupation is one where the induction rituals – both formal and informal – are in many ways misaligned with the multi-dimensional roles of our profession. This cognitive dissonance leads a growing number of us to question whether we merit the status, legitimacy and rewards that are conferred upon us as members of a hyper-competitive scholarly community.

We read their quote in a different way – we must also ask, what is it about the business school environment that breeds insecurity and questions/attacks self-worth? The system of status, legitimacy and rewards and the working environment must be brought into question.

Although the notion of readiness is linked to privilege and 'the rules of the game', we observe that no doctoral candidate is exempt from the experience of failure (even though it is apparent that some may be more likely to benefit from how success factors are measured and how policy is structured). One aspect of mentoring that remains under-explored in many business schools is preparing candidates 'to learn to fail' and, as supervisors, being willing 'to acknowledge our own capacity for failure' (Rostron, 2021, p. 191). The cultures of many universities, and business schools, are focused on rewarding 'winners' with funding and time buyouts from workloads, for example, with seemingly little regard for those who fail to win 'the prize'. In the doctorate, discussions of risk and failure tend to be tiptoed around or side-stepped but the nature of doctoral examination is such that the risk of failure or not achieving an outright pass exists. This pressure to succeed (Wass et al., 2018 cited in Rostron, 2021) is acknowledged by Rostron (2021) who recounts experiencing feelings of failure despite receiving minor amendments in the doctoral viva. We note how such a response may be influenced by the hyper-competitive and resource-limited nature of academia (Reed, 2019) and the context of a doctoral study that exposes candidates to academic culture and values over a number of years. We return to this theme in Chapter 5. Fallibility in management learning and education is picked up by Hay (2022, p. 1) who identifies it to be 'an integral yet silenced aspect of the lived experience of managing'. We note the value in adopting a processual lens that places emphasis on 'becoming' rather than failing in relation to supporting candidate experiences of the business doctorate.

We have already acknowledged changes to the delivery of business and management doctoral programmes in Chapter 1. 'Fast-track' or accelerated doctorates that can be completed in two years are offered by the UK-accredited online DBA which is jointly awarded by: the School of Business & Technology London (UK); the Open University of Switzerland; the University of Dabrowa Górnicz (Poland); and Taras National University (Ukraine). This is also the case for the online PhD at the Swiss School of Management and for online DBA and business and management PhD programmes in many universities across the USA. These relatively short doctoral programmes raise questions over the quality of supervision and candidates' readiness and integration into a learning community. There appears to be a dichotomy between attending to professional socialisation, preparedness and readiness (Helm, Campa, & Moretto, 2012) and offering candidate flexibility in terms of overall fees/affordability and length of award/completion time. However, as Russell (2021) who is based at Capella University (USA) has demonstrated, an implementation of the Design, Development, Implementation, and Support (DDIS) protocol to support the development of advanced cognitive processes, academic writing skills, and functional knowledge can facilitate the work of online doctoral candidates to ensure a robust experience. The idea of developmentally phased synchronous interactions throughout the doctorate (Russell, 2021) draws attention to the importance of human relations in the doctoral experience.

The potential impact of a lack of socialisation in an extended research community, provision of socio-professional support, and 'agentic reflexivity over time' is highlighted in Sun and Trent's (2020, p. 422) focus on the ongoing or continuous doctoral study process in a Chinese context. It draws attention to the need for supervisors and candidates to appreciate 'the nature of becoming a doctoral student' and explicitly acknowledge 'forces that are disruptive to the development of the doctoral-researcher identity' (Sun & Trent, 2020, p. 422). In Taiwan, Ching (2021) has located academic identity formation at the doctoral education stage. In the context of business doctorates in the USA, the influence of the developmental networks of candidates has been noted to be important to professional identity development and, ultimately, to academic success and faculty career progression (Sweitzer, 2009). Furthermore, integration into communities of practice has been observed to impact positively attrition rates and candidate persistence and the transition to becoming an independent scholar (Baker & Pifer, 2011; Baker, Pifer, & Flemion, 2013).

Doctoral Communities

Entering and integrating into a learning community is a fundamental part of the doctoral experience. It is apparent that doctoral learning communities in business schools differ in terms of size, scope and accessibility. Indeed, doctoral candidate profiles differ remarkably. Barriers to participation may be noted as linked to hierarchical cultures, imposter syndrome, and lack of equity of opportunities in the design and delivery of activities intended to strengthen the research environment. The influence of entrenched white, masculine and heteronormative values (Kelan & Jones, 2010; Ozturk & Rumens, 2014; Schleef, 2005; Shaw & Cassell, 2007) in business schools cannot be overlooked. Repeated calls for the critical and reflexive institutional transformation of business and management schools have been made (Ford, Harding, & Learmonth, 2010; Millar & Price, 2018; Parker, 2002).

This appears to reflect, at least partially, a wider prevalent academic culture where gender issues tend to be perceived as individualised rather than structural. It presents contrasting environments for industrial PhD candidates in particular (Salminen-Karlsson, 2013) and impacts not only on socialisation but also on deeper-seated identity.

Perceptions of being part of a doctoral community and progressing through the same doctoral lifecycle have been noted to differ between PhD and DBA candidates based in a UK business school context. As recognised in Chapter 2, faculty enrolled on doctorates, particularly when they have been required to study for a DBA as part of upskilling measures to meet accreditation targets, have been observed to view their positions in contrast to other doctoral candidates. Stoten (2020, p. 13) highlights how this is 'not necessarily based on an objective understanding of others' positions as PhD students, many of whom are also parents, work for the university and have extensive work experience' and this lack of appreciation of commonalities can frustrate the creation of cohesive doctoral communities, an aspiration of many doctoral programme leaders.

Integration of doctoral candidates into faculty learning communities is recognised as a key component in the building of inclusive research environments (Cox,

2004), acknowledged as a metric of doctoral candidate experience. The creation and maintenance of cohesive communities is facilitated where structured, mandatory programmes of research training and coursework are embedded in the doctoral curriculum as part of taught doctorate awards. Yet as Bowden and Green (2019) have observed, worldwide there exist inconsistencies and a lack of congruence across systems and PhD environments that have raised concerns about accountability and driven 'regulatory creep' in an attempt to standardise quality. In business and management, we have already noted the influence of business school accreditation bodies that tend to focus on key metrics including assurance of learning and time-to-thesis completion. Armstrong (2004) has additionally raised the issue of supervisor cognitive style on the quality of research supervision in management education, finding an analytical approach to have a more positive influence on doctoral candidate assessment of the teaching and learning experience. However, despite the introduction of initiatives to celebrate 'excellent' research supervision the assessment of the quality of doctoral supervision in many business schools and other university departments is not tightly monitored or regulated often due to a separation between the allocation of supervision and line management of research supervisors. This impacts on human resource management of organisational and supervisor support in research supervision work and thesis development as Wanyama and Eyamu (2021) and Bayona-Oré (2021) note.

However, it is acknowledged that the doctoral candidate's experience is shaped by multiple encounters and relationships throughout the lifecycle of doctoral studies. There has been increased interest in shifting institutional focus from the doctoral product to the process as part of doctoral education reforms in Europe and China (Bao et al., 2018). In many nations where doctoral programmes are more established, the benefits of leveraging purpose-driven approaches to doctoral candidate peer support networks have gained popularity and the rise of mentoring schemes, academic writing groups and initiatives that focus on shared candidate challenges is notable. To some extent, the attractiveness of candidate-driven support networks reflects the relative resource scarcity of postgraduate research (PGR) in comparison to other activities in many publicly funded universities. However, peer support initiatives are heavily dependent on motivated and committed champions, succession planning, and the provision of clear opportunities for all candidates to be involved as they wish and to participate freely. The work of Stoten (2020, p. 1), situated in an English Business School notes 'the bifurcation of students' doctoral journey into two possibilities: the idea of the lone scholar, isolated and unsupported, or that of the student as being part of a community (Lee, 2008)'.

A lack of porosity between different types of business school doctoral candidates in terms of opportunities for connection between those not studying in the same mode or who entered the doctorate at the same time has been noted (Pilbeam & Denyer, 2009). The idea of keeping students in cohorts fits well with undergraduate and taught postgraduate ethos of neat groupings to create course identity. However, as we have already acknowledged, doctoral candidates are diverse and messy in terms of characteristics, progression, and time-to-end point.

There are very few published or documented examples of attempts to bring together professional doctorate and PhD doctoral candidates in business and management. We are able to draw on our experiences of leading business school doctoral community-building activities. The introduction of combined PhD and DBA programme annual residential weekends by Sheffield Business School (UK) between 2011 and 2017 succeeded in engaging different business school doctoral candidates to those attending on-campus training events. Furthermore, the weekends enabled the building of soft and hard skills (including critical thinking, teamwork, communication, problem-solving and abstract writing), and encouraged candidate-led skills development sessions and peer-to-peer learning (Palmer, 2019).

There is scope to explore further the potential benefits of connecting doctoral candidates from different types of award programme to enhance the doctoral candidate experience and facilitate broader skills development. Greener (2021) has noted that difficulties are faced by business and management doctoral candidates in locating a supportive research community due to the diversity of disciplines and methodologies. Furthermore, it has been argued that 'social isolation among doctoral students can contribute to non-completion and withdrawal' (Greener, 2021, p. 100463) and the value of non-supervisory critical friend support should not be overlooked.

In business and management, the role of external doctoral communities, both online and offline, is notable across regional, national and international scales. Academic associations and networks in business and management are visible. The Academy of Management (AoM)'s Doctoral Student Development Programme offers advanced research methods training online to student members globally, for example. The European Academy of Management (EURAM)'s Doctoral Accelerator offers peer- and mentor-driven support and the Australian and New Zealand Academy of Management (ANZAM) organises Doctoral Student Workshops across management subject groupings and institutions. There are also university-driven networks aimed at business school PhD candidates such as the Northern Advanced Research Training Initiative (NARTI) kick-started with Economic and Social Research Council (ESRC) funding in the UK, European Summer School opportunities for doctoral candidates provided by Varna University of Management in Bulgaria, and a range of doctoral colloquia and doctoral researcher conference streams are identifiable.

However, the extent to which candidates are aware of professional academic networks and are integrated into them appears to be dependent, at least to some extent, on supervisor participation. In this regard, supervisors (or 'thesis advisors') may be identified as conduits or 'propagation actors' that can help to facilitate researcher mobility, collaboration and network formation (Horta, Birolini, Cattaneo, Shen, & Paleari, 2021) contributing to human and social capital in research systems. Moreover, 'doctoral supervision equips doctoral students with the right arsenal to be able to competently operate within their field and prepares them for their future research or professional career that demands a high level of discipline expertise' (Gube, Getenet, Satariyan, & Muhammad, 2017, p. 1) and integration into discipline-specific research communities bolsters this grounding.

The potential benefits of being networked for individual doctoral candidates are considered further in Chapter 4. Effective mentorship across identities in doctoral education is explored later in this chapter with reference to the role that the supervisor and candidate relationship can have on the business doctorate experience.

In relation to developing research independence during the doctorate, we acknowledge that this requires building social capital and collegiality such as a willingness to review others' papers and volunteer to organise or participate in scholarly activities. Van de Ven (at an AIMS workshop in Cardiff, UK) talked about taking executives on doctoral programmes to Academy of Management meetings and he would go with them to trade conferences – each side was perplexed by the different norms at these events, but they would be valuable sources of scholarly insights and access to empirical data.

Progression, Quality Assurance and Assessment

Progression points on the doctorate offer opportunities for funders and programme managers to chart the road to completion and return-on-investment. The latter point is an issue that we return to in Chapter 4 when we consider the outcomes of the business school doctorate.

Measurement of candidate progress is often linked to performance at designated doctoral assessment points that are approved at an institutional level and are intended to support assessments of quality. Despite efforts to use entry criteria to predict success, we note that there are numerous internal and external variables that impact on candidate progression and completion. Lekhetho offers valuable insights into the context surrounding PhD completion rates of Ethiopian candidates studying with Unisa, 'the oldest distance education institution in Africa and one of the mega-universities in the world' (Lekhetho, 2022, p. 25):

> A PhD at Unisa is research-based and designed to take roughly three years. However, in most cases, students take longer since they study part-time and lack the academic writing skills required at this level, as most of them are blacks who have been excluded from elite, private school systems that cater for Western preparations (Manyike, 2017; Martirosyan et al., 2019). Such deficits might be exacerbated by the supervisors' insufficient knowledge and guidance skills (van Rooij et al., 2019). (Lekhetho, 2022, p. 26)

Rigler, Anastasia, El-Amin, and Throne's (2021) observations on the peripheral identity of part-time doctoral candidates suggest that with agency comes an ability to move to the centre of a doctoral learning community. Agency, involving intentional choices or actions, is assumed to enable a positive doctoral experience, supporting candidate persistence and attrition rates. Indeed, when Pyhältö and Keskinen (2012, p. 142) explored doctoral candidates' sense of relational agency in terms of their scholarly communities and the relationship to study persistence and experienced socio-psychological well-being, they reported that 'Students who perceived themselves as active relational agents experienced less lack of interest in their studies, less negative emotions, and less often considered abandoning their studies than students who perceived themselves as passive objects in their communities'.

Smith-McGloin's (2021, p. 383) reflections on the contrast and interplay between fixed institutional-level progression frameworks and candidate navigation through space that 'enables and facilitates intellectual freedom, creativity, becoming and adventure' draw attention to the risk of structures stifling agency, intellectual and professional freedom and contributing to candidate pressures and heightened anxiety. The idea that more attention might be paid to candidate definition and evaluation of progression is worthy of further consideration. In an Australian context, Mewburn, Cuthbert, and Tokareva (2014) have questioned the fairness of progress reporting mechanisms in terms of their effects and application as management tools for all types of doctoral candidates. More recently, Dowle (2020) has provided an in-depth investigation into the factors that influence progress, submission, and eventual completion of a doctoral degree in the UK, acknowledging, among other issues, the ability of major structural factors in the doctoral experience to enable or constrain progress. Likewise in a Canadian context, Skakni (2018, p. 927) has noted both the formal and tacit organisation of doctoral programmes to involve an 'enduring perception of doctoral studies as an "initiatory trial" '.

There is a sizeable body of literature investigating gender equity and doctoral attrition, highlighting gender-specific challenges of the doctoral experience including tensions between cultural expectations, social relationships and academic performance metrics. Carter, Blumenstein, and Cook (2013) have argued identity transformation over the course of the doctorate is especially problematic for women. Beňová's (2014) autoethnographic account of a part-time female's PhD story in Slovakia indicates how distant the everyday reality of the doctorate versus the institutional policy view can be. The doctoral experience as involving learning to be an academic, keeping a place at university, commitment towards a part-time workplace, a private life and parenthood barrier, as well as a tool for intellectual growth is highlighted. Furthermore, Lantsoght's (2021) international study of doctoral candidates across a range of academic fields highlighted the particular influence of sociodemographic aspects of candidate identity on the experience of the final examination or 'defense'. These studies bring into question the extent to which doctoral programme design has been based on a vision of a particular standardised type of candidate that shapes or influences institutional regulatory expectations and behaviours. This theme is one that has captured the attention of many higher education commentators. In a USA context, the American Psychological Association (APA, 2015) has reported higher faculty responsiveness to white males in almost every academic discipline, with those in business and management (Jaschik, 2014) and at private universities displaying more bias in this regard and Greenfield (2022) has noted that across Web of Science white males remain privileged with more freedom over research choice.

The endemic nature of sexism in business schools is apparent and there is little evidence from a review of reports in Poets&Quants, EFMD's Global Focus and AACSB International's BizEd/AACSB Insights that this is being dealt with in any of its forms – belligerent, benevolent, ambivalent and oblivious. There is a need for business schools to reform themselves to 'gain substantive legitimacy as effective role models' (Yarrow & Davies, 2022, p. 1). This is important in terms of reputation-building as places that are attractive for everyone 'to do business' with, be they external business partners or doctoral candidates wishing to engage with 'the business of learning'.

Attention to issues of diversity in business school recruitment has increased over time and is encouraged by accreditation providers such as AACSB. Yet it is apparent that underlying preconceptions of what doctoral candidates look like still result in policies and practices that do not always reflect the diversity of graduate management education around the world (AACSB, 2022). There have been efforts to address racial diversity and inclusion. Since 1994, AACSB has been a sponsor of The PhD Project that offers measures to increase diversity and inclusion in management education to advance workplace diversity ultimately. It has been reported that:

> Since its inception, The PhD Project has been responsible for the increase in the number of Black/African Americans, Latinx/Hispanic American and Native Americans earning a business PhD from 294 to 1,517, of whom 1,303 are teaching in U.S. colleges and universities today. There are close to 300 underrepresented minorities currently enrolled in doctoral programs, who will take their place at the front of the classroom over the next few years. (AACSB, 2023a, p. 1)

The PhD Project has recently extended its focus to welcoming Deferred Action for Childhood Arrivals (DACA) recipients (individuals who have arrived in the USA as illegal immigrants) in their applications to PhD study as a means of deferral from deportation (AACSB, 2023b). The extent to which these initiatives pay attention to potential challenges in progression and attainment linked to pathways from childhood to adulthood, self-efficacy, individual life experiences and intersectionality requires exploration. We are mindful of Morgenshtern and Novotna's (2011) identification of '(In)(Out)Sider(s)'.

Influences on the Shape of the Doctorate

With respect to doctoral training, Sin, Soares, and Tavares (2021) noted an increased trend to include coursework as an integrated part of doctoral programmes. This has largely been unquestioned in terms of value-added and relevance, particularly in the context of industrial doctorates in Portugal. They have called for increased flexibility and personalisation of a heavily prescriptive doctoral training curriculum. In contrast, it has been argued that increased standardisation of training is desirable across doctoral programmes in the USA and across Europe because it provides some degree of quality assurance in the placement of doctoral graduates in academic positions at other universities, facilitates the potential transfer of candidates between programmes, and enables professional exchanges between academic institutions. The cultural affinity and standardisation of Nordic business education for national markets described by Engwall (2000) and Širaliova and Angelis (2006) extend to doctoral training approaches in Denmark, Finland, Norway and Sweden where common curricula are in place. 'Foreign influence' (Engwall, 2000), 'mimetic behaviour' (Engwall, 2007), and Americanisation is apparent (Engwall, 2004; Juusola, Kettunen, & Alajoutsijärvi, 2015). A traditional predisposition to quantitative research inherited from management science has started to shift and there is more acceptance of qualitative and mixed methods in academic management journals. However, assessment standards in doctoral education *per se* may be critiqued on the basis of being designed to meet the needs of funded full-time candidates divorced from caring responsibilities and work commitments, neglecting barriers to doctoral education (Lindner, 2020) and, controversially, representing attempts to standardise knowledge production (Ruano-Borbalan, 2022). Returning to our ideas around the globalisation of the business doctorate in Chapter 1, this holds implications for the dominance and reproduction of particular educational paradigms and the *status quo*.

In a New Zealand context, Spronken-Smith et al. (2018) have reported that, within a research-intensive university, high PhD submission rates are aligned with being a full-time candidate funded through a three-year scholarship, with business candidates tending to submit their doctoral theses in the fastest times. Full-time candidate status has also been documented to impact positively on doctoral completion rates in the UK (Booth & Satchell, 1996) and Australia (Bourke, Holbrook, Lovat, & Farley, 2004; Rodwell & Neumann, 2008). However, we note that through their review of USA-based cases, Horta, Cattaneo, and Meoli (2019) have found that funding may reduce research productivity and increase time-to-completion. From our experiences, completion of the business school doctorate is not automatically reflective of the candidate's mode of study. Time-to-degree may be affected by departmental practices and policies, particularly where in-programme coursework or examinations require preparation, as Nerad and Cerny (1993) have observed. Furthermore, motivations to gain a doctorate may have a substantial influence on the rate and pace of completion. Kelley and Salisbury-Glennon (2016) have proposed that completion of the doctoral dissertation might be vitally linked to self-regulated learning and active monitoring of progress by candidates. Additionally, we note the potential influence of structural factors; it may be argued that many doctoral programmes operate to meet the needs of certain types of candidates as we have already noted. In this regard, Douglas' (2021) 'dimensions of fit' regarding the (mis)alignment of candidate learning identities with the supervisory, programme and institutional support appear to hold relevance.

Concerns of part-time doctoral candidates about fitting the mould of a 'traditional' doctoral candidate (Gardner & Gopaul, 2012) and constraints experienced by women doctoral candidates relating to their capacity to 'work the system' (Maher, Ford, & Thompson, 2004) draw attention to barriers to doctoral community participation. In the context of business and management, we note the implicit bias that comes with the selection of new candidates often subject to consideration of existing strengths and specialisations of research-active faculty members (EIASM, 2015).

Deem and Brehony (2000) have argued that part-time and international candidates have the most difficulty in accessing peer cultures and academic cultures. Self-funding international PhD candidates in business schools have received little academic attention to date, despite the internationalised nature of business school doctorate provision. As Mogaji, Adamu, and Nguyen (2021) have noted, this group has been assumed to possess agency due to the lack of funder requirement constraints and the freedom that this offers. Yet, self-funding international doctoral candidates often face structural constraints including visa rules and lack of public funding entitlement that are under-acknowledged stressors on candidate experience and progression. Despite self-funding full-time international PhD candidates being among the most dominant groupings of business school doctoral candidates worldwide, it is apparent that, as with other groups of business school doctoral candidates, a more informed understanding of individual circumstances and needs is required. The precarity identified by Mogaji et al. (2021, p. 100543) highlights 'the role of university administrative systems, supervisors, fellow PhD students, social networks, families, and self-funded PhD students as key stakeholders shaping students' learning experiences and maintaining their engagement, influencing completion rates, and affecting post-graduation outcomes'.

Implications of Funded PGRs

In some institutions, funding for doctoral candidates in business schools includes free tuition for five years on a competitive basis for advertised full-time studentships (e.g., Harvard Business School, HEC Paris, London Business School, Warwick Business School). Stipends/bursaries are tax-free. In some countries, doctoral candidates are employees (e.g., Denmark and France). There may be requirements or opportunities to be paid as a graduate teaching assistant (GTA). Funding may also be provided for doctoral candidates on studentships to participate in additional training, language courses, international conferences and for data collection in some cases. Government funding is available for national studentships allocated to different universities to support the knowledge economy (Neuman & Tan, 2011). For example, UKRI funding in the UK is linked to research council training requirements (Park, 2005). Doctoral candidates in business schools may be funded by a specific research project grant although this is less likely than in STEM disciplines where there is big science. In Denmark, the Ministry of Science, Innovation and Higher Education funds 50% of an individual's salary to enable Industrial Research Fellows to undertake PhD study at Copenhagen Business School while they remain employed half-time in an organisation. Doctoral candidates in business and management studies may also be fully funded by their employer or by their home country government for scholarships abroad (e.g., the Kingdom of Saudi Arabia). Others benefit from a combination of scholarships: university; business school; government loans; and employer contributions. Self-funded PhDs/DBAs where the candidate chooses their own topic of study is a different model from a STEM student joining a large externally funded research team where the topic is pre-allocated (and where there may be shared resources in place to benefit the research of many researchers).

Mellors-Bourne et al. (2016, p. 41) found that '[f]or those participating in DBA programmes, employer support or demand seemed to be very variable' in the UK as the DBA was seen as niche and more expensive than traditional PhD programmes. Indeed, we are reminded of the Cambridge Judge Business School example provided in Chapter 2 where the premium-priced four-year BusD enrols a very small number of executives filtered out by their long-standing leadership experience. There is seemingly little regard for the implications of this type of pricing strategy. What are the challenges for a young management scholar who is supervising a doctoral candidate who is paying such huge fees?

Power asymmetries are interesting in supervisory relationships where a business school is reliant on high fees from executives or international candidates, yet the supervisor feels the candidate is not producing work of a sufficiently high standard. Curiously enough, rather than focusing on how a business school doctorate will accelerate your career promotion, Davies et al. (2019) noted that late-career DBA candidates were using the professional doctorate to wind down or escape from the demands of their jobs and, for some learners, this can affect levels of motivation, effort and urgency.

Doctoral supervisors need to be aware of funding arrangements as these can affect candidates' expectations, milestones and completion times. For example, a candidate who receives sufficient funding to live with their family for seven years overseas might be in no rush to complete as they want their children to finish school in that country. In some institutions, doctoral candidates delay submitting their thesis or arrange vivas to give them more time to publish in peer-reviewed academic journals, thereby enhancing their job prospects. We have seen cases of self-funded candidates from low-income countries with families left behind being overly anxious about finishing their PhD in two years while working part-time so that they can quickly find full-time paid work. In contrast, doctoral candidates in full-time work where the doctorate does not really affect their careers and/or achieving promotions during doctoral studies may feel little pressure to complete their dissertations on time. The value of the doctorate might be called into question here.

Clearly, doctoral candidates' financial circumstances may change. Financial hardship can affect a student's morale and ability to concentrate on the doctorate. During the COVID-19 pandemic, international students were stuck in Australia financially desperate (Johnson et al., 2020). Candidates who needed to work to support their studies and those with family and other responsibilities had to deal with anxieties in addition to the pressures of doctoral study. International candidates may also have to contend with currency fluctuations and cost-of-living rises are another factor to consider.

In their study of self-funded international PhD candidates in UK business schools, Mogaji et al. (2021) make important points about multiple forms of precarity. For instance, some candidates need to earn their fees while they are studying and may struggle to meet this financial liability, others experience visa restrictions on their rights to work. A doctoral supervisor may be supervising different candidates who need different levels of support because financial concerns are causing candidates to be anxious and socially isolated. By comparison, executives on part-time DBA programmes who are working full-time may have access to a rich range of resources and support in their organisations. In other scenarios, doctoral candidates in well-endowed business schools may be very well supported financially but highly pressured to publish (see, e.g., Horta & Li, 2022).

Issues of funding also relate to mobility. Self-funded or government-funded doctoral candidates from low-income countries may have different expectations from rich international candidates who have better living conditions and more discretionary funds to pay for research assistance and enjoy their free time. A doctoral candidate who is stressed from working several jobs and worried about employability when they complete their studies will have a different attitude from an academic who has a guaranteed job to return to on completion.

Working While Completing a Doctorate

What does working while completing a doctorate entail? Maloshonok and Terentev (2019) identified barriers to completion of doctorates at Russian universities including a lack of funding and a need for doctoral candidates to have paid work. Bekova (2021) questioned whether employment during doctoral training reduces the PhD completion rate, finding a negative association between off-campus employment and completion and increased chances to defend the thesis through the skills acquired during on-campus employment. The employment status of business school doctoral candidates varies between national educational systems and within certain countries.

In the USA, the recruitment of PhD candidates to serve partially as teaching assistants has resulted in the formation of graduate student unions and Nerad (2004, p. 183) has noted how the University of California, Berkeley, New York University, Yale, University of California San Diego, University of Wisconsin, University of Washington have formed unions 'linked to large US union organisations such as the American Automobile and Transportation Union'. Bauman (2020) has also reported striking by University of California Santa Cruz Graduate Teaching Assistants in response to a failure of monthly stipends to keep pace with the standard of living costs in the local area. It is argued that for many candidates this has impacted positively on the doctoral experience, encouraging institutions to improve learning and working environments (Bauman, 2020).

The casualisation of academic work in Australia has captured the interest of researchers such as May (2013, p. vii) who has noted 'poor conditions, lack of career path and no job security' reflective of the economic imperative of university missions. Pre COVID-19, Yasukawa and Dados (2018, p. 257) observed that:

> Casualisation of the academic workforce in Australia has increasingly become a pointed issue of contestation between university managements and the union, the National Tertiary Education Union.

Hogan, Kortt, and Charles (2020) have noted that low levels of graduate satisfaction linked to high casualisation could increase the vulnerability and international competitiveness of Australian business schools, bringing challenges to candidate recruitment.

Doctoral candidate status holds implications not only for the rights of candidates and responsibilities of the institution, but as we have seen in Chapter 2, it can also impact on recruitment and retention patterns. The status of doctoral candidates differs around the world. In the UK, for example, doctoral candidates are counted as students by the Higher Education Statistics Agency (HESA) and institutional data but tend to have an ambiguous 'in between' student/staff status (Szadkowski, 2014) with respect to university policies. In the Netherlands and Scandinavia, the employee status of doctoral candidates typically provides social rights to the standards of every worker in that country (Fry, Tress, & Tress, 2006). Many PhD candidates in Sweden, for example, are recognised as staff and hold employment contracts (Bennett, 2022a) either from the start of their doctoral funding or transferring part-way through. Precarity can inevitably impact upon the doctoral candidate's experience not least in terms of power relations (ESRC, 2021).

A recent campaign by the University and College Union (UCU) in the UK has focused on fighting for staff status for PGRs (UCU, n.d.). One key argument here has centred on the potential for the exploitation of PhD candidates as a lower-paid, casualised teaching resource. A decrease in university internal labour costs has been noted as a side effect of increased doctoral candidate enrolment in Poland by Szadkowski (2014). National-level higher education reform modifying the status of Polish PhD candidates from quasi-students to future faculty has been observed by Pyrzyńska (2020). This has been accompanied by a universal scholarship system across Polish Doctoral Schools whereby since October 2020 candidates are funded for the maximum PhD registration period of four years, exempt from tax, but subject to pension and retirement contributions (University of Warsaw, 2022).

Hockey (1994) has noted that adjustment to doctoral student status may result in different types of social interactions with faculty. Watts (2009) has acknowledged the challenges of status transition for post-experience candidates becoming PGR students in terms of a shift in professional standing and identity. For PhD candidates who teach, the experience of liminality and laminal space has been noted whereby the teaching role is peripheral or marginalised in status and a teaching identity and 'sense of ownership' is often absent (Davis, 2018). However, it must be acknowledged again that opportunities to teach as part of professional skills development during the doctorate are not available for all candidates, even in the business school environment where a heavy emphasis is placed on the doctorate as a route into the academy and a means of reproducing faculty. In this regard, equality impact assessments (EIAs) are lacking, and many universities stop short of requiring and being able to guarantee teaching opportunities for all candidates given deviations in the amount of teaching available each year when undergraduate recruitment levels are open to variance. Even where student numbers are steady, the processes by which teaching is allocated and the extent of support available to doctoral candidates new to teaching differ markedly. As Austin (2002, p. 95) suggests:

> Although teaching and research responsibilities surely can provide training opportunities for the future faculty, these assistantship roles sometimes are structured more to serve institutional or

faculty needs than to ensure a high quality learning experience for graduate students.

It is also important to acknowledge that in the context of business and management doctorates teaching opportunities are not always desired by part-time and professional doctorate candidates. The motivations of candidates and sponsors must be acknowledged. The nature of business doctorates means that varied career experiences exist and these challenge assumptions of the doctorate as a route to academic careers.

The Doctoral Examination

Consideration of the final examination format used to assess doctorates has tended to reflect an analysis of the purpose and process of doctoral education (Charity, 2010; Erwee & Perry, 2018; Houston, 2007). The business doctorate has already been identified as an award that, by virtue, might be expected to meet the needs of industry. Institutional expectations of the DBA are currently noted to vary in relation to contributions to knowledge and practice. Davies, McGregor, and Horan (2019) have argued for greater recognition and evidencing of the personal, practical and scholarly published impacts that arise from DBA research. Maxwell and Kupczyk-Romanczuk (2009) have proposed that a portfolio of work of equivalent quality offers a legitimate alternative to the thesis for the final examination of the professional doctorate. To date, it is apparent that whilst there exist commonalities of PhD structures, standards and assessment points, professional doctorates vary in terms of structure, curriculum and even examiner expectations. There is a lack of overarching co-ordination of DBA curricula in comparison to the PhD. However, this is not to disregard the existence of regional bodies such as the DBA Association Switzerland, an organisation that exists to represent common interests and increase the awareness of this type of doctoral programme, bringing together current and completed DBA candidates alongside DBA educators (see http://www.dba-as.ch/). The National DBA Society based in the USA similarly promotes the interests of scholarly practitioners (see https://www.dbasociety.org/) and, with respect to external oversight of quality, we have already acknowledged the AMBA-accredited DBA programmes that exist in Europe, South America, South Africa and Russia.

The doctoral examination of the DBA has received attention in Australia in terms of consistency of understanding of the difference between DBA and PhD awards at the examination stage (Sarros, Willis, Fisher, & Storen, 2005) and a need to standardise examination criteria to provide common frames of reference for candidates, supervisors, and examiners (Perry & Cavaye, 2004). Additionally, the relationship between PhD and DBA assessment methods has been questioned in a UK context (Ruggeri-Stevens, Bareham, & Bourner, 2001) from a quality assurance and levelness perspective. Focusing on the terminal assessment of work-based doctorates, Johnson (2005) has identified a mismatch of interests between higher education awarding institutions and sponsoring organisations in research and developmental aspects respectively. In the USA, Pina, Maclennan,

Moran, and Hafford (2016) have concluded, through an analysis of 107 doctoral degree programmes, that similar preparation and requirements exist for DBA and PhD candidates but mixed messages about the value of the awards arise from inconsistent national doctoral degree classifications.

The business school PhD examination experience is not without question. Doloriert and Sambrook (2011) draw attention to UK traditional business school research practices and the role of supervisor and examiner discretion in final judgements of thesis quality where contemporary approaches are employed by candidates. Despite a variety of types of support to prepare for the viva experience offered by doctoral schools, programme leaders, supervisors and convenors, the subjectivity involved in the examination system of British PhD theses using closed vivas has been questioned on the grounds of quality assurance and equality (Morley, Leonard, & David, 2010). The idea of 'searching for doctorateness' (Wellington, 2013) and parity of esteem (Burgess & Wellington, 2010; Park, 2005) across an increasing range of types of the doctorate (Poole, 2018) has preoccupied many discussions of viva practice. In relation to this, Wilkins, Neri, and Lean (2019) have noted a traditional preoccupation with the use of theory to make an original contribution to knowledge in business and management and a call to consider the doctoral competence implications of this is pertinent given the relevance of insider action research undertaken in an organisation or community by part-time PhD and DBA candidates (Coghlan, Coughlan, & Shani, 2019). As Rigg, Ellwood, and Anderson (2021, p. 100497) argue, 'a philosophy of knowledge that makes explicit the iterative entanglement of practice and knowledge' is needed. This holds implications for institutional, supervisor and examiner understandings. Building on the work of Raineiri (2013) that reflects on how knowledge production practices within the business school PhD straddle conformity and reflexivity, we recognise a need to explore further the business school doctoral process and the role of academic advisors and supervisors in candidate support.

The Role of Academic Advisors and Supervisors in the Business Doctorate

We have witnessed an increase in online doctoral programmes in business and management, following a trend for online MBA programmes and recognising the executive market for advanced and terminal degrees (see, e.g., the DBA offered by ESCE, France, where online attendance is available for non-European candidates). However, a rise in online programmes in management education *per se* has not come without bias against a perceived inability to recreate 'the kind of interaction, collaboration, and learning outcomes that are necessary to support a quality business education' (Redpath, 2012, p. 125). Supervising candidates from a distance brings challenges and Deshpande (2016) has observed the absence of human interaction to impact on the online DBA candidate experience of a doctoral programme offered by a UK university. Lack of in-person cohort interaction places greater pressure on the quality of relationships developed with instructors, academic advisors, and supervisors and not least in terms of expectations around the provision of socialising opportunities for candidates (Deshpande, 2016). Burkholder (2022) has noted how, linked to widening access agendas, an increase in mentoring doctoral candidates in online environments brings with it a need to examine and disentangle the roles of supervisors from targeted services requirements. This highlights the importance of reviewing institutional expectations of the role of supervisors (and their support needs). In the context of business doctorates, Okoli (2019) has noted how there has been an increased focus on research supervision by many institutions and funders as part of attempts to make all stakeholders accountable for candidate attrition rates but there is more to understand about supervisor relationships in low-income or lesser developed countries.

The idea of supervisors playing a role in researcher development has been explored in terms of contributions to particular mindsets, behaviours and research productivity (Jazvac-Martek, Chen, & McAlpine, 2011). Linked to this, McAlpine, Paulson, Gonsalves, and Jazvac-Martek (2012) have emphasised the value of pedagogies that are relational and focus on an ethic of care. In the face of an affective turn in the social sciences, it is important to acknowledge the emotional dimensions of social relations that impact upon everyday life happenings, including the doctoral experience. There is a need to acknowledge relationship building as emotional scaffolding (Mahn & John-Steiner, 2002) and the supervisory relationship by virtue of its intensity and prolonged nature is key in terms of emotional support for candidates to complete on time (Ahmad, 2020). McCray and Joseph-Richard (2021) have observed there to be an over-reliance on the supervisory team for managing doctoral candidate well-being in UK business schools. Similarly, Stoten's (2022a) exploration of British and Dutch part-time DBA candidate experiences located supervisory support as pivotal to equipping candidates with coping strategies.

Benmore's (2016) work on boundary management and the negotiation and transition of doctoral supervisor roles in a UK business school has categorised physical, emotional and relational role aspects as secondary to temporal and cognitive dimensions. With respect to the latter, we note the fundamental role that supervisors play in professional skills development and candidate appreciation of training based on disciplinary practices (Crossouard, 2013). The idea that supervisors are 'stewards of the discipline' and responsible for inducting candidates into the disciplinary community (Walker, Baepler, & Cohen, 2008) and introducing threshold concepts may be seen to hold relevance in the context of business school doctorates.

Whether or not supervisors are directly involved in the assessment of the doctorate, there is power to be exercised in terms of progress monitoring of candidates and progression panel recommendations. Supervisors also impact on candidate progression through doctoral studies in business and management in terms of overseeing candidate progress and offering a frontline key support interface and potentially signposting to a range of support services on offer within an institution. Supervisor knowledge of institutional and wider discipline-related support systems is important in terms of being able to respond to the inter-linked institutional, professional, societal and private domains that impact on doctoral-researcher learning experiences (Elliot, Bengtsen, Guccione, & Kobayashi, 2020). The notion of a 'doctoral learning ecosystem' holds value and is a topic recognised by doctoral programme leaders at the 2022 EFMD Doctoral Programmes Conference hosted by Vlerick Management School, Belgium. In the conceptualisation of business school doctoral ecosystems, interactive, dynamic and agentic forces are recognised. This is notable in relation to supervisor practices and behaviours. Indeed, Saunders and Fortin (2023, p. 29) acknowledge how the doctoral supervisor-supervisee relationship is dyadic and involves vulnerability whereby demonstration of 'trust and trustworthiness are ... crucial for both supervisees and supervisors'. Denicolo (2004) has questioned the nature of the relationship where supervisors and candidates may be colleagues (as is the case in some business schools with significant numbers of faculty on doctorates to meet doctorally qualified accreditation scheme quotas) and where practices and performances may be open to increased scrutiny by institutions. Attention is drawn to an aspect of doctoral supervision that remains under-examined: supervisor-candidate relationships whereby research and work contexts are not dissociated and whereby 'safe' rather than creative or innovative research may be co-produced as a result (Denicolo, 2004). The notion of trustworthiness in such cases may be especially complex, unstable and fragile.

Supervisors and candidates can be overloaded with work and delays in providing timely submissions and feedback can result in poor-quality engagement and dissertation supervision (Bahtilla, 2022). The opposite challenge may be micromanagement which indicates a lack of trust (Gorup & Laufer, 2020). It is vital, therefore, to pay attention to dyadic relationships and respective responsibilities in building and sustaining trust in supervisor-candidate relationships (Guccione, 2016). There should be a reliable follow-up to meetings (Saunders & Fortin, 2023) and trust to enable the candidate's voice and resilience (Robertson, 2017) through structure and support (Gatfield & Alpert, 2002).

As we have acknowledged earlier in this chapter, doctoral study involves negotiating multiple identities (McAlpine & Lucas, 2011). Faculty who are pursuing doctoral degrees experience a particular sense of liminality in transitions to PhD status, with interesting intersectional characteristics at play such as age, race, gender, ethnicity, supervisor relations, and challenges over time and where they are located in the academy (Breier et al., 2020). The dual status of faculty who are doctoral students involves code-switching and different levels of agency, with emotional challenges where they are supervised by their colleagues (Billot et al., 2021).

Carter et al. (2021, p. 284) encourage:

> critical exploration of the various borderland journeys that different forms of doctoral education open up – novice growing into expert, professional combining practice with critical study, individual joining a team, supervisor reinventing themselves, student working within a new culture, discovery of the world of scholarly publication and so on.

Gravett (2021) draws on Deleuze and Guattari's (1987) concept of a rhizome rather than a linear path to completion with the potential for creativity, innovation and joy once regulatory boundaries are clarified.

As today's doctoral candidates will be influential in educating future generations it is clearly important that we support them in what can be a lonely experience (Greener, 2021). It is also important that we understand the different perspectives of DBA candidates who have much to offer in terms of making practical impacts in organisations and professions (Breese et al., 2021). Especially in the case of formalised industry-academic doctoral partnerships, self-reflections on 'liminal selves' and help to understand the identities of candidates and supervisors (Hardwicke et al., 2018). Autoethnographies of doctoral candidates and supervisors provide some insights into the lived experiences of doctoral journeys (e.g. Doloriert & Sambrook, 2009).

Structured full-time PhD programmes in the USA typically last 4–6 years and involve dissertation qualifying examinations following on from in-programme research training and personal and professional development requirements (Bennett, 2022b). Use of the term 'all but thesis' or 'all but dissertation' (ABD) in business and management to denote doctoral candidates who have completed all coursework but not the final thesis is common in institutional and accreditor assessment of the quality of doctoral provision (see Chapter 2). Mujtaba, Scharff, Cavico, and Mujtaba (2008) reported a tendency for 30–70% of doctoral candidates in the USA to become ABDs, varying by discipline area. Expanding on earlier work in the USA by Mah (1986) that found perceived enhancement of the advisor–candidate relationship to play a key part in reducing ABD attrition, Hanson, Loose, and Reveles (2022). however, have drawn attention to the need to reform formal programme structures to improve candidate retention and completion rates. Anastasia and Burrington (2022) have stressed the importance of recognising training needs relating to the supervision of practitioner doctorate dissertations even for experienced research supervisors. They argue that distinct DBA mentoring is needed for scholar-practitioners. The extent to which bespoke supervisor training is provided in this area across business schools is open to question and not well documented. Our experiences suggest that this level of focused training is not widely accessible.

Mouzughi and Davies (2016) claimed that professional doctorate supervision adds a layer of complexity to understanding candidate-supervisor relationships and the DBA. There are specific challenges relating to the characteristics of professional doctoral candidates who may be working in highly influential professional roles with a wealth of experience in their chosen fields. In relation to the tailoring of mentorship to specific doctoral identities, there also remains a need for a deeper understanding of socio-cultural and geographically contextual sensitivities. For example, Davies (2016, p. 1) has advised DBA supervisors to 'transcend the Anglo-American model inherent in DBA curricula' and 'guard against neo-colonial mind sets' when working with candidates from Gulf Cooperation Council (GCC) states given the potential application of the doctorate in different nation-building contexts.

Hall and Burns (2009) locate the supervisor as a potential role model influencing the professional researcher identity formation of their candidates. They argue that 'the success or marginalization that students experience may depend on the extent to which they attempt to enact identities that are valued by their mentors'

(Hall & Burns, 2009, p. 49). Fit between mentors and protégés can be crucial (Baker, Pifer & Griffin, 2014) and is something that is often under-explored in mentoring scheme matching processes. For under-represented groups, a lack of appreciation and understanding of struggles faced (Zambrana et al., 2015) can be seen to be problematic in business schools where lack of diversity of faculty and/or heteronormative, gendered and racialised research environments are dominant as previously acknowledged earlier in this chapter. To this end, it is apparent that there is a need to design, support, and enact mentoring and supervision in a way that is intentionally mindful of equity and power issues (Bettencourt, Friedensen, & Bartlett, 2021) and pay attention to agentic and structural aspects relating to identity in doctoral supervision (Wilkin, Khosa, & Burch, 2022).

The Business Doctorate as Doctoral Training for Whom?

We have already noted how there is a need for the traditional business school model to evolve to meet a more complex student and employer context in mature countries especially and that its reproduction is linked to the recruitment of talent to ease faculty shortages. Within this context, training acquired through doctoral studies has been acknowledged to provide a key role in developing 'quality faculty' (Zimmerman, 2001) and 'qualified faculty' (Hawawini, 2005), particularly in relation to academic rigour (Schoemaker, 2008). In this vein, expectations for business school doctoral training to benefit faculty provision and the sustainability of the business school education model may be acknowledged.

In the context of European doctoral education, Baschung's (2010) study of a Norwegian PhD programme in finance acknowledged the influence of the Neo-Weberian-State (NWS) in the development, coordination and integration of doctoral training across universities by the state in the early 2000s. However, this was shaped by internationalisation of the doctorate in response to a national goal to achieve an internationally competitive PhD programme, swayed by the 1990s USA approach to doctoral education reform driven by US leaders of business and industry (Golden & Dore, 2001 in Matas, 2012). Linked to this, and the relinquishing of institutional autonomy, the quality of business school doctoral training has been found to be related to the heavy influence of rankings and external business school accreditation bodies.

Matas (2012, p. 163) identified in-programme doctoral training internationally as being part of an (ongoing) debate on what doctoral education should look like associated with preparing early-stage researchers with 'transferable or generic skills, as well as specific skills, in order to educate active and sustainable researchers for the competitive international knowledge-based societies of the 21st century'.

However, as acknowledged repeatedly in Chapter 2, there is a need to recognise the value of preparing candidates before they embark on the doctorate. Willison and Buisman-Pijlman (2016, p. 63), for example, have drawn attention to how, for doctoral candidates progressing to doctoral study through continuous education routes, research skills development from undergraduate programmes may be seen as part of the preparation for the doctorate in terms of 'deepening metacognition of research processes' and 'assisting students towards acting and thinking like researchers'. They refer to the value of a Researcher Skills Development framework (RSD7), based on the work of Willison and O'Regan (2008, 2015 as cited in Willison & Buisman-Pijlman, 2016) used with undergraduate students in Australian, Canadian, Irish and Dutch universities across disciplines, including business and management.

In the UK, the Vitae Researcher Development Framework (RDF) (Vitae, n.d.) is used to describe the knowledge, behaviour, and attributes of successful researchers. The Vitae RDF is widely used by UK universities and higher education institutions with research staff and PGRs to support development needs analysis in line with the concept of continuous professional development (CPD). Yet in the context of the professional doctorate, candidate perceptions of their development needs have been observed to differ, reflecting a need to revisit competencies in bringing together theory and practice during doctoral studies. This has resulted in the integration of a bespoke Researching Professional Development Framework into The Open University's EdD programme (Lindsay, Kerawalla, & Floyd, 2018).

It is notable that the positioning of the DBA as 'executive education' by some business schools is distinctive *vis-à-vis* many PhD programmes, signalling portfolio differentiation (see, e.g., Aston University, n.d.; ESCE–INSEEC, 2020; ISB, n.d.). Banerjee and Morley's (2013) focus on DBA programmes in the UK and Australia acknowledges the development of professional doctorates in response to the recognition of different modes of knowledge production and criticism surrounding the lack of PhD research relevance to practice. Use of the term 'executive' in PhDs in Belgium, France, India and the USA reflects the targeting of a particular market for the award, part-time professionals in the workplace. This exclusivity, in terms of positioning, is potentially open to a lack of equity of opportunity, however. For example, we have noted the issue of employer approval in Chapter 2 at the applications stage. The support of employers for part-time candidates can play an integral role in terms of funding and study time. Both types of support can impact greatly on candidate progress and completion rates, particularly in view of the existence of fewer funding options available for professional doctorates in comparison with other doctoral provisions (Stoten, 2020).

Additionally, the ways in which doctoral candidates are supported in-programme have been noted to impact on happiness and satisfaction. Bekova and Dzhafarova (2019, p. 87), focusing on PhD students enrolled in Russian universities, have reported that 'balancing work and study can benefit both the academic performance and professional experiences of PhD students, but only insofar as the topic of one's PhD thesis research is closely aligned with what they do in the workplace'. The alignment or fit of doctoral training with part-time doctoral candidates in employment requires further attention. We note the challenges of DBA and part-time PhD candidates in the workplace with employment positions that may change over the timeframe of programme completion and present challenges to doctoral supervisors and programme managers (Bourner, 2016), affect candidate performance, and ultimately, threaten attrition rates. To some extent, the lack of formal institutional responses to these types of trials is reflective of 'a gap in the literature in terms of a comparative approach that reports on the variety of experiences of PhD and PD students' (Stoten, 2022b, p. 321) but it also illustrates a normative approach to doctoral education management in many institutions that is centred on the full-time monograph PhD route. In many business schools, however, we note that, increasingly, the majority of doctoral candidates will not be studying for full-time PhDs.

We acknowledged some of the enduring divisions between business education and practice in Chapter 1. In the context of business doctorate recruitment, relational management education and co-production agendas have not only been identified as interventions for impact (Anderson, Ellwood, & Coleman, 2017) but offer opportunities for re-positioning of the doctorate (Crossouad, 2010). Some commentators such as Thomas (2007, p. 306) have gone so far as to argue that:

> The classic PhD degree does not belong in an applied social science such as marketing, but the less well-known Doctor of Business Administration (DBA) does. Those who pursue it will emerge better qualified to teach this real-world subject, without compromising their second role as researchers into the knowledge base. Every institution calling itself a 'business school' should therefore prefer the DBA as the route to establishment/tenure and promotion.

This viewpoint links to Banerjee and Morley's (2013) ideas relating to the development of professional doctorates in an attempt to meet changes in the context and content of a shifting knowledge economy and criticisms about traditional PhD relevance.

Roolaht's (2015) focus on industrial PhD programmes in Estonia, Assbring and Nuur's (2017) case study on collaborative doctoral education in Sweden, and Tavares, Sin, and Soares (2020) exploration of industry–university collaboration in industrial doctorates present fresh approaches to the recruitment and exploitation of doctoral talent. The idea of adding value to the business school doctorate offer through reflexive learning (Paton, Chia, & Burt, 2014) is also welcomed. Yet, to date, the scope for value creation rather than value addition has tended to be overlooked. As Smith (2018, p. 19) has observed 'co-funded academic-industrial doctoral programmes provide a framework for an engagement at both the institutional and individual level, although they are underdeveloped in business and management compared to engineering and the hard sciences'. This appears to be a missed opportunity in view of the scope for industrial PhD programmes to be policy tools for business schools and the wider university (Roolaht, 2015) and the powerful role of business-university collaborations in addressing productivity challenges (NCUB, 2022).

Where business and management industrial PhD programmes appear to have thrived, the establishment of explicit and embedded reciprocal long-term relationships may be identified as critical success factor. In Italy, the International Doctoral School in Human Capital Formation and Labor Relations, supported by private and public funding, has strategically used PhD scholarships in the promotion of academic and scientific exchange between universities and enterprises to meet business demand: 'doctoral students may be asked over the academic year to carry out specific project research and to undertake an internship at the company/institution funding their scholarship' (ADAPT, n.d., p. 1). Notably partnerships are prioritised with institutions (including non-profit), organisations and businesses funding the Doctoral School. As observed in Chapter 1, funding models affect the ability of business schools to detach themselves from national priorities to establish themselves as sector leaders. With respect to the university–industry interface, Thune (2009) has observed that our knowledge of the influence of industry collaboration on doctoral candidate experience, training, research, and subsequent careers is little understood.

Changes During the COVID-19 Pandemic and Future Prospects

The impact of the COVID-19 pandemic on business school doctoral education has evolved since 2020. Davies, Palmer, Braccia, Clegg, and Smith (2021) noted the challenges and opportunities presented by an unprecedented need to support doctoral programmes during a global pandemic, reflecting on initial and immediate business school responses in different European contexts.

Across the PGR sector, the issue of financial support during the COVID-19 pandemic has gained attention. Burke and Matthews (2021) critiqued Germany's Bäfog system of financial support based on it reaching less than one in five students affected by curtailing part-time employment opportunities due to lockdowns and acknowledged the need for government emergency loans to be arranged. Donohue, Lee, Simpson, and Vacek (2021) emphasised a need for institutions in the USA to be aware of the 'impacts of a crisis' and 'systemic strain' on doctoral candidates and to plan contingency assistance mechanisms in the areas of research design, access to resources, workload, mental health and finances. In many countries, institutional levels of support offered to doctoral candidates have focused on extensions to funding, assessment deadlines, and registration times, with a varied response notable between institutions reflecting reactive, emergency decision-making.

Progress and well-being have been identified as key issues for PhD candidates (Pyhältö, Tikkanen, & Anttila, 2022) but as Brandau, Vogt, and Garey (2022) noted, pressure has been placed on faculty to rapidly transition to unfamiliar teaching methodologies, at a cost to faculty mental health and well-being. Indeed, in the USA, 'clinically significant burnout' resulting from the pandemic has been reported, highlighting the importance of workplace relationships in terms of support (Leigh & Edwards, 2021). Tucker, Wilson, Hannibal, Lawless, and Qu's (2021) reflections on the ways in which an internationalised DBA programme at Liverpool Business School (UK) has had to adapt due to the COVID-19 pandemic draws attention to challenges in aligning doctoral-level teaching and learning strategies to the nature of the PGR candidate. Mandawali et al. (2022, p. 15) have argued that 'Doctoral supervision, including supervision at a distance, is a pedagogical activity, and critical reflection offers a useful tool to understand how the pedagogy is working and to consider how it might be adjusted'.

As a result of the pandemic, contrasts have been noted in terms of disrupted supervision versus 'business as usual' (Börgeson et al., 2021). Exploration of the impact of a shift to online supervision has identified better prospects for sustaining one-to-one rather than team-based interactions between doctoral candidates and supervisors (Torka, 2021). Ultimately, self-determination and level of dependency on guidance provided by advisers or supervisors have been found to affect doctoral candidate attrition during the pandemic (Hurt, Woods Ways, & Holmes, 2022).

Commentators have questioned the extent to which all doctoral candidates have been equally affected. In Belgium, van Tienoven, Glorieux, Minnen, Te Braak, and Spruyt (2022) have noted PhD candidates beginning their doctorates and those with family responsibilities have reported lower supervisor satisfaction scores as a result of the first and second national lockdowns. In Finland, Pyhältö et al. (2022) have identified candidates at the 'mid-phase of their studies to be at the greatest risk of being negatively impacted by the COVID-19 pandemic'. It is apparent that until the pandemic many institutions have paid little regard to candidate susceptibility to uncertainties due to status or personal circumstances. In the context of business schools, Leigh and Edwards (2021) drawing on the observations of Brammer and Clark (2020) have remarked that students were the stakeholders most impacted by the COVID-19 pandemic, with international students susceptible to isolation due to travel restrictions and border closures. Where doctoral programmes offer international and transnational provisions, it has been cautioned that there is a risk of shifts to online-only supervision compounding power distribution complexities and inequalities (Price & Martin, 2021).

Summary

- Preparedness for entry to doctoral studies appears to be overlooked in expectations relating to the time taken to complete. Two-year doctoral programmes may appear attractive but it is vital that an institution provides a solid grounding for doctoral students. The Design, Development, Implementation, and Support (DDIS) protocol is a useful tool.
- Integration into doctoral communities is variable. It is very important, however, that doctoral candidates are provided with opportunities to engage in discipline-level networks through research workshops and conferences, special interest groups, and become independent learners in a particular field.
- The progression and achievements of doctoral candidates depend on multiple factors such as country, institutional, and domestic contingencies but, additionally, we cannot overlook the existence of conservative culture in business schools and resistance to progressive agendas that are viewed as 'antithetical to free-market enterprise' (Jordan Peterson cited in Rhodes, 2022, p. 1).
- Opportunities to develop academic skills for teaching positions are not provided on a level playing field. While some postgraduate teaching assistantships are valuable and well-supported learning opportunities, others appear to exploit doctoral candidates as low-paid casual labour.
- Connections between self-identity transitions and the value of mentoring can be explored in greater depth.

- There is scope for further exploration and sharing of the practice of the extent to which doctoral training meets and might satisfy the expectations and needs of business school doctorate stakeholders.
- The University of Sydney's Vice-Chancellor has emphasised the need for co-located universities to collaborate (Scott, 2021) and we support this for business school doctoral programmes, not least in view of PGR resource challenges.

Questions you might like to consider:

- What does building a collegial community of doctoral candidates entail and how do we measure success for the individual, provider, and funder/employer?
- How do we orientate doctoral candidates, create a collaborative and open environment, and achieve success for all?
- How should we develop doctoral researcher identities within business schools?
- How do supervisory structures impact on the doctoral candidate's experience in business and management?
- How do we measure not just the progression of doctoral candidates but the 'distance travelled' and 'learning gained'?
- To what extent do external codes and standards set by accreditation bodies and quality assurance agencies affect the business school doctoral candidate experience?

References

AACSB. (2022). Diversity: The story in the stats. Retrieved from https://www.aacsb.edu/insights/articles/2022/04/diversity-the-story-in-the-stats. Accessed on September 10, 2022.

AACSB. (2023a). The PhD Project. Retrieved from https://www.aacsb.edu/about-us/advocacy/diversity-and-inclusion/the-phd-project. Accessed on March 25, 2023.

AACSB. (2023b, February 27). People and places. Retrieved from https://www.aacsb.edu/insights/articles/2023/02/people-and-places-february-7-2023. Accessed on March 25, 2023.

ADAPT. (n.d.). Human capital formation and labour relations. Retrieved from https://studylib.net/doc/5270684/human-capital-formation-and-labour-relations. Accessed on September 11, 2022.

Ahmad, T. (2020). Proposing student support model for postgraduate research education. *World Journal of Entrepreneurship, Management and Sustainable Development*, *17*(1), 125–139.

Anderson, L., Ellwood, P., & Coleman, C. (2017). The impactful academic: Relational management education as an intervention for impact. *British Journal of Management*, *28*(1), 14–28.

APA. (2015). Faculty in doctoral programs more responsive to white male prospective students. *Study finds*. Retrieved from https://www.apa.org/news/press/releases/2015/04/doctoral-white-male. Accessed on September 10, 2022.

Armstrong, S. J. (2004). The impact of supervisors' cognitive styles on the quality of research supervision in management education. *British Journal of Educational Psychology*, *74*(4), 599–616.

Assbring, L., & Nuur, C. (2017). What's in it for industry? A case study on collaborative doctoral education in Sweden. *Industry and Higher Education*, *31*(3), 184–194.

Aston University (n.d.). Executive DBA. Retrieved from https://studyonline.aston.ac.uk/programmes/executive-doctor-business-administration-dba. Accessed on September 11, 2022.

Austin, A. E. (2002). Preparing the next generation of faculty: Graduate school as socialization to the academic career. *The Journal of Higher Education*, *73*(1), 94–122.

Baker, V. L., & Pifer, M. J. (2011). The role of relationships in the transition from doctoral student to independent scholar. *Studies in Continuing Education*, *33*(1), 5–17.

Baker, V. L., Pifer, M. J., & Flemion, B. (2013). Process challenges and learning-based interactions in stage 2 of doctoral education: Implications from two applied social science fields. *The Journal of Higher Education*, *84*(4), 449–476.

Baker, V. L., Pifer, M. J., & Griffin, K. A. (2014). Mentor-protégé fit: Identifying and developing effective mentorship across identities in doctoral education. *International Journal for Researcher Development*, *5*(2), 83–98.

Banerjee, S., & Morley, C. (2013). Professional doctorates in management: Toward a practice-based approach to doctoral education. *Academy of Management Learning & Education*, *12*(2), 173–193.

Bao, Y., Kehm, B. M., & Ma, Y. (2018). From product to process: The reform of doctoral education in Europe and China. *Studies in Higher Education*, *43*(3), 524–541.

Baschung, L. (2010). Changes in the management of doctoral education. *European Journal of Education*, *45*(1), 138–152.

Bauman, D. (2020). Do graduate assistants earn a living wage? Not in these cities. Retrieved from https://www.chronicle.com/article/do-graduate-assistants-earn-a-living-wage-not-in-these-cities/. Accessed on September 10, 2022.

Bayona-Oré, S. (2021). Perceptions of postgraduate students on the relationship between thesis development and performance of a supervisor. *Journal of Turkish Science Education*, *18*(4), 559–573.

Bekova, S. (2021). Does employment during doctoral training reduce the PhD completion rate? *Studies in Higher Education*, *46*(6), 1068–1080.

Benmore, A. (2016). Boundary management in doctoral supervision: How supervisors negotiate roles and role transitions throughout the supervisory journey. *Studies in Higher Education*, *41*(7), 1251–1264.

Bennett, M. (2022a). PhD study in Sweden: A guide for 2022. Retrieved from https://www.findaphd.com/guides/phd-study-in-sweden. Accessed on September 10, 2022.

Bennett, M. (2022b). PhD study in the USA: A guide for 2022. Retrieved from https://www.findaphd.com/guides/phd-study-in-usa. Accessed on September 10, 2022.

Beňová, K. (2014). Research (er) at home: Auto/ethnography of (my) PhD. *European Journal of Higher Education*, *4*(1), 55–66.

Bettencourt, G. M., Friedensen, R. E., & Bartlett, M. L. (2021). Re-envisioning doctoral mentorship in the United States: A power-conscious review of the literature. *International Journal of Doctoral Studies*, *16*, 237.

Booth, A. L., & Satchell, S. E. (1996). British PhD completion rates: Some evidence from the 1980s. *Higher Education Review*, *28*(2), 48–56.

Börgeson, E., Sotak, M., Kraft, J., Bagunu, G., Biörserud, C., & Lange, S. (2021). Challenges in PhD education due to COVID-19-disrupted supervision or business as usual: A cross-sectional survey of Swedish biomedical sciences graduate students. *BMC Medical Education*, *21*(1), 1–11.

Bothello, J., & Roulet, T. J. (2019). The imposter syndrome, or the mis-representation of self in academic life. *Journal of Management Studies*, *56*(4), 854–861.

Bourdieu, P. (1977). *Reproduction in education, society and culture*. London: Sage.

Bourke, S., Holbrook, A., Lovat, T., & Farley, P. (2004, November). Attrition, completion and completion times of PhD candidates. In *AARE annual conference*, Melbourne, Victoria (Vol. 28, pp. 2–14).

Bourner, T. (2016). *A guide to professional doctorates in business and management* (pp. 294–298). Boca Raton, FL: CRC Press.

Bowden, J. A., Green, P. J., (2019). *Establishing integrity in doctoral research training. Playing the PhD game with integrity: Connecting research, professional practice and educational context* (pp. 225–255). Berlin: Springer.

Brammer, S., & Clark, T. (2020). COVID-19 and management education: Reflections on challenges, opportunities, and potential futures. *British Journal of Management, 31*(3), 453–456.

Brandau, M., Vogt, M., & Garey, M. L. (2022). The impact of the COVID-19 pandemic and transition to distance learning on University Faculty in the United States. *International Education Studies, 15*(3), 14–25.

Burgess, H., & Wellington, J. (2010). Exploring the impact of the professional doctorate on students' professional practice and personal development: Early indications. *Work Based Learning E-Journal, 1*(1), 160–176.

Burke, F., & Matthews, D. (2021). What Germany's new government means for research and innovation. Retrieved from https://sciencebusiness.net/news/what-germanys-new-government-means-research-and-innovation. Accessed on September 11, 2022.

Burkholder, G. J. (2022). Mentoring doctoral students in a distance learning environment. In D. Stein, H. R. Glazer, & C. Wanstreet (Eds.), *Driving innovation with for-profit adult higher education online institutions* (pp. 142–172). Hershey, PA: IGI Global.

Carter, S., Blumenstein, M., & Cook, C. (2013). Different for women? The challenges of doctoral studies. *Teaching in Higher Education, 18*(4), 339–351.

Charity, I. (2010). *PhD and professional doctorate: Higher degrees of separation?* DBA thesis, University of Northumbria, Newcastle.

Ching, G. S. (2021). Academic identity and communities of practice: Narratives of social science academics career decisions in Taiwan. *Education Sciences, 11*(8), 388. https://10.3390/educsci11080388

Clance, P. R., & Imes, S. A. (1978). The imposter phenomenon in high achieving women: Dynamics and therapeutic intervention. *Psychotherapy: Theory, Research & Practice, 15*(3), 241–247.

Coghlan, D., Coughlan, P., & Shani, A. B. (2019). Exploring doctorateness in insider action research. *International Journal of Action Research, 15*(1), 9–10.

Costley, T. (2008). You are beginning to sound like an academic: Finding and owning your academic voice'. In C. P. Casanave & X. Li (Eds.), *Learning the literacy practices of the graduate school: Insiders' reflections on academic enculturation* (pp. 74–87). Ann Arbor, MI: University of Michigan Press.

Cotterall, S. (2013). More than just a brain: Emotions and the doctoral experience. *Higher Education Research & Development, 32*(2), 174–187.

Cox, M. D. (2004). Introduction to faculty learning communities. *New Directions for Teaching and Learning, 2004*(97), 5–23.

Crossouard, B. (2013). Conceptualising doctoral researcher training through Bernstein's theoretical frameworks. *International Journal of Researcher Development, 4*(2), 72–85.

Davis, D. (2018). The laminal space occupied by a PhD student teacher. In *29th International networking for healthcare education conference* (pp. 4–6), Cambridge.

Davies, J. (2016). DBAs for GCC citizens: A call to acknowledge cultural origins and supervisors' impacts on nation building. In *UKCGE 5th international conference on professional doctorates*, March 15–16, Huddersfield. (Unpublished)

Davies, J., McGregor, F., & Horan, M. (2019). Autoethnography and the doctorate in business administration: Personal, practical and scholarly impacts. *The International Journal of Management Education, 17*(2), 201–213.

Davies, J., Palmer, N., Braccia, E., Clegg, K., & Smith, M. (2021). Supporting doctoral programmes during a global pandemic: Crisis as opportunity. *EFMD Global Focus, 1*(15), 20–24.

Deem, R., & Brehony, K. J. (2000). Doctoral students' access to research cultures: Are some more unequal than others? *Studies in Higher Education, 25*(2), 149–165.

Denicolo, P. (2004). Doctoral supervision of colleagues: Peeling off the veneer of satisfaction and competence. *Studies in Higher Education, 29*(6), 693–707.

Deshpande, A. (2016). A qualitative examination of challenges influencing doctoral students in an online doctoral program. *International Education Studies, 9*(6), 139–149.

Doloriert, C., & Sambrook, S. (2011). Accommodating an autoethnographic PhD: The tale of the thesis, the viva voce, and the traditional business school. *Journal of Contemporary Ethnography, 40*(5), 582–615.

Donohue, W. J., Lee, A. S. J., Simpson, S., & Vacek, K. (2021). Impacts of the COVID-19 pandemic on doctoral students' thesis/dissertation progress. *International Journal of Doctoral Studies, 16*, 533.

Douglas, A. S. (2021). Dimensions of fit for doctoral candidates: Supporting an academic identity. *Research Papers in Education, 37*(6), 1–21.

Dowle, S. (2020). *Retheorising doctoral completions: Exploring the role of critical events, structure and agency.* PhD thesis, Royal Holloway, University of London, Egham.

Easterby-Smith, M., Jaspersen, L. J., Thorpe, R., & Valizade, D. (2021). *Management and business research.* Newcastle upon Tyne: Sage.

Engwall, L. (2000). Foreign role models and standardisation in Nordic business education. *Scandinavian Journal of Management, 16*(1), 1–24.

EIASM. (2015). Guidelines for doctoral programs in business and management. Retrieved from https://www.eiasm.org/UserFiles/European%20Code%20of%20Practice%20-%20Revised%20(shorter)%20version%20-%20Sept%202015.pdf. Accessed on September 10, 2022.

Elliot, D. L., Bengtsen, S. S., Guccione, K., & Kobayashi, S. (2020). A 'Doctoral Learning Ecology Model'. *The Hidden Curriculum in Doctoral Education, 97*–111.

Engwall, L. (2004). The Americanization of Nordic management education. *Journal of Management Inquiry, 13*(2), 109–117.

Engwall, L. (2007). The anatomy of management education. *Scandinavian Journal of Management, 23*(1), 4–35.

Erwee, R., & Perry, C. (2018). Examination of doctoral theses: Research about the process and proposed procedures. *Postgraduate Education in Higher Education, 359*–374.

ESRC. (2021, October 5). Review of the PhD in the social sciences. Retrieved from https://www.ukri.org/what-we-offer/developing-people-and-skills/esrc/esrc-review-of-the-phd-in-the-social-sciences/. Accessed on March 24, 2023.

Ford, J., Harding, N., & Learmonth, M. (2010). Who is it that would make business schools more critical? Critical reflections on critical management studies. *British Journal of Management, 21*, s71–s81.

Fry, G., Tress, B., & Tress, G. (2006). PhD students and integrative research. In *From landscape research to landscape planning: Aspects of integration, education and application* (Vol. 12, pp. 193–205). Berlin: Springer.

Gardner, S. K., & Gopaul, B. (2012). The part-time doctoral student experience. *International Journal of Doctoral Studies, 7*, 63.

Greener, S. L. (2021). Non-supervisory support for doctoral students in business and management: A critical friend. *The International Journal of Management Education, 19*(2), 100463.

Greenfield, N. M. (2022). White men have more freedom over research choice: Study. Retrieved from https://www.universityworldnews.com/post.php?story=2022011407030929. Accessed on September 10, 2022.

Gube, J. C. C., Getenet, S. T., Satariyan, A., & Muhammad, Y. (2017). Towards 'operating within' the field: Doctoral students' views of supervisors' discipline expertise. *International Journal of Doctoral Studies, 12*, 1–16.

Hall, L., & Burns, L. (2009). Identity development and mentoring in doctoral education. *Harvard Educational Review, 79*(1), 49–70.

Hanson, J., Loose, W., & Reveles, U. (2022). A qualitative case study of all-but-dissertation students at risk for dissertation noncompletion: A new model for supporting candidates to doctoral completion. *Journal of College Student Retention: Research, Theory & Practice, 24*(1), 234–262.

Hawawini, G. (2005). The future of business schools. *Journal of Management Development, 24*(9), 770–782.

Hay, A. (2022, December 18). On the neglect of fallibility in management learning and education: From perfect to adequate managers. *Academy of Management Learning & Education.* Retrieved from https://doi.org/10.5465/amle.2022.0032. Accessed on March 25, 2023.

Helm, M., Campa, H., III, & Moretto, K. (2012). Professional socialization for the Ph.D.: An exploration of career and professional development preparedness and readiness for Ph.D. candidates. *The Journal of Faculty Development, 26*(2), 5–23.

Hockey, J. (1994). New territory: Problems of adjusting to the first year of a social science PhD. *Studies in Higher Education, 19*(2), 177–190.

Hogan, O., Kortt, M. A., & Charles, M. B. (2020). Standing at the crossroads: The vulnerabilities of Australian business schools. *Education+ Training, 62*(6), 707–720.

Horta, H., Birolini, S., Cattaneo, M., Shen, W., & Paleari, S. (2021). Research network propagation: The impact of PhD students' temporary international mobility. *Quantitative Science Studies, 2*(1), 129–154.

Horta, H., Cattaneo, M., & Meoli, M. (2019). The impact of Ph.D. funding on time to Ph.D. completion. *Research Evaluation, 28*(2), 182–195.

Houston, D. (2007). TQM and higher education: A critical systems perspective on fitness for purpose. *Quality in Higher Education, 13*(1), 3–17.

Hurt, S., Woods Ways, E., & Holmes, B. (2022). Wait! Don't quit! Stay with your doctoral program during the global pandemic: Lessons learned from program completers. *The Journal of Advancing Education Practice, 3*(1), 2.

INSEEC. (2020). 1st Year: DBA. Retrieved from https://www.inseec.education/1st-year-dba/. Accessed on March 25, 2023.

ISB. (n.d.). ISB doctoral programmes. Retrieved from https://www.isb.edu/en/study-isb/doctoral-studies.html. Accessed on March 25, 2023.

Jaschik, S. (2014). The bias for white men. Retrieved from https://www.insidehighered.com/news/2014/04/24/study-finds-faculty-members-are-more-likely-respond-white-males-others. Accessed on September 10, 2022.

Jazvac-Martek, M., Chen, S., & McAlpine, L. (2011). Tracking the doctoral student experience over time: Cultivating agency in diverse spaces. *Doctoral education: Research-based strategies for doctoral students, supervisors and administrators* (pp. 17–36).

Johnson, D. (2005). Assessment matters: Some issues concerning the supervision and assessment of work-based doctorates. *Innovations in Education and Teaching International, 42*(1), 87–92.

Juusola, K., Kettunen, K., & Alajoutsijärvi, K. (2015). Accelerating the Americanization of management education: Five responses from business schools. *Journal of Management Inquiry, 24*(4), 347–369.

Kamler, B., & Thomson, P. (2014). *Helping doctoral students write: Pedagogies for supervision.* Oxfordshire: Routledge.

Keefer, J. M. (2015). Experiencing doctoral liminality as a conceptual threshold and how supervisors can use it. *Innovations in Education and Teaching International, 52*(1), 17–28.

Kelan, E. K., & Jones, R. D. (2010). Gender and the MBA. *Academy of Management Learning & Education, 9*(1), 26–43.

Kelley, M. J., & Salisbury-Glennon, J. D. (2016). The role of self-regulation in doctoral students' status of all but dissertation (ABD). *Innovative Higher Education, 41*(1), 87–100.

Lantsoght, E. O. (2021). Students' perceptions of doctoral defense in relation to sociodemographic characteristics. *Education Sciences, 11*(9), 463.

Lee, A., & Murray, R. (2015). Supervising writing: Helping postgraduate students develop as researchers. *Innovations in Education and Teaching International, 52*(5), 558–570.

Leigh, J. S., & Edwards, M. S. (2021). Drowning on dry land: Looking back and learning from COVID-19. *Journal of Management Education, 45*(6), 823–833.

Lindner, R. (2020). Barriers to doctoral education. Retrieved from https://www.grad.ucl.ac.uk/strategy/barriers-to-doctoral-education.pdf. Accessed on September 10, 2022.

Lindsay, H., Kerawalla, L., & Floyd, A. (2018). Supporting researching professionals: EdD students' perceptions of their development needs. *Studies in Higher Education, 43*(12), 2321–2335.

Lindsay, S. (2015). What works for doctoral students in completing their thesis? *Teaching in Higher Education, 20*(2), 183–196.

Mah, D. M. (1986). *The process of doctoral candidate attrition: A study of the all but dissertation (ABD) phenomenon.* Seattle, WA: University of Washington.

Maher, M. A., Ford, M. E., & Thompson, C. M. (2004). Degree progress of women doctoral students: Factors that constrain, facilitate, and differentiate. *The Review of Higher Education, 27*(3), 385–408.

Mahn, H., & John-Steiner, V. (2002). The gift of confidence: A Vygotskian view of emotions. In *Learning for life in the 21st century: Sociocultural perspectives on the future of education* (pp. 46–58). Hoboken, NJ: Blackwell Publishers.

Maloshonok, N., & Terentev, E. (2019). National barriers to the completion of doctoral programs at Russian universities. *Higher Education, 77*(2), 195–211.

Mandalawi, S. M., Henderson, R., Huijser, H., & Kek, M. Y. C. A. (2022). Issues of belonging, pedagogy and learning in doctoral study at a distance. *Journal of University Teaching & Learning Practice, 19*(4), 15.

Matas, C. P. (2012). Doctoral education and skills development: An international perspective. *REDU: Revista de Docencia Universitaria, 10*(2), 163.

Maxwell, T. W., & Kupczyk-Romanczuk, G. (2009). Producing the professional doctorate: The portfolio as a legitimate alternative to the dissertation. *Innovations in Education and Teaching International, 46*(2), 135–145.

May, R. (2013). An investigation of the casualisation of academic work in Australia. PhD dissertation, Griffith University, Australia.

McAlpine, L., Paulson, J., Gonsalves, A., & Jazvac-Martek, M. (2012). 'Untold' doctoral stories: Can we move beyond cultural narratives of neglect? *Higher Education Research & Development, 31*(4), 511–523.

McCray, J., & Joseph-Richard, P. (2021). Doctoral students' well-being in United Kingdom business schools: A survey of personal experience and support mechanisms. *The International Journal of Management Education, 19*(2), 100490.

Metcalfe, J., Wilson, S., & Levecque, K. (2018). *Exploring wellbeing and mental health and associated support services for postgraduate researchers.* Vitae in partnership with the Institute of Employment Studies (IES) and the University of Ghent. Retrieved from https://www.vitae.ac.uk/doing-research/wellbeing-and-mental-health/HEFCE-Report_Exploring-PGR-Mental-health-support/view. Accessed on March 27, 2023.

Mewburn, I., Cuthbert, D., & Tokareva, E. (2014). Experiencing the progress report: An analysis of gender and administration in doctoral candidature. *Journal of Higher Education Policy and Management, 36*(2), 155–171.

Millar, J., & Price, M. (2018). Imagining management education: A critique of the contribution of the United Nations PRME to critical reflexivity and rethinking management education. *Management Learning*, *49*(3), 346–362.

Mogaji, E., Adamu, N., & Nguyen, N.P. (2021). Stakeholders shaping experiences of self-funded international PhD students in UK business schools. *The International Journal of Management Education*, *19*(3), 100543.

Morgenshtern, M., & Novotna, G. (2012). (In)(Out) Sider (s): White immigrant PhD students reflecting on their teaching experience. *Social Work Education*, *31*(1), 47–62.

Morley, L., Leonard, D., & David, M. (2002). Variations in vivas: Quality and equality in British PhD assessments. *Studies in Higher Education*, *27*(3), 263–273.

Mouzughi, Y., & Davies, J. (2016, July 4–5). A call for supervisors with split personalities: An exploration of PhD and Prof Doc supervision roles. In *Achieving excellence in Masters and Doctoral education*. Huddersfield: University of Huddersfield.

Mujtaba, B. G., Scharff, M. M., Cavico, F. J., & Mujtaba, M. G. (2008). Challenges and joys of earning a doctorate degree: Overcoming the 'ABD' phenomenon. *Research in Higher Education Journal*, *1*, 9.

NCUB. (2022). State of the relationship 2022. Analysing trends in UK university-business collaborations. National Centre for Universities and Business. Retrieved from https://www.ncub.co.uk/wp-content/uploads/2022/12/NCUB_State_of_the_Relationship_2022-digital.pdf. Accessed on December 1, 2022.

Nerad, M. (2004). The PhD in the US: Criticisms, facts, and remedies. *Higher Education Policy*, *17*(2), 183–199.

Nerad, M., & Cerny, J. (1993). From facts to action: Expanding the graduate division's educational role. In L. L. Baird (Ed.), *New directions for institutional research* (Vol. 80, pp. 27–39). San Francisco, CA: Jossey-Bass.

Okoli, M. (2019). *Doctoral research supervision experiences of business education students in Nigeria*. Ph.D. thesis, University of KwaZulu-Natal, Durban.

Ozturk, M. B., & Rumens, N. (2014). Gay male academics in UK business and management schools: Negotiating heteronormativities in everyday work life. *British Journal of Management*, *25*(3), 503–517.

Palmer, N. (2019). *Case study 2: Application to senior fellowship of the higher education academy*. AdvanceHE. Unpublished.

Park, C. (2005). New variant PhD: The changing nature of the doctorate in the UK. *Journal of Higher Education Policy and Management*, *27*(2), 189–207.

Parker, M. (2002). Queering management and organization. *Gender, Work & Organization*, *9*(2), 146–166.

Paton, S., Chia, R., & Burt, G. (2014). Relevance or 'relevate'? How university business schools can add value through reflexively learning from strategic partnerships with business. *Management Learning*, *45*(3), 267–288.

Perea, E., & Brady, M. (2017). Research rigor and the gap between academic journals and business practitioners. *Journal of Management Development*, *36*(8), 1052–1062.

Perry, C., & Cavaye, A. (2004). Australian universities' examination criteria for DBA dissertations. *International Journal of Organisational Behaviour*, *7*(5), 411–421.

Pilbeam, C., & Denyer, D. (2009). Lone scholar or community member? The role of student networks in doctoral education in a UK management school. *Studies in Higher Education*, *34*(3), 301–318.

Pina, A. A., Maclennan, H. L., Moran, K. A., & Hafford, P. F. (2016). The DBA vs. Ph.D. in US business and management programs: Different by degrees? *Journal for Excellence in Business & Education*, *4*(1), 6–19.

Poole, B. (2018). Doctorateness and the DBA: What next? *Higher Education, Skills and Work-based Learning*, *8*(2), 211–223.

Price, M., & Martin, R. (2021). Co-constructed transnational learning in postgraduate research supervision: Exploring issues of power and trust. *African Perspectives of Research in Teaching and Learning*, 5(1), 158–165.

Pyhältö, K., & Keskinen, J. (2012). Doctoral students' sense of relational agency in their scholarly communities. *International Journal of Higher Education*, 1(2), 136–149.

Pyhältö, K., Tikkanen, L., & Anttila, H. (2022). The influence of the COVID-19 pandemic on PhD candidates' study progress and study wellbeing. *Higher Education Research & Development*, 1–14.

Pyrzynska, A. (2020). Selected problems regarding the status of PhD Student. *Bialstockie Studia Prawnicze*, 25, 111.

Raineri, N. (2013). The PhD program: Between conformity and reflexivity. *Journal of Organizational Ethnography*, 2(1), 37–56.

Ramirez, E. (2017). Unequal socialization: Interrogating the Chicano/Latino (a) doctoral education experience. *Journal of Diversity in Higher Education*, 10(1), 25.

Redpath, L. (2012). Confronting the bias against on-line learning in management education. *Academy of Management Learning & Education*, 11(1), 125–140.

Reed, M. (2019). Hypercompetitive and Resource Limited. *InsiderHE*. Retrieved from https://www.insidehighered.com/blogs/confessions-community-college-dean/hyper-competitive-and-resource-limited. Accessed on April 6, 2023.

Rhodes, C. (2022). 'Woke' business schools? The reality is quite the opposite. *Times Higher Education*, February 3 Retrieved from https://www.timeshighereducation.com/blog/woke-business-schools-reality-quite-opposite/. Accessed on March 25, 2023.

Rigg, C., Ellwood, P., & Anderson, L. (2021). Becoming a scholarly management practitioner–Entanglements between the worlds of practice and scholarship. *The International Journal of Management Education*, 19(2), 100497.

Rigler, K. L., Jr, Anastasia, C. M., El-Amin, A., & Throne, R. (2021). Scholarly voice and academic identity: A systematic review of doctoral student agency. In *Handbook of research on developing students' scholarly dispositions in higher education* (pp. 63–89). Hershey, PA: IGI Global.

Rodwell, J., & Neumann, R. (2008). Predictors of timely doctoral student completions by type of attendance: The utility of a pragmatic approach. *Journal of Higher Education Policy and Management*, 30(1), 65–76.

Roolaht, T. (2015). Enhancing the industrial PhD programme as a policy tool for university—Industry cooperation. *Industry and Higher Education*, 29(4), 257–269.

Rostron, A. (2021). Failing better: Learning from failure and learning to fail in the Doctorate of Business Administration. In *Organisation studies and human resource management* (pp. 191–201). Oxfordshire: Routledge.

Ruano-Borbalan, J. C. (2022). Doctoral education from its medieval foundations to today's globalisation and standardisation. *European Journal of Education*, 57(3), 367–380.

Ruggeri-Stevens, G., Bareham, J., & Bourner, T. (2001). The DBA in British universities: Assessment and standards. *Quality Assurance in Education*, 9(2), 61–71.

Russell, D. L. (2021). Design, development, implementation, and support (DDIS): Supporting online nontraditional doctoral candidates. *Higher Learning Research Communications*, 11(1), 14–26.

Salminen-Karlsson, M. (2013). Choosing between academy and industry: Industrial PhDs and their supervisors speak about gendered research environments. *GEXcel Work in Progress Report*, XVIII(11), 45.

Sarros, J. C., Willis, R. J., Fisher, R., & Storen, A. (2005). DBA examination procedures and protocols. *Journal of Higher Education Policy and Management*, 27(2), 151–172.

Saunders, M. K., & Fortin, M. (2023). Building and maintaining trust in doctoral supervisor/supervisee relationships. *EFMD Global Focus*, 2(17), 28–33.

Schleef, D. J. (2005). *Managing elites: Socializaton in law and business schools*. Lanham, MD: Rowman & Littlefield Publishers.

Schoemaker, P. J. (2008). The future challenges of business: Rethinking management education. *California Management Review*, *50*(3), 119–139.

Scott, M. (2021). Prof. Mark Scott AO, Vice Chancellor, The University of Sydney. *YouTube*. Retrieved from https://www.youtube.com/watch?v=jhuB9-TF-JU. Accessed on September 8, 2021.

Shaw, S., & Cassell, C. (2007). 'That's not how I see it': Female and male perspectives on the academic role. *Women in Management Review*, *22*(6), 497–515.

Sin, C., Soares, D., & Tavares, O. (2021). Coursework in industrial doctorates: A worthwhile contribution to students' training? *Higher Education Research & Development*, *40*(6), 1298–1312.

Širaliova, J., & Angelis, J. J. (2006). Marketing strategy in the Baltics: Standardise or adapt? *Baltic Journal of Management*, *1*(2), 169–187.

Skakni, I. (2018). Doctoral studies as an initiatory trial: Expected and taken-for-granted practices that impede PhD students' progress. *Teaching in Higher Education*, *23*(8), 927–944.

Smith, M. (2018). The battle for doctoral talent. *EFMD Global Focus*, *2*(3). Retrieved from https://www.globalfocusmagazine.com/wp-content/uploads/2018/05/Issue_2_2018_3_battle_doc_talent.pdf/. Accessed on September 10, 2022.

Smith McGloin, R. (2021). A new mobilities approach to re-examining the doctoral journey: Mobility and fixity in the borderlands space. *Teaching in Higher Education*, *26*(3), 370–386.

Spronken-Smith, R., Cameron, C., & Quigg, R. (2018). Factors contributing to high PhD completion rates: a case study in a research-intensive university in New Zealand. *Assessment & Evaluation in Higher Education*, *43*(1), 94–109.

Stoten, D. W. (2020). How do doctoral students interpret the idea of being part of a doctoral community at an English business school? *Qualitative Research Journal*, *20*(1), 1–18.

Stoten, D. W. (2022a). 'I've been in a box too long and I didn't even realise that I was.' How can we conceptualise the subjective well-being of students undertaking a part-time DBA? The IICC model. *The Journal of Continuing Higher Education*, 1–18.

Stoten, D. (2022b). Conceptualising subjective well-being through Social Ecology Systems theory: A comparison of PhD and Professional Doctorate students' experiences. *Innovative Practice in Higher Education*, *4*(3), 321–354.

Sun, X., & Trent, J. (2020). Ongoing doctoral study process to live by: A narrative inquiry into the doctoral identity construction experiences—A Chinese case. *Frontiers of Education in China*, *15*(3), 422–452.

Szadkowski, K. (2014). The long shadow of doctoral candidate status: Case study-Poland. *Social Work & Society*, *12*(2).

Tavares, O., Sin, C., & Soares, D. (2020). Building bridges between industry and academia: What is the profile of an industrial doctorate student? *Structural and Institutional Transformations in Doctoral Education: Social, Political and Student Expectations*, 347–373.

Thomas, M. J. (2007). Is your doctorate really necessary? *Marketing Intelligence & Planning*, *25*(4), 306–307.

Thune, T. (2009). Doctoral students on the university–industry interface: A review of the literature. *Higher Education*, *58*(5), 637–651.

Torka, M. (2021). The transition from in-person to online supervision: Does the interaction between doctoral advisors and candidates change? *Innovations in Education and Teaching International*, *58*(6), 659–671.

Tucker, M. P., Wilson, H., Hannibal, C., Lawless, A., & Qu, Z. (2021). Delivering professional doctorate education: Challenges and experiences during the COVID-19 pandemic. In *SHS web of conferences* (Vol. 99), Les Ulis.

University of Warsaw. (2022). Scholarships for PhD students and social matters. Retrieved from https://welcome.uw.edu.pl/scholarships-for-phd-students/. Accessed on September 10, 2022.

UCU. (n.d.). PGRs as staff. Retrieved from https://www.ucu.org.uk/PGRs-as-staff. Accessed on March 25, 2023.

van Tienoven, T. P., Glorieux, A., Minnen, J., Te Braak, P., & Spruyt, B. (2022). Graduate students locked down? PhD students' satisfaction with supervision during the first and second COVID-19 lockdown in Belgium. *Plos One*, *17*(5), e0268923.

Vitae. (n.d.). About the Vitae Researcher Development Framework. Retrieved from https://www.Vitae.ac.uk/researchers-professional-development/about-the-Vitae-researcher-development-framework/. Accessed on March 24, 2023.

Walker, J. D., Baepler, P., & Cohen, B. (2008). The scholarship of teaching and learning paradox: Results without rewards. *College Teaching*, *56*(3), 183–190.

Wanyama, S. B., & Eyamu, S. (2021). Perceived organizational support, graduate research supervision and research completion rate. *Employee Relations: The International Journal*, *43*(6), 1414–1430.

Watts, J. H. (2009). From professional to PhD student: Challenges of status transition. *Teaching in Higher Education*, *14*(6), 687–691.

Wellington, J. (2013). Searching for 'doctorateness'. *Studies in Higher Education*, *38*(10), 1490–1503.

Wilkin, C. L., Khosa, A., & Burch, S. (2022). Identity in doctoral supervision: Perspectives on agency and structure. *The Journal of Higher Education*, *94*(2), 1–35.

Wilkins, S., Neri, S., & Lean, J. (2019). The role of theory in the business/management PhD: How students may use theory to make an original contribution to knowledge. *The International Journal of Management Education*, *17*(3), 100316.

Willison, J., & Buisman-Pijlman, F. (2016). PhD prepared: Research skill development across the undergraduate years. Retrieved from https://www.emerald.com/insight/content/doi/10.1108/IJRD-07-2015-0018/full/html. Accessed on May 9, 2016.

Willson, R. (2022). Identifying and leveraging collegial and institutional supports for impact. In W. Kelly (Ed.), *The impactful academic: Building a research career that makes a difference* (pp. 13–28). Leeds: Emerald.

Wrigley, C., Wolifson, P., & Matthews, J. (2021). Supervising cohorts of higher degree research students: Design catalysts for industry and innovation. *Higher Education*, *81*(6), 1177–1196.

Yasukawa, K., & Dados, N. (2018, January). How much is this number worth? Representations of academic casualisation in Australian universities. In *Higher education research and development society of Australasia annual international conference*, Hammondville, Australasia.

Zambrana, R. E., Ray, R., Espino, M. M., Castro, C., Douthirt Cohen, B., & Eliason, J. (2015). 'Don't leave us behind': The importance of mentoring for underrepresented minority faculty. *American Educational Research Journal*, *52*(1), 40–72.

Zimmerman, J. L. (2001). Can American business schools survive? Retrieved from https://papers.ssrn.com/sol3/papers.cfm?abstract_id=283112. Accessed on September 11, 2001.

Chapter 4

Employability, Career Management and Postdoctoral Outcomes in Business and Management

Overview

The Organisation for Economic Co-operation and Development's (OECD, 2020) identification of the worst jobs crisis since the Great Depression and the United Nations' (2022) concerns over gaining and regaining footholds in the future job market signify global economic disruption. More recently, forecasts that global unemployment would be pushed over 200 million in 2022 due to the impacts of the COVID-19 pandemic (United Nations, 2021) were overturned within one month when the International Labour Organisation's (2021) World Employment and Social Outlook Trends 2022 report stated that employment growth to make up for the losses was not expected to catch up until 2023. We did see some signs of economic recovery in early 2023 but Capital Economics (2023) has reported that resilience will give way to recession with cautious optimism for recovery in the short- to medium-term. It is with this in mind that we explore employability and employer links at the postgraduate research (PGR) level in business schools and the potential that closer alignment to business has for better business and management doctoral experiences, graduate outcomes, stronger links between industry and academia, and leading-edge creative practices.

Brain Drain, Brain Gain and Business Doctorate Mobility: The Academic Career Market

Little has been formally written about employability and employer links at doctoral level in business schools. We have repeatedly acknowledged that there are expectations that the PhD plays a key role in the training and recruitment of new faculty in business schools across the globe. There have been sustained reports of a shortage of business school professors and predictions that this shortage may continue in the USA (AACSB, 2007; Daly & Weber, 2021; Gardiner, 2011), India (McCullough & Wooten, 1984; Merritt, 2004; Neelam, Sheorey, Bhattacharya, & Kunte, 2020; QS Contributor, 2014; University World News, 2011),

Business and Management Doctorates World-Wide: Developing the Next Generation, 103–124
Copyright © 2024 by Nicola J. Palmer, Julie Davies and Clare Viney
Published under exclusive licence by Emerald Publishing Limited
doi:10.1108/978-1-78973-499-720231004

UK (Ivory, Miskell, Neely, Shipton, & White, 2007), China (Bradshaw, 2014), and Australia (Mather & Lebihan, 2008). This contrasts with many reports of an over-production of PhD graduates versus academic career opportunities in some academic disciplines (e.g., CCA, 2021; Ganning, 2022), and high levels of unfulfilled preference among doctoral degree candidates for academic careers (e.g., in the UK – Grove, 2021 – and in other parts of Europe – Hnatkova, Degtyarova, Kersschot, & Boman, 2022).

Multiple reasons exist for a shortage of business school faculty. In parts of Africa, Asia, the Middle East, and the Caribbean 'brain drain' reflecting a trend towards studying overseas to complete PhDs and not returning has been documented (Brissett, 2021; Nabawanuka, 2011; Song, 1997; Tansel & Demet Güngör, 2003; Zweig, 2006). The strategy of encouraging doctoral candidates to train overseas with the goal of bringing back knowledge to develop faculty at home appears to be unrealised or at least open to question. Indeed, Brentschneider and Dai (2017) have questioned the extent to which returning home is made more attractive through science infrastructure. Furthermore, Kahn and MacGarvie (2020) have highlighted visa and immigration policies and processes that challenge opportunities for permanent residency status, particularly in relation to East–West mobilities in academic employment. Chen (2006) has drawn attention to a need to understand international graduate student mobility in relation to outcomes for graduates plus the strategic contribution of doctoral education to national economies. She (Chen, 2006) noted a desire among Chinese, Hong Kong, Japanese, Korean, and Taiwanese graduate students graduating from Canadian universities in China, Hong Kong, Japan, Korea, and Taiwan to work in North American universities and argued that:

> international students benefit from possible future career enhancements and improved job prospects in an international setting. Finally, those who intend to emigrate to North America gain opportunities to explore the best environment for their studies and future careers through these international activities. This also benefits Canada, as Canada would like to attract and retain the best and brightest international students as immigrants. (Chen, 2006, pp. 100–101)

In the context of business schools, 'brain gain', linked to the circulation of global talent as a result of international doctoral candidates deciding to remain in their countries of study, may be linked to business school status as perceived by academics, students and business community stakeholders, and a closed hierarchical system (D'Aveni, 1996). One outcome of this for business school academic careers is 'homosocial reproduction of senior faculties and social isolation and immobility for certain PhD graduates' (D'Aveni, 1996, p. 166), limiting competition and business school academic employment opportunities. Linked to this is a shortage of business school faculty diversity in terms of racialised backgrounds as noted in a USA context by Burrell,

Finch, Dawson, Rahim, and Williams (2012). Bedeian et al. (2010) noted that graduates from more prestigious doctoral programmes benefitted from better initial and subsequent academic career prospects. Inevitably, there are links between financially well-endowed or generous business schools and doctoral alumni mobility. Doctoral programmes must support candidates' employability beyond traditional academic career options (Paolo & Mañé, 2016). It is particularly important to avoid a 'drop out crisis' (Wollast et al., 2023) from doctoral programmes or situations where candidates accrue significant debts and do not graduate.

Although a status hierarchy of business schools has been noted, there are some opportunities for doctoral graduates from lower-ranking business schools to secure academic careers at higher-ranking institutions. A focus on where PhD graduates are 'placed' in relation to league tables such as the global *Financial Times* business school rankings reflects a broader, global academic system that 'gauges programme excellence by placing graduate students at research universities' (Posselt, 2016, p. 5). The outputs of doctoral programmes in terms of academic employment tend to be based on prestige linked to research rather than teaching skills (Armstrong & Sperry, 1994). What this means for Graduate Teaching Assistants (GTAs) in business and management, who are forced to reconcile teaching and researcher roles (Collins, Brown, & Leigh, 2021) has yet to be explored in relation to the academic job market. Earlier considerations of the role of GTAs in North America and the UK prompted the question of whether American business schools were beginning to focus on increasing teaching excellence (Butler, Laumer, & Moore, 1994). However, it has been observed that the GTA model attempts to meet multiple institutional teaching and learning, and research objectives, leaving GTAs feeling like 'donkeys in the department' (Park & Ramos, 2002). More recently, attention has turned to the employability value of formal teacher training for GTAs as a transferable skill to enhance PhD employability within or outside academia (Barr & Wright, 2019).

Role Modelling Business School PhD Graduate Careers

Back in 1968, George J. Gore, writing in the *Academy of Management Journal*, questioned the number of new PhDs in business and management entering the field without any prior direct or meaningful contact with the business world (Gore, 1968). This prompted a myriad of responses in a still ongoing debate. Wren, Atherton, and Michaelsen (1978), for example, contended that a typical management professor has 12 years of managerial experience and seven years of non-managerial experience, arguing that it is not a simple case of 'the blind leading the blind'. Yet the currency of that experience may be questioned. Picking up on Gore's (1968) point about the need for meaningful contact with the business world, Bolton and Stolcis (2003), Darabi, Saunders, and Clark (2020), Santini, Marinelli, Boden, Cavicchi, and Haegeman (2016), Simba and Ojong (2017), and Wilkerson (1999) maintain there is a need to enhance the relevance of business and management research to practitioners. This requires reducing the gap between thinkers and doers, paying attention to engaged scholarship, and increasing professors' managerial work exposure.

The aforementioned debate on business relevance and managerial experience of business school faculty does not acknowledge the existence of the 'pracademic', a term popularised by Posner (2009). Yet, we might observe that someone who is both an academic and an active practitioner in their subject area is explicitly recognised and welcomed by international business school accreditation systems. For example, AACSB's 'practice academic' (PA) category, albeit often interpreted as linked to the deficit – normally doctorally qualified or doctorally prepared faculty members who do not publish – rather than its intended acknowledgement of practice community engagement contributions (Bryant, 2019).

In many traditional North American and European state-owned universities, a structurally imposed division between different academic contracts and permitted contributions may be outlined at an institutional level. This can translate into rules on who can supervise doctoral researchers or not. In some UK research-intensive Russell Group universities and North American universities, including those outside the Ivy League, for example, research supervision is an activity that can only be undertaken by 'research and teaching' academics and not 'teaching and scholarship' academics; the implications of this are often overlooked when considering the potential to provide business relevant doctorates. Indeed, 'the added value that they [pracademics] bring to the student experience by drawing on their practitioner knowledge, skills, experience and values, and accessing employer networks' (Dickinson, Fowler, & Griffiths, 2020, p. 1) appears to be potentially lost to many supervised doctoral candidates.

Notably, in business and management, there have been calls to reject 'an overly narrow definition of research as the only legitimate avenue to further knowledge' (CELTS, 2021, p. 1) in line with Boyer's (1996) ideas on engaged scholarship – to end the subdivision of faculty work into distinct and separate teaching, research, and service tasks (Beaulieu, Breton, & Brousselle, 2018). Linked to this, over the past decade, we have witnessed clear attempts to transform management practice in business schools and this has highlighted difficulties for critical management studies, in particular (see, e.g., King & Learmonth, 2015). Does the marketisation of higher education offer increased opportunities for business schools to harness stronger and more explicit business-education links?

We note that UK business schools currently remain less dependent on commercial sponsorships and academic–practitioner–policy-maker exchanges than their USA and other European counterparts. Additionally, we observe that in business and management, a scarcity of second-career academics, 'experienced and qualified business practitioners … recruited to assume the role of academics' (Ong, 2021, p. 11003), has been identified. In contrast, in the field of accountancy where doctoral-level faculty recruitment challenges have been especially noted due to AACSB practitioner/academic distinctions, Boyle, Carpenter, and Hermanson (2015) highlighted the potential for non-traditional doctoral programmes, such as DBAs, to offer a potential solution for smaller, non-doctoral institutions to provide doctorally qualified educators. Business school faculty may be required to complete DBAs to maintain their employment if they have joined a university without a doctorate and this raises ethical challenges. The qualification can provide career enhancement to individuals, increase the number of doctorally qualified full-time permanent faculty on a par with the requirements of STEM disciplines, and supports AACSB accreditations. However, there may be conflicts of interest when colleagues supervise each other and job loss anxiety if a DBA faculty member fails an assignment.

Business School PhD Graduate Careers Beyond Academia

The labour market relevance of the doctorate has been questioned in relation to over-qualification, employer/employee satisfaction, award purpose, and value within the climate of the global knowledge economy (Boulos, 2016; Bryan & Guccione, 2018; Pitt, 2008). In a European context, the number of PhD graduates employed outside of higher education has been found to vary by geographic area, the level of economic development within a country, employment sector, the type of work, and field of research (Hnatkova et al., 2022). Unlike in Canada and the USA, there is currently no granular EU-wide data on doctorate-level employment and careers.

Despite this lack of worldwide intelligence, an opportunity for yet more ranking has been seized, in relation to conflating 'the most popular business schools with employers' with measures of 'time to employment offer from time of graduation' and 'median base salary' (Smith, 2018). On the face of it, you can gain employment the fastest and be the highest paid with a business and management degree from Harvard, The University of Cambridge, or the Massachusetts Institute of Technology (MIT).

Jackson's (2013) challenging of a career destination approach in favour of employability enhancement in the context of business school graduates draws attention to the value of considering multiple stakeholder perspectives on employability, particularly the viewpoint of the graduate. In relation to doctoral graduates, Young, Kelder, and Crawford (2020) highlight an excessive focus to date on problematising doctoral employability as reflecting doctoral programme deficiencies in preparing candidates for employment. They propose a solutions-focused approach to addressing a persistent industry-academia gap in terms of candidate preparedness. Linked to this need for an outlook-oriented strategy is the idea that we move away from reactively preparing candidates to fill labour market gaps and recognise that there is scope to be more innovative and creative, in line with fundamental ideals of the role of research and development in the knowledge economy. Among the most innovative doctoral programmes highlighted by Burrell et al. (2012, p. 21) are those that have been 'developed with the understanding that the fastest growing population of doctoral students is working adults'.

Understanding of part-time and post-experience PhDs in business and management plus business school staff on doctorates has tended to focus on the challenges presented through a need to balance work and study in part-time contexts. These candidates, described by Bates and Goff (2012) as 'invisible students', have often had to fit into systems that have been essentially designed with the needs of full-time, young PhD candidates lacking in employment experiences (Pearson, Evans, & Macauley, 2004). It is perhaps no surprise then that acknowledgement of employability at the doctoral level tends to provoke institutional discussions centred on the provision of transdisciplinary work-integrated learning in PhDs (albeit this being an under-explored research theme to date – Valencia-Forrester, 2019).

In the provision of many business and management PhDs, effectively an 'academic internship' is perceived to be ongoing in terms of working with a Business Professor to gain socialisation into academia. There are some notable pockets of innovative practice. However, Norges Bank's (2020) established salaried PhD internship programme is open to economics and finance PhD candidates who are resident outside Norway and seeks to align doctoral research interests with those of Norges Bank. It aims to forge academic and industry sector research collaborations and to pursue co-authorship and joint international academic journal publication opportunities with Norges Bank staff. The Internship Programme of German Business (https://www.djindjic-stipendienprogramm.de/applicants) aimed at applicants from countries of the Western Balkans is intended to close academic knowledge-labour market implementation gaps and fits with an ethos of 'try before you buy' talent (NTU, 2021), providing candidates with opportunities to decide on favourable and unfavourable professional career directions. Furthermore, the programme extends beyond internship to alumni networking to mitigate against the short-term, temporary nature of internships.

The issue of supporting the transition of candidates out of the doctoral study into work is picked up through the ideas of Gioli and Ricardo (2022). They consider the skills offered through PhD programmes *vis-à-vis* labour market requirements in Italy, Malaysia, and Portugal, finding that career pathways are open to change and disruption, not least due to economic shifts. In the specific case of French PhD candidate paths to private sector employment, Canolle and Vinot (2018) have questioned the suitability of professionalisation and skills training approaches. Less attention has been paid to the transition from work into doctoral study and the situating of PhD candidates among a range of peers equipped with previous and/or current industry experience (as we touched on in Chapter 3) that might be harnessed to support doctoral programme employability goals and meaningful, collaborative conversations around career development beyond academia.

Business school graduate destinations are often considered as part of the national-level monitoring of career outcomes in publicly funded education systems. However, the measurement of this is open to scrutiny and critique. For example, the UK Grad Programme census information on PhD career outcomes within 18 months of graduation has been critiqued by Nerad (2006) not least based on a lack of information on graduate motivations and job progression opportunities. Linked to developing a more holistic view of doctoral graduate outcomes, Nerad (2006) has highlighted the scope for further understanding of PhD careers in relation to job search experience; job satisfaction; retrospective analyses of the quality and usefulness of the doctoral education; recommendations for current students and current programmes. Neumann and Tan (2011) have also called for a better understanding of doctoral career trajectories. We note the work of Vitae (2022) provides insights into what researchers do. In addition to this, we would highlight that, in the case of business and management doctoral graduates, there is a need to acknowledge that the career outcomes of the PhD study are not readily discernible given the potential impact of employment experiences pre-, during, and post-doctorate. Additionally, the destinations of international PhD candidates, highly visible in business and management and whose futures are often limited by host country visa and immigration policies, receive little attention in terms of formal monitoring of career outcomes.

Career-Oriented Researcher Development Needs

Given the positioning of the PhD in many business schools around the world as a route to academic careers and expectations that 'today's doctoral students will have a major role in educating tomorrow's students' (Greener, 2021, p. 100463), the insights into a cross-section of PGRs who teach in an Irish context provided by Noonan (2020) are interesting. The experiences of the PGRs teaching in business within Noonan's (2020) sample draw attention to the business school doctorate potentially being viewed by candidates who have previously worked in the industry as 'a proven means to an end'. In this case, the endpoint is an academic teaching career whereby teaching is seen as 'making a contribution' as much as, if not more so, than research. Furthermore, we note the idea of the doctorate is a 'rite of passage' (Maniss, 1997; Raineri, 2015; Shapiro, Briggs-Kenney, Robinson, & De Jarnette, 1997) towards the completion of a thesis where power sits with the awarding institution of which candidates are aware. However, awareness of power imbalance appears to be accompanied by perceptions by candidates that they possess some degree of agency and choice that may suit their development needs (Noonan, 2020). Less consideration has been given to the 'rite of passage' towards an academic career, surprisingly so in business and management, given a commonly observed purpose of the PhD as a means of reproducing the academy.

Discussions around a need to prepare doctoral candidates for a diversity of career paths should acknowledge the aspirations of candidates alongside future prospects for research and innovation and promote greater porosity between academia and industry. We note however that there are very different career-oriented support needs for doctoral candidates in business and management, reflecting candidate diversity in terms of employment history.

A candidate who takes two years off from working in financial services in the City of London to complete a PhD in finance and then returns to a highly paid job in the city would clearly be in a very different situation from a self-funded young candidate who is relying on financial support from multiple family members and working several jobs. Moreover, financial prospects postgraduation might also affect morale. We also are aware that doctoral supervisors from whom candidates might solicit career advice do not tend to be business school faculty members with the greatest levels of non-academic employment experience.

Green's (2005, p. 153) observation that 'doctoral education is as much about identity formation as it is about knowledge production' has stimulated debate on PGR identity which, in turn, has raised questions about candidate status. Compton and Tran's (2017) exploration in a UK context has drawn attention to 'a triality' of identity (researcher, student, and often teacher) with variance in how candidates view themselves and 'self-label' within the academic community during their candidature and navigate multiple selves. This contrasts with other countries/geographical contexts, reflecting different formal statuses and treatment of doctoral candidates and the extent to which they are positioned betwixt and between roles within universities.

In the context of business schools, Petriglieri and Petriglieri's (2010) identification of their function as identity workspaces that might through management education support managers in understanding and shaping who they are provides an interesting angle to consider DBA identity and status within a research environment.

DBA Impact on Careers – Key Challenges

While DBA programmes can support job satisfaction, organisational performance, career transitions, and career changes, DBA candidates tend to be left to their own devices without dedicated career support. Moreover, we argue that business schools are missing out on realising mutual long-term benefits from applied research in DBA theses. In the context of a turbulent post-pandemic labour market, we call for ongoing support for DBA candidates and graduates and for clearer communications about the real benefits of professional doctorates in business schools.

Building on insights from EFMD doctoral programme conferences, careers fairs, and case studies of practices across the global EFMD community, we highlight the value of the DBA for careers in academia, policy, and practice.

Importantly, as DBA programmes have a dual purpose of requiring candidates to contribute to business theory and to develop their professional practice and/or contribute to professional knowledge in organisations, business schools typically require candidates to demonstrate significant experience in strategic leadership. There are multiple motivations for individuals to embark on a DBA and it might be assumed that as candidates are usually at work, they do not require support from a business school careers service. Cranfield School of Management states that its DBA alumni progress to senior positions, sometimes move into government or start a consultancy, and may combine these activities with part-time teaching.

We have found some candidates who are completing the DBA to enhance their status, as a hobby, or to give them and their families some time to gain a visa to live and study abroad. These candidates may have limited if any, expectations about the business school facilitating a career move for them in the same way that a full-time PhD candidate who wishes to be a full-time academic might expect their supervisor to help them gain their first academic job. For instance, government-funded civil servants on DBAs may feel that internal promotion will be guaranteed when they complete their DBA. Long-serving CEOs pre-retirement who feel stale in the saddle may see the DBA as a sabbatical. The DBA may enable time for them to wind down before leaving their organisations or handing over a family firm to a successor without the expectation of career advancement.

In contrast, it might be assumed that others with aspirations for promotion are able to figure out their own next steps with the help of an executive search firm consultant or private coach. Why include careers advice at all then in a business school for DBA candidates, especially if they continue to work?

We suggest this approach ignores the considerable talent among DBA candidates in an age of lifelong learning and the increasing scholarly research impact agenda. Rather than letting DBA graduates fend for themselves, we argue that career services should be available to counsel DBA candidates throughout and beyond their studies, if not before programme application. Additionally, a lack of support for DBA candidates can result in many lost in the system who never graduate.

There is a risk of treating the DBA as an executive qualification only without integrating the DBA into a business school's research and knowledge exchange strategy. The Executive DBA Council (EDBAC) was founded in 2011 to promote DBA degrees as business or executive qualifications, rather than as academic qualifications. On its website that advises on choosing a DBA programme, no mention is made of career prospects. Instead, it focuses on the convenience to travel to the business school, face-to-face contact, tuition fee, class sizes, how long the programme has existed, graduation rates, accreditations, and student profiles in terms of diversity, experience, and entry requirements.

Impactful DBA Programmes

In a UK study, Davies, McGregor, and Horan (2019), evaluated DBA impact statements according to Vitae's Researcher Development Framework (RDF) (Vitae, n.d.) to gain insights into how the degree benefitted students. We also examined UK business school DBA websites to explore expectations. We found that the DBA student journal was seen as personally highly rewarding in developing reflective practices and websites emphasised candidates' contributions to practice. Disappointingly, one did mention that DBA candidates would be encouraged to publish in academic journals. Clearly, busy executives may not appreciate the publish-or-perish culture in which their supervisors may be operating, however, we suggest that if their ideas are merely confined to their thesis in the business school this is a lost opportunity.

Interest in the scholarly research impact agenda is intensifying in a polarised society where business schools are seeking greater legitimacy by supporting, for example, the United Nations' Sustainable Development Goals and pandemic recovery. The outputs of DBA research can support professional developments in particular sectors and fields, improve organisational-level practices, and enhance individual competencies to support strategy development and implementation.

The annual EFMD Global Careers Fair showcases the achievements of DBAs to recruiters. It includes a wide range of international companies and alumni. The virtual careers fair provides a single platform globally for talented students and graduates to access employers to discuss job prospects. The fair offers live CV clinics, with careers consultants providing feedback on CVs, which compensates for the lack of explicit local support in business school careers services which may be geared more towards undergraduates.

Key challenges currently are about the lack of integration of DBA candidates in the fabric of business schools and an appreciation that the DBA can provide an alternative to an established corporate career, for example, into self-employment. DBA candidates are often recruited from senior corporate positions and study part-time. They are, therefore, a valuable source of accessible data and industry insights with experiences of career moves. This does not necessarily mean they know how to market themselves on completing the DBA. Careers and employability services in business schools may be focused on national metrics for the career destinations of undergraduate students. DBA graduates may aspire to move into consulting, start their own businesses, or change careers after their DBA. They may feel overqualified and unsure about their career trajectories and how to sell their new degree in the long term.

DBA candidates/graduates need career support because they may not realise how to sell their applied research skills, they may be too busy working to consider different options or to reflect on how they might network and prepare for interviews with an updated CV. They may be out-of-touch with tools such as LinkedIn or Xing, be unfamiliar with opportunities to work in academia, or simply be unsure about their new identities and how to focus their energies after they have successfully defended their thesis.

Thanks to EFMD's annual careers fairs, business schools can support DBA candidates' careers in a range of companies and academic settings. Reverse mentoring activities in business schools with faculty members and students can offer mutual benefits. Critically, we would hope that DBA alumni are lifelong learners who can actively engage in or support research impact agendas and support others' careers. As practitioner–scholars, DBA candidates and alumni can help to bridge the 'great divide' between practice and theory. Several business schools offer career advice to alumni. As the world of work is changing, a terminal degree like the DBA should not be the end of formal learning and we note that alumni grapple with new ways of working and new types of careers that are opening up. Despite the lack of wide recognition given to the value of DBAs, we return to our earlier analogy from Chapters 1 and 2 and hope that like Cinderella, the DBA can emerge triumphantly and successfully in a context where serious research and organisational leadership are important counterpoints to fake news and a crisis of leadership.

Impacts that Hit Multiple Policy Agendas

Attendees of EFMD doctoral conferences over the years will have noted a common focus on the doctorate as a response to national knowledge economy agendas. This is more explicit in some nations than others; we have already acknowledged how Dimitris Assimakopoulos, Guangzhong Li, and Yusra Mouzughi (in Palmer, 2018), for example, have highlighted an explicit direct relationship between the PhD and national development growth in European, Middle East, and China contexts.

This theme is not unique to the business and management doctorate. More broadly, Halse and Mowbray (2011, p. 513) have stated how:

> Doctoral research plays a 'crucial role in driving innovation and growth' of nation-states, and is a significant contributor to national and international knowledge generation and research outputs. (Smith, 2010, p. 4)

However, Halse and Mowbray (2011, p. 513) further observe that 'there is a striking absence of systematic research into the multidimensional impact of the doctorate'.

As we reflect on the World Bank's (2021) and Capital Economics' (2023) forecasts of uneven and unstable post-recession recovery and the potential for business schools to respond proactively to this challenge, it is timely to examine the multidimensional impact of business and management doctorates in particular. Alim (2020) has noted an opportunity for a more equitable post-COVID world order to be re-imagined, including stewardship of a more inclusive economy. The potential contributions to be made by business schools in terms of shifting away from neoliberalist tenets to integrate stakeholder capitalism principles into the curriculum, speak about power (and political economy) more openly, and recognise the societal and ecological impacts of business decisions have been acknowledged (Markovitz, 2020). Waddock (2020, p. 1) advocates a new conceptualisation to:

> include collaboration and competition, stewardship of the whole system, a cosmopolitan to local sensibility, and recognition of humanity's deep embeddedness and connection with other people, other beings, and nature.

Kalika (2019) has previously drawn attention to how, since the 2008 financial crisis, the impact of business schools has received much attention. There is evidence of the growing international importance of the notion of impact for business schools on society. The French Foundation for Management Education (Fondation nationale pour l'enseignement de la gestion des entreprises – FNEGE) together with EFMD launched the Business School Impact System (BSIS) in 2014 aimed at helping schools to assess their economic and social impact on 'the world around' (Bradshaw, 2014; EFMD, 2014 cited in Kalika, 2019, p. 1). The American Association to Advance Collegiate Schools of Business (AACSB) has also updated its business accreditation standards to include the notion of impact (AACSB, 2020) and, aligned to this, has published a paper specifically focused on AACSB and societal impact (AACSB, 2023).

However, as Kalika (2019) has argued, there has traditionally been a tendency for business schools to continually frame impact as 'economic impact' and there is a need to also consider knowledge impact and responsibility impact. There have been some concerted attempts to broaden the focus of impact, particularly through the Responsible Research in Business and Management (RRBM) initiative, 'dedicated to inspiring, encouraging, and supporting credible and useful research in the business and management disciplines' (Mijnhart, 2019).

Zaheer (2021), however, has questioned how business schools are preparing PhD candidates to examine the relationships between business and the institutional context rigorously and systematically in their work. Zaheer calls for fieldwork to enable a deeper understanding of the business context and critical problems facing society. Targeted funding support is emerging to respond to a need to address global grand challenges through responsible research in business and management. The 2021 RRBM 'Dare to Care' doctoral scholarships, sponsored by the International Association for Chinese Management Research, specifically respond to a broader, macro-level impact agenda in line with the United Nations' Sustainable Development Goals. Eight $10,000 awards have been offered to business school doctoral candidates whose research focuses on economic inequality, racial, gender, or other forms of social justice in organisations.

The Chartered Association of Business Schools (CABS), representing UK business schools, has stated the case for acknowledging multiple stakeholders in terms of impact and being clearer about what it is business schools deliver for the public good (CABS, 2021). As Cools (2021, p. 1) has pointed out, 'calls for responsible research – and by extension, doctoral education – are not new, as discussions on impact and science as service to society already date back many years'. There is, nevertheless, a need to dig deeper to 'discuss how to put this into action and really bring transformative change in doctoral education and business schools at large' (Cools, 2021, p,1). Here, the EMFD doctoral programmes community provides a unique and progressive vehicle of value in the doctoral education field.

Anderson and Gold's (2019, p. 1) exploration of the value of the research doctorate argues that there is a need to recognise applied, personal, and organisational outcomes to move away from a situation where 'current norms in doctoral education privilege the assumptions of the academic community at the expense of the practice community'.

In comparison to the PhD, the DBA award has been repeatedly acknowledged for its innovation capacity (Erwee, 2004; Pearson, 1999; Robinson, Morgan, & Reed, 2016). It is an award cognisant as a 'product' aligned to business relevance and macro-level economic development policies with industrial strategy. Yet, we must not overlook established practices of industrial PhDs, common across northern Europe in particular. As Palmer (2018, p. 1) observes, 'it is here that a normative Responsible Research in Business and Management (RRBM) agenda offers some clear opportunities in helping to guide the production of research that enables businesses to contribute to a better world/making lives better'.

The potential value of business school doctorates has been a key theme for discussion among business school doctoral educators. The 2016 EFMD Doctoral Programmes Conference focused specifically on innovation and impact in doctoral education and the importance of bringing the practitioner experience into the faculty was noted as part of an exploration of innovative delivery models. The scope for value creation and income generation in a model of combining the logic of academia with the logic of society was postulated. There was an appetite to assess and discuss this at a meso-level via EFMD. In one particular French model of doctoral study, PhD candidates are hired by companies, partly funded by the state, and contracted within research labs (under the *Conventions industrielles de formation par la recherche* - CIFRE - programme).

At the 2018 EFMD Doctoral Programmes Conference, Jordi Diaz (cited in Palmer, 2018) emphasised the need for business school doctoral programmes to be agile and to proactively sustain innovation. This reminds us that the time to innovate was already here pre-COVID. We were already witnessing a clear divide between traditional, conservative business schools and those displaying pioneering approaches to embracing the future. The latter is exemplified not least by the Guanghua Thought Leadership Platform of Peking University's School of Management and the sustainable development business model of Rotterdam School of Management. We had already started to engage in proactive conversations about disrupting doctoral education in business and management with the goal of being 'fit for the future'. Within our conversations at the 2018 EFMD Doctoral Programmes Conference, we began to acknowledge the importance of not only endorsing individualised acts of innovation. We identified the scope to develop collaborations between our institutions. This is something that we have continued to pursue throughout the COVID-19 pandemic, sharing practice, for example, through the 2020 EFMD doctoral community webinar on 'Supporting business school doctoral programmes during the pandemic and post lockdown'. New developments with the greater use of ChatGPT and other iterations require the community of business school doctoral providers to reflect on changing dynamics.

Back in 2004, Erwee identified opportunities to collaborate between Australian and American universities to share insights about best practices in the management of DBA programmes. There remain opportunities for collaboration across doctorate providers in business and management. The nature of the highly ranked business school arena means that competitive collaboration offers an appropriate strategy for knowledge management. There is further opportunity for us to shape the future of business school doctoral education through developing and sustaining a community of practice. We should recognise the strength of forging multidisciplinary relationships in business school doctoral education in response to theories of Mode 2–4 knowledge production.

Structural and Agentic Influences on the Impacts of Business Doctorates

Doctoral research is, ideally, a driver of innovation and growth (Smith, 2010). The impacts of the doctorate are multidimensional (Halse & Mowbray, 2011) and not limited to macro-level economic and societal effects. Understanding the 'returns' on investing in doctorates in business and management stretches beyond traditional analyses of degree choice and earnings potential (Altonji, Arcidiacono, & Maurel, 2016). It extends to professional identities, socialisation settings, and processes, and requires recognition of meso- and micro-level effects.

Breese, Issa, and Tresidder (2021) have begun to explore how completion of the DBA impacts on management practice at organisational and individual levels. They emphasise a wide range of workplace impacts reported by DBA alumni. Impacts of the business doctorate have been considered largely in relation to the professional and the personal with DBA pathways to impact reflecting entanglements between the worlds of industry and academia, practice, and scholarship (Rigg, Ellwood, & Anderson, 2021). This is linked to wider debates about the relevance, legitimacy, and impacts of business schools (Pettigrew & Starkey, 2016; Redgrave, Grinevich, & Chao, 2022). Contributions to management practice following completion of a doctorate, however, require more longitudinal investigation and tracking and evaluation of programme impacts before, during, and on completion (McSherry et al., 2019). This would help us to understand the extent to which impacts reflect specific outcomes of the doctoral thesis *vis-à-vis* 'the capacity-building effect of the doctorate' (Boud, Costley, Marshall, & Sutton, 2021). The latter is linked to programme design, curricula, and supervision in particular (Okeke-Uzodike, 2021). It is interesting that Creaton and Anderson (2021, p. 100461) have highlighted the social construction of professional doctoral impact 'through negotiation between student, employer and professional networks'.

PhD impact beyond contribution to the advancement of academic knowledge has not been systematically considered. Indeed, it is apparent that there has been a lack of construct clarity in relation to doctoral research impact. It is often bundled up with 'doctorateness', 'originality', 'relevance' and 'innovation' (Baptista et al., 2015). In a UK context, Laundon (2017) has presented a case for the integration of research impact and engagement into PhD training, noting a tendency for the conflation of impact with dissemination. In an attempt to avoid impact being treated as a bolt-on to doctoral research, there are examples in business and management of the embedding of impact statements into doctoral award structures (see Davies et al., 2019).

There is scope for further exploration of the potential connections between impact and career development. We also need to look at the extent to which engagement with people outside academia is valued in business school doctorates. The DBA is recognised to present opportunities in terms of providing 'informing channels between practice and industry' (Gill & Hoppe, 2009, p. 27). However, part-time PhD candidates with industry experience, knowledge and contacts, and an understanding of research partner and end-user needs (Laundon, 2017) are present in many business schools and there is a need to appreciate the variety and diversity of business and management doctoral candidates. There is a tendency for part-time PhDs in business and management to be promoted as 'study while you work' opportunities. Yet relatively little is known about the motivations for and outcomes of the part-time PhD. It is often assumed that family circumstances and a desire for career advancement are drivers of part-time learning. However, the extent to which part-time PhD motivations differ from professional doctorates (Grabowski & Miller, 2015) and part-time mature learners in business and management programmes at other levels of study (Swain, Hammond, & Jamieson, 2007) is open to question. What is clear is that PhD programmes tend to be based on norms that leave part-time candidates indicating feelings of dissatisfaction with many aspects of the doctoral experience (Turner, 2021), and norm-critical perspectives are needed to 'raise awareness of privileges, power imbalances, and the exclusion that some norms create' (Davies & Vieker, 2023, p. 39).

Changes During the COVID-19 Pandemic and Reflections for the Future

It has been reported that fewer tenure-track academic positions will be available in the USA as a result of COVID-19. Researchers have already begun to explore how PhD candidates' career aspirations and priorities have shifted in response, finding no clear patterns to date (e.g., Haas, Gureghian, Díaz, & Williams, 2022). In relation to non-academic career paths, an observation that 'poor labor market conditions lead to a substitution from full-time enrolment to part-time enrollment' across genders (Johnson, 2013, p. 122) perhaps reinforces a need to acknowledge the effects of the recession. This is not only on doctoral candidate enrolments but also on employability, talent and career management, and postdoctoral outcomes. As we head into 2024 'thriftiness' appears to be shifting from a marketing buzzword to a necessary lifestyle choice for institutions, organisations and individuals alike. The consequences of this remain to be seen

Summary

Some key observations we make on employability, career management, and postdoctoral outcomes in business and management are:

- There is a dichotomy between reported shortages of business school faculty and academic employment opportunities for business school doctoral graduates. This reflects status hierarchies and factors that impact on postgraduates' career opportunities and mobility.
- PhD candidate in-programme exposure to business school faculty members with experience in practice may be limited by doctoral policies and regulations. This can impact on career role modelling.
- It is surprising that there is so little data to track business school PhD graduate destinations outside academia. This would provide potential quick wins in securing business school-wide benefits linked to this highly qualified alumni group in the industry. Similarly, a lack of exploitation of DBA candidate links with industry is remarkable.

Questions you might like to consider:

- How might business and management doctorates facilitate more effective and sustainable connections between business schools and industry?
- Should all doctoral research in business and management make an impact beyond academic impact or 'contribution to knowledge'?
- How can we track career trajectory and post-doctoral outcomes in business and management?
- What might this mean for the design and delivery of business school doctorate programmes?
- Do we systematically collate the impacts of business and management doctorate research? Should we?

References

AACSB. (2007). *Becoming a business professor*. Tampa, FL: AACSB International, Association to Advance Collegiate Schools of Business.

AACSB. (2020). *2020 Guiding principles and standards for business accreditation*. Retrieved from https://www.aacsb.edu/-/media/documents/accreditation/2020-aacsb-business-accreditation-standards-jul-1-2022.pdf. Accessed on 18 December, 2022.

AACSB. (2023). *AACSB and Societal Impact: Aligning with the AACSB 2020 Business Accreditation Standards*, February 2023. AACSB Accredited.

Alim, A. (2020). Why business schools can't 'return to normal' after the COVID-19 pandemic. Retrieved from https://www.weforum.org/agenda/2020/06/why-business-schools-can-t-return-to-normal-after-the-covid-19-pandemic/. Accessed on December 10, 2021.

Altonji, J. G., Arcidiacono, P., & Maurel, A. (2016). The analysis of field choice in college and graduate school: Determinants and wage effects. In E. A. Hanushek, S. Machin, & L. Woessmann (Eds.), *Handbook of the economics of education* (Vol. 5, pp. 305–396). Amsterdam, Netherlands: Elsevier.

Anderson, V., & Gold, J. (2019). The value of the research doctorate: A conceptual examination. *The International Journal of Management Education, 17*(3), 100305.

Armstrong, J. S., & Sperry, T. (1994). The ombudsman: Business school prestige—Research versus teaching. *Interfaces, 24*(2), 13–43.

Baptista, A., Frick, L., Holley, K., Remmik, M., Tesch, J., & Âkerlind, G. (2015). The doctorate as an original contribution to knowledge: Considering relationships between originality, creativity, and innovation. *Frontline Learning Research, 3*(3), 55–67.

Barr, M., & Wright, P. (2019). Training graduate teaching assistants: What can the discipline offer? *European Political Science, 18*(1), 143–156.

Bates, P., & Goff, L. (2012). The invisible student: Benefits and challenges of part-time doctoral studies. *Alberta Journal of Educational Research, 58*(3), 368–380.

Beaulieu, M., Breton, M., & Brousselle, A. (2018). Conceptualizing 20 years of engaged scholarship: A scoping review. *PloS One, 13*(2), e0193201.

Bedeian, A. G., Cavazos, D. E., Hunt, J. G., & Jauch, L. R. (2010). Doctoral degree prestige and the academic marketplace: A study of career mobility within the management discipline. *Academy of Management Learning & Education, 9*(1), 11–25.

Bolton, M. J., & Stolcis, G. B. (2003). Ties that do not bind: Musings on the specious relevance of academic research. *Public Administration Review, 63*(5), 626–630.

Boud, D., Costley, C., Marshall, S., & Sutton, B. (2021). Impacts of a professional practice doctorate: A collaborative enquiry. *Higher Education Research & Development, 40*(3), 431–445.

Boulos, A. (2016). The labour market relevance of PhDs: An issue for academic research and policy-makers. *Studies in Higher Education, 41*(5), 901–913.

Boyer, E. L. (1996). The scholarship of engagement. *Journal of Public Service & Outreach, 1*(1),11–20.

Boyle, D. M., Carpenter, B. W., & Hermanson, D. R. (2015). The accounting faculty shortage: Causes and contemporary solutions. *Accounting Horizons, 29*(2), 245–264.

Bradshaw, D. (2014). Meet the dean: Sarah Dixon, International Business School Suzhou. *Financial Times*, January 17.

Breese, R., Issa, S., & Tresidder, R. (2021). Impact on management practice after completing the DBA. Retrieved from https://papers.ssrn.com/sol3/papers.cfm?abstract_id=3944827. Accessed on October 20, 2021.

Brentschneider, S., & Dai, Y. (2017). *Why do foreign citizens with US PhD degrees return home?* Arizona State University: Center for Organization Research and Design. Retrieved from https://cord.asu.edu/sites/default/files/wpcontent/uploads/2017/03/Why-do-foreigncitizens-with-US-PhD-CORD-website-version-.pdf.

Brissett, N. O. (2021). 'I left because…': Caribbean high-skilled emigrants' reasons to migrate to the US. *Compare: A Journal of Comparative and International Education, 53*(2), 235–252.

Bryan, B., & Guccione, K. (2018). Was it worth it? A qualitative exploration into graduate perceptions of doctoral value. *Higher Education Research & Development, 37*(6), 1124–1140.

Bryant, S. (2019, April 5). *Myths 7 and 8. About AACSB* accreditation standards: *Faculty* qualifications. AACSB Retrieved from https://www.aacsb.edu/insights/2019/April/myths-7-8-aacsb-accreditation-standards-faculty-qualifications. Accessed on July 10, 2021.

Burrell, D. N., Finch, A., Dawson, M., Rahim, E., & Williams, K. A. (2012). A solution oriented assessment of the positive role that non-traditional doctoral programs can have in developing diverse and valuable business school facility. *Journal of International Business Management & Research-JIBMR, 1*(2), 1–29.

Butler, D. D., Laumer, J. F., Jr, & Moore, M. (1994). Graduate teaching assistants: Are business schools focusing on increasing teaching excellence? *Marketing Education Review, 4*(2), 14–19.

CABS. (2021). *Business Schools and the public good: A chartered ABS task force report,* June 2021 (pp. 1–68). Retrieved from https://charteredabs.org/wp-content/uploads/2021/06/Chartered-ABS-Business-Schools-and-the-Public-Good-Final-1.pdf. Accessed on March 28, 2023.

Canolle, F., & Vinot, D. (2018). *French PhDs' paths to employment in the private sector: Are professionalisation and skills training the least acceptable compromise possible? An exploratory research.* (No. hal-01876767). Paris: Ministry of Higher Education and Research.

Capital Economics. (2023). Q3 2023 Global Economic Outlook Report. *Capital Economics Ltd.,* London. Retrieved July 25, 2023 from https://www.capitaleconomics.com/global-economy-outlook?utm_source=google&utm_medium=cpc&utm_name=outlook_leadgen_prospect_glbec_glb_june2023_q3globaleconomicoutlook&utm_term=europe_global_outlook&utm_content=responsive&salesforce_campaign_id=7014H0000002cVdQAI&gad=1&gclid=Cj0KCQjwiIOmBhDjARIsAP6YhSUKbjLgMqS9ZYN3OWiQEcxJbj63dsqErhhq8C1ceYC1oJhHM18v3fgaAk7HEALw_wcB

CCA. (2021, January 26). *Degrees of success.* Council of Canadian Academies. Retrieved from https://www.cca-reports.ca/reports/the-labour-market-transition-of-phd-graduates/. Accessed on October 2, 2022.

CELTS. (2021). *The scholarship of engagement.* Centre for Engaged Learning Teaching and Scholarship, Loyola University Chicago. Retrieved from https://www.luc.edu/celts/engaged_scholars.shtml/. Accessed on March 17, 2023.

Chen, L. H. (2006). Attracting East Asian students to Canadian graduate schools. *Canadian Journal of Higher Education, 36*(2), 77–105.

Collins, J., Brown, N., & Leigh, J. (2021). Making sense of cultural bumps: Supporting international graduate teaching assistants with their teaching. *Innovations in Education and Teaching International, 59*(2), 511–521.

Compton, M., & Tran, D. (2017). Liminal space or in limbo? Post Graduate Researchers and their personal pie charts of identity. *Compass: Journal of Learning and Teaching, 10*(3). doi:10.21100/compass.v10i3.620

Cools, E. (2021). The responsibility turn: Building responsible doctoral programmes for a responsible future. *RRBM Blog Post.* Retrieved from https://www.rrbm.network/the-responsibility-turn-building-responsible-doctoral-programmes-for-a-responsible-future-eva-cools/. Accessed August 1, 2021.

Creaton, J., & Anderson, V. (2021). The impact of the professional doctorate on managers' professional practice. *The International Journal of Management Education, 19*(1), 100461

D'Aveni, R. A. (1996). A multiple-constituency, status-based approach to interorganizational mobility of faculty and input–output competition among top business schools. *Organization Science, 7*(2), 166–189.

Daly, A., & Weber, J. (2021). The accounting faculty shortage: Understanding masters of accounting students' interest in pursuing careers as accounting professors. *Journal of Education for Business, 96*(3), 167–175.

Darabi, F., Saunders, M. N., & Clark, M. (2020). Trust initiation and development in SME-university collaborations: Implications for enabling engaged scholarship. *European Journal of Training and Development, 45*(4/5), 320–345.

Davies, J., McGregor, F., & Horan, M. (2019). Autoethnography and the doctorate in business administration: Personal, practical and scholarly impacts. *The International Journal of Management Education, 17*(2), 201–213.

Davies, J., & Vieker, K. (2023). Building diverse and inclusive doctoral ecosystems. Special supplement: Towards healthy doctoral systems in business schools, *Global Focus, 2*(17), 34–40.

Dickinson, J., Fowler, A., & Griffiths, T. (2020, July 3). Pracademic expertise and its value to higher education. Advance HE. Retrieved from https://www.advance-he.ac.uk/news-and-views/pracademic-expertise-and-its-value-higher-education/. Accessed on July 10, 2023.

EFMD Global. (2018). *Annual Report 2016* (pp. 1–52). Retrieved from https://efmdglobal.org/wp-content/uploads/efmd_annualreport_2016.pdf. Accessed on April 4, 2023.

Erwee, R. (2004). Professional doctorates and DBAs in Australia: Dilemmas and opportunities to innovate. *International Journal of Organisational Behaviour, 7*(3), 394–400.

Ganning, J. (2022). Doctoral education and the academic job market in planning. Retrieved from https://core.ac.uk/download/pdf/216955388.pdf. Accessed September 7, 2018.

Gardiner, B. (2011). Faculty jobs go begging at business schools. *The Wall Street Journal.* Retrieved from https://www.wsj.com/articles/SB10001424052970204224604577032232809553166. Accessed on May 4, 2021.

Gill, G., & Hoppe, U. (2009). The business professional doctorate as an informing channel: A survey and analysis. *International Journal of Doctoral Studies, 4*, 27.

Gioli, G., & Ricardo, R. (2022). *Employability and PhD curricula. The case studies of Italy, Malaysia and Portugal.* Adult Learning and Education in International Contexts: Future Challenges for its Professionalization (p. 103).

Gore, G. J. (1968). The management internship. *Academy of Management Journal, 11*(2), 163–176.

Grabowski, L. J., & Miller, J. (2015). Business professional doctoral programs: Student motivations, educational process, and graduate career outcomes. *International Journal of Doctoral Studies, 10*, 257.

Green, B. (2005). Unfinished business: Subjectivity and supervision. *Higher Education Research & Development, 24*(2), 151–163.

Greener, S. L. (2021). Non-supervisory support for doctoral students in business and management: A critical friend. *The International Journal of Management Education, 19*(2), 100463.

Grove, J. (2021). UKRI to review 'one principal investigator per grant' rule. *Times Higher Education*, May 19.

Haas, N., Gureghian, A., Díaz, C. J., & Williams, A. (2022). Through their own eyes: The implications of COVID-19 for PhD students. *Journal of Experimental Political Science, 9*(1), 1–21.

Halse, C., & Mowbray, S. (2011). The impact of the doctorate. *Studies in Higher Education, 36*(5), 513–525.

Hnatkova, E., Degtyarova, I., Kersschot, M., & Boman, J. (2022). Labour market perspectives for PhD graduates in Europe. *European Journal of Education, 57*(3), 395–409.

International Labour Organization. (2021). *World employment and social outlook trends 2022 Report*, January 17, 2022. ILO: Geneva, Switzerland.

Ivory, C., Miskell, P., Neely, A., Shipton, H., & White, A. (2011). *The future of business school faculty*. Delhi: Advanced Institute of Management Research.

Jackson, V. (2013). *Investigating employability: The perspective of the business school graduate*. Ph.D. thesis, University of Liverpool, Liverpool, UK.

Johnson, M. T. (2013). The impact of business cycle fluctuations on graduate school enrollment. *Economics of Education Review, 34*, 122–134.

Kahn, S., & MacGarvie, M. (2020). The impact of permanent residency delays for stem PhDs: Who leaves and why. *Research Policy, 9*, 103879.

Kalika, M. (2019, February 25). The impact of Business Schools: Increasing the range of strategic choices. *EFMD Global*. Retrieved from https://blog.efmdglobal. org/2019/02/25/the-impact-of-business-schools-increasing-the-range-of-strategic-choices/. Accessed on December 10, 2021.

King, D., & Learmonth, M. (2015). Can critical management studies ever be 'practical'? A case study in engaged scholarship. *Human Relations, 68*(3), 353–375.

Laundon, M. (2017). *PhD students should be taught more about research impact and engagement.LSE*. Retrieved from https://blogs.lse.ac.uk/impactofsocialsciences/2017/12/18/phd-students-should-be-taught-more-about-research-impact-and-engagement/. Accessed on March 22, 2023.

Maniss, S. (1997). *Female students' experience of the rite of passage of doctoral education: A phenomenological feminist study*. San Antonio, TX: St. Mary's University.

Markovitz, G. (2020, January 15). *Top risks are environmental, but ignore economics and they'll be harder to fix*. World Economic Forum. Retrieved from https://www.weforum.org/agenda/2020/01/what-s-missing-from-the-2020-global-risks-report/. Accessed on December 10, 2021.

Mather, J., & Lebihan, R. (2008, April 28). Brained by the PhD shortage. *Financial Review*. Retrieved from https://www.afr.com/policy/economy/brained-by-the-phd-shortage-20080428-jcses. Accessed on July 20, 2022.

McCullough, C. D., & Wooten, B. E. (1984). Shortage of business professors threatens quality instruction. *The Journal of Business Education, 59*(5), 193–197.

McSherry, R., Bettany-Saltikov, J., Cummings, E., Walker, K., Ford, K., & Walsh, K. (2019). Are you measuring the impacts and outcomes of your professional doctorate programme? *Studies in Continuing Education, 41*(2), 207–225.

Merritt, J. (2004). PhD shortage sparks debate over who's teaching business. *Business Week*, February 28.

Mijnhart, W. (2019, July 26). *RSM hosts the first global responsible research summit*. Rotterdam School of Management. Retrieved from https://www.rsm.nl/news/detail/14776-rsm-hosts-the-first-global-responsible-research-summit/. Accessed on July 26, 2019.

Nabawanuka, J. W. (2011). *Brain drain at African higher education institutions: The case of Makerere University*. Ph.D. thesis, University of Georgia, Athens, GA.

Neelam, N., Sheorey, P., Bhattacharya, S., & Kunte, M. (2020). Organization for economic co-operation and development guidelines for learning organization in higher education and its impact on lifelong learning: Evidence from Indian business schools. *VINE Journal of Information and Knowledge Management Systems, 50*(4), 569–596

Nerad, M. (2006). Defining and measuring successful PhD career outcomes. In *Presentation at UKCGE European summer conference new dimensions for doctoral programmes in Europe: Training, employability and the European knowledge agenda*. Florence:University of Florence.

Neumann, R., & Tan, K. K. (2011). From PhD to initial employment: The doctorate in a knowledge economy. *Studies in Higher Education, 36*(5), 601–614.

Noonan, G. (2020). '*Restor (y) Ing Their Position in the Spotlight, Please Welcome Back on Stage… Postgraduate Students Who Teach… or Graduate Teaching Assistants… or Teaching Postgrads… Or…*'. Ph.D. thesis, National University of Ireland, Maynooth.

Norges Bank. (2020). PhD internship program. Retrieved from https://www.norges-bank. no/en/topics/Research/Phd-internship/. Accessed on October 2, 2022.

NTU. (2021). NTU's graduate internship scheme sets a precedent for 8 years of successful collaboration. Retrieved from https://www.ntu.ac.uk/about-us/news/news-articles/2021/04/diversity-case-study. Accessed on June 27, 2022.

OECD. (2020). Employment outlook 2020. Facing the jobs crisis. Retrieved from https://www.oecd.org/employment-outlook/2020/. Accessed on July 20, 2022.

Okeke-Uzodike, O. E. (2021). Postgraduate supervision in a South African transforming academic environment: A reflexivity approach. *Issues in Educational Research, 31*(4), 1175–1194.

Ong, L. T. (2021). Overcoming shortage of second-career academics in business schools. In *SHS web of conferences* (Vol. 124, p. 11003). Les Ulis: EDP Sciences.

Palmer, N. (2018). Are our doctoral programmes fit for purpose and the future?*EFMD Global*. Retrieved from https://blog.efmdglobal.org/2018/05/16/are-our-doctoral-programmes-fit-for-purpose-and-the-future/. Accessed on February 2, 2023.

Paolo, A. D., & Mañé, F. (2016). Misusing our talent? Overeducation, overskilling and skill under-utilisation among Spanish PhD graduates. *The Economic and Labour Relations Review, 27*(4), 432–452.

Park, C., & Ramos, M. (2002). The donkey in the department? Insights into the graduate teaching assistant (GTA) experience in the UK. *Journal of Graduate Education, 3*(2), 47–53.

Pearson, M. (1999). The changing environment for doctoral education in Australia: Implications for quality management, improvement and innovation. *Higher Education Research & Development, 18*(3), 269–287.

Pearson, M., Evans, T., & Macauley, P. (2004). The working life of doctoral students: Challenges for research education and training. *Studies in Continuing Education, 26*(3), 347–353.

Petriglieri, G., & Petriglieri, J. L. (2010). Identity workspaces: The case of business schools. *Academy of Management Learning & Education, 9*(1), 44–60.

Pettigrew, A., & Starkey, K. (2016). From the guest editors: The legitimacy and impact of business schools—Key issues and a research agenda. *Academy of Management Learning & Education, 15*(4), 649–664.

Pitt, R. (2008). The PhD in the global knowledge economy: Hypothesising beyond employability. Retrieved from https://www.academia.edu/4258179/The_PhD_in_the_global_knowledge_economy_Hypothesising_beyond_employability.

Posner, P. L. (2009). The pracademic: An agenda for re-engaging practitioners and academics. *Public Budgeting & Finance, 29*(1), 12–26.

Posselt, J. R. (2016). *Inside graduate admissions: Merit, diversity, and faculty gatekeeping.* Cambridge, MA: Harvard University Press.

QS Contributor. (2014). *India's business school faculty crisis.* Retrieved from https://www.topmba.com/where-to-study/asia/india/indias-business-school-faculty-crisis. Accessed on April 17, 2022.

Raineri, N. (2015). Business doctoral education as a liminal period of transition: Comparing theory and practice. *Critical Perspectives on Accounting, 26*, 99–107.

Redgrave, S. D. J., Grinevich, V., & Chao, D. (2022). The relevance and impact of business schools: In search of a holistic view. *International Journal of Management Reviews, 25*(3), 1–50.

Rigg, C., Ellwood, P., & Anderson, L. (2021). Becoming a scholarly management practitioner–Entanglements between the worlds of practice and scholarship. *The International Journal of Management Education, 19*(2), 100497.

Robinson, G., Morgan, J., & Reed, W. (2016). Disruptive innovation in higher education: The professional doctorate. *International Journal of Information and Education Technology, 6*(1), 85.

Santini, C., Marinelli, E., Boden, M., Cavicchi, A., & Haegeman, K. (2016). Reducing the distance between thinkers and doers in the entrepreneurial discovery process: An exploratory study. *Journal of Business Research, 69*(5), 1840–1844.

Shapiro, J. P., Briggs-Kenney, M., Robinson, R. W. J., & De Jarnette, P. M. (1997). Autobiographical stories of rites of passage of Caucasian and African–American female doctoral students in educational administration. *Journal of School Leadership, 7*(2), 165–193.

Simba, A., & Ojong, N. (2017). Engaged scholarship: Encouraging interactionism in entrepreneurship and small-to-medium enterprise (SME) research. *Journal of Small Business and Enterprise Development, 24*(4), 1009–1027.

Smith, A. K. (2010). *The delicate balance of organizational leadership: Encouraging learning and driving successful innovation.* Ph.D. thesis, Case Western Reserve University, Cleveland, OH.

Smith, R. (2018). World Economic Forum. Retrieved from https://www.weforum.org/agenda/2018/04/these-are-the-most-popular-business-schools-with-employers/. Accessed on March 25, 2023.

Song, H. (1997). From brain drain to reverse brain drain: Three decades of Korean experience. *Science, Technology and Society, 2*(2), 317–345.

Swain, J., Hammond, C., & Jamieson, A. (2007). *The benefits of part-time study for mature students: Findings from interviews with Birkbeck graduates.* Centre for the Wider Benefits of Learning, Institute of Education and Birkbeck, University of London.

Tansel, A., & Demet Güngör, N. (2003). 'Brain drain' from Turkey: Survey evidence of student non-return. *Career Development International, 8*(2), 52–69.

Turner, H. A. (2021). *I'm still valid: An explanatory sequential mixed-methods study of part-time PhD students' motivation and satisfaction:ThinkIR*, University of Louisville's Institutional Repository.

United Nations. (2021). *COVID crisis to push global unemployment over 200 million mark in 2022.* UN News, June 2. Retrieved from https://www.news.un.org/en/story/2021/06/1093182. Accessed on December 3, 2021.

United Nations. (2022, September 1). World economic situation and prospects: September 2022 Briefing, No. 164. Retrieved from https://www.un.org/development/desa/dpad/wp-content/uploads/sites/45/publication/Monthly_Briefing_164.pdf

University World News. (2011, May 8). India: Business schools face faculty crisis. Retrieved from https://www.universityworldnews.com/post.php?story=20110507085555179. Accessed on July 20, 2022.

Valencia-Forrester, F. (2019). Internships and the PhD: Is this the future direction of work-integrated learning in Australia? *International Journal of Work-Integrated Learning, 20*(4), 389–400.

Vitae. (2022). What do researchers do? Retrieved from https://www.Vitae.ac.uk/events/Vitae-international-researcher-development-conference-2022/Vitae-zone-2022/wdrd-2022-report.pdf. Accessed on March 24, 2023.

Waddock, S. (2020). Will businesses and business schools meet the grand challenges of the era? *Sustainability, 12*(15), 6083.

Wilkerson, J. M. (1999). On research relevance, professors' 'real world' experience, and management development: Are we closing the gap? *Journal of Management Development, 18*(7), 598–613.

Wollast, R., Aelenei, C., Chevalère, J., Van der Linden, N., Galand, B., Azzi, A., Frenay, M., & Klein, O. (2023). Facing the dropout crisis among PhD candidates: The role of supervisor support in emotional well-being and intended doctoral persistence among men and women. *Studies in Higher Education*, 1–16.

World Bank. (2021). The Global Economy: On track for strong but uneven growth as COVID-19 still weighs. *Feature Story*, June 8. Retrieved from https://www.

worldbank.org/en/news/feature/2021/06/08/the-global-economy-on-track-for-strong-but-uneven-growth-as-covid-19-still-weighs. Accessed on December 10, 2021.

Wren, D. A., Atherton, R. M., & Michaelsen, L. K. (1978). The managerial experience of management professors: Are the blind leading the blind? *Journal of Management*, *4*(1), 75–83.

Young, S. M., Kelder, J. A., & Crawford, J. (2020). Doctoral employability: A systematic literature review and research agenda. *Journal of Applied Learning & Teaching*, *3*(1), 1–11.

Zaheer, S. (2021). Bring context back in for impact. *RRBM Daily Archives*. Retrieved from https://www.rrbm.network/2021/06/17/. Accessed on March 10, 2022.

Zweig, D. (2006). Competing for talent: China's strategies to reverse the brain drain. *International Labor Review*, *145*, 65.

Chapter 5

Research Environment, Culture, Capacity, Capabilities and Connectivity

Overview and Context

Increasingly there has been greater recognition of the importance of the research environment and culture on doctoral programmes and how they affect doctoral education policy, structures, candidates' experiences, outcomes, and destinations. Diversity in academic cultures and institutional systems worldwide has been recognised, bringing challenges in terms of doctoral education access and knowledge provision (Nerad et al., 2022).

In this chapter, we draw attention to some of the key thematic developments for doctoral programme management and their implications. These include publishing practices; trust and research integrity; professionalisation of doctoral supervision; well-being and the emotional impact of doctoral studies; interdisciplinarity and team science. First, we consider business school research environments as objective domains which significantly impact research culture and performance and then we explore subjective aspects. The chapter progresses to consider key issues that have underpinned our observations in this book so far and ones that hold implications for the future of business school doctorates: capacity; capabilities; and connectivity.

Business School Research Environments

The reputation and prestige of a business school are major factors in student choice (Armstrong & Sperry, 1994; Dubois & Walsh, 2017; Hogan, Kortt, & Charles, 2020; Pfeffer & Fong, 2002; Vidaver-Cohen, 2007). Around the globe, correlations between research environments and academic research productivity have been noted. Before the COVID-19 pandemic, there was an emphasis on the relevance of faculty members' working environment (Way, Morgan, Larremore, & Clauset, 2019); specific policies and practices (Eagan, Jaeger, & Grantham, 2015); research self-efficacy beliefs (Pasupathy & Siwatu, 2014); collaborative and prosocial behaviours (Ryazanova & McNamara, 2016); the interaction of individual and institutional leadership (Bland, Center, Finstad,

Business and Management Doctorates World-Wide: Developing the Next Generation, 125–151
Copyright © 2024 by Nicola J. Palmer, Julie Davies and Clare Viney
Published under exclusive licence by Emerald Publishing Limited
doi:10.1108/978-1-78973-499-720231005

Risbey, & Staples, 2005); and national characteristics (Heng, Hamid, & Khan, 2020). Contextual complexities have been acknowledged, frustrating the identification of 'the characteristics of research-favourable environments' (Ajjawi, Crampton, & Rees, 2018, p. 936).

Heng et al.'s (2020, p. 965) observations that the research engagement and productivity of academics in developing countries are influenced by external pressures and the 'publish or perish' dictum is interesting when considering business school research environments. Differences in commitment to professions versus organisations have been emphasised in Becker, Kernan, Clark, and Klein's (2018) study of tenured management professors in the USA, with intrinsic motivations to engage in research being linked to being an academic rather than employment at an individual university. Commitment to the organisation (university) as extrinsically motivated and linked to non-research job components (Becker et al., 2018) reflects the nature of research-related rewards and incentives (linked to a scientific model – Bennis & O'Toole, 2005) that are open to question in terms of research integrity. Pyne (2017) has drawn attention to the rewards of publishing in predatory journals at a small business school in Canada, noting positive correlations between internal research awards and these types of 'low barrier' publications. However, Pyne's (2017) work has been challenged based on erroneous claims and reproducibility issues (Tsigaris & Teixeira da Silva, 2020). Notwithstanding this, the extent to which individualism and self-interest are promoted and incentivised in business school research, largely reflecting wider university academic reward systems, has been observed, particularly in relation to the USA (see, e.g., the work of Chen, Gupta, & Hoshower, 2006; Oviatt & Miller, 1989; Stremersch, Winer, & Camacho, 2021). More recently, we note Horta and Li's (2022, p. 1) observations of publishing becoming 'the overriding goal' of PhD students studying in mainland China, Hong Kong, and Macau and their claims that 'Publication pressure is perceived to be filtering down into doctoral education worldwide'. This is reported to result in doctoral journeys that are 'publishing-centred' and a shift in doctoral candidate behaviours:

> […] it causes doctoral students to commodify knowledge production, devalues coursework, conference participation, and teaching assistantships, encourages students to regard their supervisors as publishing facilitators and their peers as rivals rather than collaborators, and marginalises engagement with external stakeholders. (Horta & Li, 2022, p. 1)

The implications of this for candidates on business doctorates are not transparent nor expected to be uniform in a global context. Business school reputation and research rankings tend to focus on aggregated publications performance (Baden-Fuller, Ravazzolo, & Schweizer, 2000). This reflects inter-institutional competition, notable in the North American context:

> U.S. business schools are locked in a dysfunctional competition for media rankings that diverts resources from long-term knowledge

creation, which earned them global pre-eminence, into short-term strategies aimed at improving their ranking. (De Angelo et al., 2005, p. 1)

As Hogan et al. (2020, p. 715) have noted when considering the vulnerability of Australian business schools,

[w]hile some rankings are beginning to measure teaching quality and impact, they are ... predominantly driven by research outcomes and can reportedly be gamed by individual business schools. (Clarke et al., 2013)

Throughout the discourse on business school research performance focused on academic research outputs and rankings, we note the extent to which research environment and culture are under-explored, especially in relation to the potential implications for business and management doctorates.

Pratt, Margaritis, and Coy's (1999) examination of the development of research culture into an inclusive, independent learning and intellectually inquiring academic environment in a New Zealand-based university's School of Management Studies demonstrated the importance of leadership in transforming and instilling cultural values. Levels of support for staff to 'develop their research capabilities, including conference and research funding, supervision, payment of doctorate fees, computing facilities, journal, and online database resources, and appropriately timed sabbatical leave' (Pratt et al., 1999, p. 43) are indicators of a progressive research culture. In their example, the propensity for academic staff to move to other institutions after completion of their doctorates was recognised to present 'a coming of age for the school' in terms of doctoral graduate placement and it facilitated 'a network of research relationships' (Pratt et al., 1999, p. 54). This perspective that the academic destinations of business school doctorate graduates are valued by business schools as a programme outcome measure and indicator of quality is important. It adds to Bryan and Guccione's (2018) cross-disciplinary work on UK doctoral graduate perceptions whereby career value was identified as a domain of doctoral value. In the context of business school doctorates, we note an explicit element of shared interest/investment in the academic career value of the doctorate. Jean-Alexis Spitz (JAS) has been active in promoting EFMD Global Careers Fairs for doctoral candidates (Pouza, 2022) – events that provide an opportunity for job-seeking PhD students or graduates to meet with recruiters from international business schools.

Uneven patterns of researcher output and capacity by geographical region cannot be overlooked. Simon Kay's (The Association of Commonwealth Universities, 2020) reflections on challenges facing African early career researchers draw attention to a lag in research outputs and governmental investment (Ezeh & Lu, 2019). Despite the emergence of centres of research and training excellence across Africa, many researchers who are seeking a high-quality (and high-ranked) research environment need to travel overseas. This can then lead to a second major life-changing decision whether to return to Africa or build a career and life outside the continent. A return to an African institution will depend on their ability to pursue their research interests, attract funding, and to deal with the third challenge of impossible teaching loads because of high student enrolments which leave them with little if any, time for research. Additionally, with relatively weak research management support, a researcher in Africa faces heavy administrative loads that elsewhere in the world might be performed by research services teams. Moreover, the absence of clear research career pathways in poorly endowed institutions is a challenge while international funders tend to focus on the top 20 leading African institutions for funding, knowledge, and data sharing. Much of the literature and discussion on building research capacity in sub-Saharan Africa in particular takes place at a structural and institutional level, far removed from the needs and motivations of young researchers themselves. Mtwisha et al.'s (2021) research has illuminated the strategic career choices facing early- and mid-career transition to research leadership in African countries, compounded by difficult personal decisions.

Different types of research environments inevitably hold different levels of attraction for different doctoral graduates. There is a lot of difference to note. We have already acknowledged the appeal of North American research environments as places for East Asian graduate students to pursue careers (Chen, 2006). Brexit prompted fears of a staff exodus from UK business schools with business school leaders unable to compete with the attractiveness of US salaries to EU faculty (Jack, 2019). However, we are also very aware that the personal circumstances of some doctoral researchers limit their pursuit of geographically dispersed research career opportunities and their ability to experience different research environments.

Cultural Paradigms and the Business School Doctoral Research Environment

Gardner's (2010, p. 658) observation that '[i]nstitutional prestige is an inherent part of the higher education culture in the United States' is mirrored in the culture of business schools, which have been heavily influenced by North American models focused on shareholder value. MBA programmes and accreditation schemes are unequivocally linked to the idea of prestige and, as we have noted so far in this book, the highly competitive nature of business schools is sustained through the reproduction of the elite, research-intensive model. European business schools have tended to focus more on the public sector and stakeholder value (Antunes & Thomas, 2007).

Most recently, business schools have embraced the United Nations' Sustainable Development Goals (Weybrecht, 2022) and business school accreditation bodies such as AACSB actively support evidence of societal impact (Gupta & Cooper, 2022). The need to evidence responsible management in doctoral research is continuing to gain traction (McKiernan & Tsui, 2019) with a view to evidencing wider impact. At the same time, calls in the UK for more inclusive internal cultures have grown (Berry & Davidson, 2022) with concerns about how individual researchers were affected particularly during the pandemic and beyond in relation to equality issues (Davies & Berry, 2022).

James and Mihov's (2023) assertion that 'transformative change starts with responsible research' alerts us to issues of research integrity associated with business school curricula and the teaching of business leaders, and the management of research-based doctoral programmes.

Doctoral candidates and supervisors must be trusted and trustworthy in society for upholding values of honesty, open communications, rigour, transparency, and accountability in addition to care and respect for individuals who are involved in and use research. Intense pressures and incentives to publish can result in research misconduct and difficulties with business schools having to deal with questionable 'grey areas' of behaviours. This might include gift authorship and collusion as the number of co-authors on academic articles increases (Hall & Martin, 2019). Moreover, with different cultural understandings of plagiarism and the growing use of AI tools like Chat GPT, Google Bard, and Microsoft Copilot (WONKHE, 2021), it is vital that business schools ensure doctoral research is conducted with high levels of integrity in a positive research environment.

Wright (2016) highlights dubious research practices in analysing and reporting in peer-reviewed journals. Chapman, Davis, Toy, and Wright (2004) observed that academic dishonesty has increased, with business students more likely to cheat than their counterparts in other disciplines, especially in marketing majors. One solution is to establish honour and integrity programmes and to find time in the curriculum to promote ethical behaviours (Eury & Treviño, 2019). Reeves (2022) argues that there are opportunities to improve research cultures and doctoral well-being by providing robust researcher development and effecting changes within structural limitations. In their article in *Nature*, Mejlgaard et al. (2020) emphasise the importance of the research environment, effective supervision and mentoring, integrity training, ethics structures, procedures for dealing with integrity breaches, data practices and management, research collaboration, declaration of interests, publication and communication guidelines. Time for research to be conducted robustly needs to be protected (Ajjawi et al., 2018). The notion of the 'lone genius' also needs to be debunked (Grove, 2021). It is vital that women in research teams are not merely grafting for men who are principal investigators and who appropriate work as their own which others generate (Davies, Yarrow, & Syed, 2020). We need to appreciate candidates' perspectives on ethics in doctoral supervision (Löfström & Pyhältö, 2020), different challenges possibly for women doctoral students (Carter, Blumenstein, & Cook, 2013), and the need for supervisors to be timely and responsive as well as constructive in providing feedback (Kuvaas, Buch, & Dysvik, 2017).

Ryan and Mulligan (2022) state that much scholarship has been dedicated to understanding doctoral supervisory praxis and the life of doctoral candidates. They view the act of supervision through the experiential lens of both a doctoral candidate and supervisor as they make sense of transformation processes happening for each of them simultaneously. Clearly, this involves various stressors such as the imposter phenomenon (Clance & Imes, 1978). Linked to these sensitivities, and given their potential mediating positions, it is important that university administrators understand the competing pressures for academics (Ching, 2021) as well as candidates. Cowling (2017) suggests that regular contact between a candidate and their supervisor is key to candidate happiness and for the candidate to develop their subject knowledge and research skills. Cultural context also matters with the need to navigate disciplinary and institutional factors over time as the supervisee–supervisor relationship matures in relation to levels of feedback, initiative, and independent research skills (Saxena, 2021). For DBA cohorts, trust can be developed within the group if candidates progress at the same time (Gough, 2019).

The impact of administrative and professional services support is remarkably overlooked in these discussions. Yet, individuals in these roles very often act as linchpins in doctoral research environments. We note, not least, that research managers who care about 'doctoral orphans' who have lost their supervisors (Wisker & Robinson, 2013) are critical indicators of a genuinely supportive research culture for doctoral candidates.

Trust, including peer-led support communities, reduces social isolation at different phases of the doctoral journey (Greener, 2021) in universities where doctoral candidates' educational transitions are often overlooked (McPherson, Punch, & Graham, 2018). Casey, Harvey, Taylor, Knight, and Trenoweth (2022, p. 850) 'recommend that supervisors and doctoral schools encourage peer support networks and open dialogue with students around the reality of postgraduate research (PGR) study, to manage expectations and reduce self-doubt'. They note the scope to develop a deeper understanding of challenges faced by candidates throughout their doctorates to enable the implementation of beneficial wellbeing interventions that are meaningful and aligned to candidates' specific needs during their transitions as researchers (McPherson et al., 2018).

Research Culture and Organisational Behaviour

The Royal Society in the UK states that

> [r]esearch culture encompasses the behaviours, values, expectations, attitudes, and norms of our research communities. It influences researchers' career paths and determines the way that research is conducted and communicated. (UKRIO, 2023, p. 1)

The Wellcome Trust's (2020) survey of UK researchers revealed that a poor research culture increases stress, anxiety, and mental health problems, strains personal relationships, and creates a sense of isolation and loneliness at work resulting in poorer quality outputs, lost public trust, and talent retention problems.

The idea that 'culture is how we do things round here' draws attention to the notion of a cultural paradigm (Johnson et al., 2011). Different models of the business school have been explored as a means of organising to attract and retain talent. Katrin Muff at the boutique Lausanne Business School experimented for a while with holacracy, a form of self-managing with decentralised decision-making, to help drive purpose (Ignite Adaptive, 2017).

We note that there remains a tendency for business schools to shy away from adoption of leadership styles according to goals faced (Rui & Chao, 2022) and learning leadership through on-the-job experience (Davies, Thomas, Cornuel, & Cremer, 2023; Thomas & Thomas, 2011) risks inheritance of behaviours that have gone before and replication of organisational culture.

Professionalisation of Doctoral Supervision

Relationships are key to the doctoral candidate experience as we have noted in Chapter 3. The UKCGE Good Supervisory Practice Framework (UKCGE, n.d.) emphasises the value of researcher and supervisor training and development (Huet & Casanova, 2022; Pearson & Brew, 2002) to enhance candidates' critical writing skills (Woodhouse & Wood, 2022) and a 'completion mindset' (Green & Bowden, 2012; Lindsay, 2015). Effective supervisors encourage candidates to disseminate findings from doctoral projects (Dinham & Scott, 2001), to communicate the benefits of doctoral students participating in conferences (Hauss, 2021), and to learn the rules of the publishing game in business and management studies (Wilkinson, 2015).

Universities in the UK where doctoral supervisors have gained full UKCGE research supervisor recognition are clearly showing a commitment to doctoral studies and the quality of supervisors, focusing on the following aspects (UKCGE, n.d., p. 1):

1. Recruitment and selection.
2. Supervisory relationships with candidates.
3. Supervisory relationships with co-supervisors.
4. Supporting candidates' research projects.
5. Encouraging candidates to write and giving appropriate feedback.
6. Keeping research on track and monitoring progress.
7. Supporting candidates' personal, professional, and career development.
8. Supporting candidates through completion and the final examination.
9. Supporting candidates to disseminate their research.
10. Reflecting upon and enhancing practice.

For instance, such practices include understanding the candidate-led selection of supervisors in business schools based on supervisors' web profiles (Marder et al., 2021). This links to the notion of the importance of individual academic reputation (and effective and efficient university staff web page information) despite our observation that at a high level business school research environments are assessed on aggregate performance. Individuals make crucial contributions to doctoral research environments (like ants in an ant colony). There is an expectation that effective supervisors develop constructive psychological contracts with their supervisees (Sambrook, 2016) and manage team supervision effectively (Watts, 2010). With respect to the latter point, we are aware that the process of appointing principals and co-supervisors has received little attention or scrutiny. In many universities, we observe that heads of department or equivalent have a powerful voice in who is included (or not) in the team. Building of capacity can be less of a challenge, and provide substantial benefits to doctoral candidates, where a more progressive and collaborative approach is enabled. The cooperation on doctoral education projects (CODOC) between Africa, Asia, Latin America, and Europe (Jørgensen, 2012, pp. 6, 9) illustrates an outwards-looking perspective on responding to 'the need to build research capacity across the world to meet global challenges' in the context of doctoral education that is recognised, at a global level to be 'knitted together in a pattern which is becoming more convergent, more complex and more inclusive'.

We identify the merits of the UKCGE Good Supervisory Practice Framework in helping to provide a useful lens on pertinent issues that are facing doctoral programmes management *per se* and those encountered by business schools beyond a UK context. The UKCGE framework is indicative of an approach to influence the national-level quality of doctoral supervision in an arena where government policy may be described as *laissez-faire*. We also note the influence of sector bodies and associations in guiding good practice in the delivery of business school doctorates. The British Academy of Management (BAM) organises a series of events aimed at business school doctoral candidates spotlighting good practices in doctoral research. One recent event (in March 2023) promised benefits to attendees in terms of a 'nuanced conceptualisation of the student-supervisor relationship' and 'robust perspectives on the realities of completing a doctorate' (BAM, n.d., p. 1).

A potential burgeoning suite of 'good practice' initiatives is in line with the increased professionalisation of doctoral education and raises questions about the extent to which dialogue and coordination exist or hold a value between organisers to provide coherence for students, supervisors, programme managers, and funders.

Business Doctoral Education and Capacity Development

The extent to which business and management doctorates are effective in the development of R&D capacity in line with the strategic aims of doctoral education (noted in Chapter 1) may be considered. Lekhetho (2022, p. 24) has noted how:

> As part of the Ethiopian government's *human development capacity programme*, Unisa has been offering postgraduate education to Ethiopian students, mostly doctoral degrees to lecturers teaching at different public universities and senior public servants since 2007.

The role of the business school PhD in the reproduction of the academy is a theme we have repeatedly acknowledged in this book. The doctorate as a means of addressing capacity needs in response to business school faculty shortages in Australia, China, India, UK, and the USA mean that (geography and mobility aside) there is scope to sustain rather than grow the academic workforce. Yet, the reproduction of the academy through the business school PhD is accompanied by concerns over replication of the *status quo* and 'homosocial reproduction' (D'Aveni, 1996, p. 166) and this threatens the diversification of talent.

AACSB (2021) accreditation standards emphasise the importance of diversity, equity, inclusion, and belonging (DEIB). The PhD Project (mentioned in Chapter 3) was established almost 30 years ago to support African Americans in business schools to complete doctorates. It is a positive development that dedicated Chief Diversity Officer (CDO) roles are being created in leading business schools. For example, since 2015 the Stockholm School of Economics (SSE) has employed a full-time Diversity, Equity, and Inclusion Manager. Harvard Business School's first Chief Diversity and Inclusion Officer was appointed in 2021, and Wharton appointed its first Chief Diversity, Equity, and Inclusion Officer in 2022. We assume that the creation of these senior positions and scholarships for women and other marginalised groups signals to doctoral students and supervisors that diversity matters.

However, it is critical that this signalling also includes embedded monitoring of demographics such as disabled and mature candidates, different socio-economic backgrounds, hardship funding, and systemic changes to prevent bias and discrimination. The topics being studied at the doctoral level also need to be considered, for example, are they contributing to civic and responsible management education (Colombo, 2023)? Are doctoral outputs making an impact? For example, how did they respond to the COVID-19 crisis, how do they enhance the legitimacy of business schools, and influence management consultants and university executives (Fleming, 2022)? Moreover, how do candidates themselves gain cultural capital to help them socialise? Business schools attract significant numbers of self-funded international students in PhD programmes and their particular needs must be considered (Mogaji, Adamu, & Nguyen, 2021). Espino (2014) highlighted the challenges for Mexican American PhD candidates in navigating and gaining different forms of capital during their studies to access career and funding opportunities in doctoral programmes. The idea that graduate school can provide socialisation to the academic career is riddled with discrepancies, not least with respect to differences between the academic workplace and academic study context (Austin, 2002). Here, the potential benefits of attenuated authentic mentorship have been identified (Dias, Freedman, Medway, & Par, 1999) to increase doctoral researchers' exposure to some of the global realities of academia.

The innovation capacity of the DBA is dependent on its alignment to business relevance and macro-level economic development and industrial strategy as we have noted in Chapters 1 and 4. However, Trkman (2019) has pointed to inertia in the business models of business schools based on implicit value propositions of teaching and research that frustrate transformation. The scope for creative, novel, and innovative doctoral research in business and management appears stifled by conservative, risk-averse culture.

Mentoring, Social Capital and Capacity-Building

The use of mentorship as a tool in business settings tends to be more established than in education environments (Zografou & McDermott, 2022). However, the evolution of higher education policy and the origins of the PhD in Germany and the USA often traced back to 'Humboldtian' principles, are linked to the idea of tacit knowledge transfer from supervisor to candidate akin to an academic apprenticeship or mentoring model. We observe a recently re-ignited discussion of the role of doctoral candidate advisors or supervisors as mentors (Berdahl, Malloy, & Young, 2022) running alongside many negative reports of academic workload time for supervision in USA and UK contexts (Clegg & Gower, 2021; Robeyns, 2019).

Expectations placed on doctoral supervisors include high levels of empathy and emotional intelligence, with arguably little consideration of how doctoral supervisors feel. Managerialism further challenges and mediates the extent to which high levels of doctoral supervision processes can be realised (Bui, 2014; Parker-Jenkins, 2018). The social practices entailed in doctoral supervision are much less visible than for mainstream undergraduate teaching (Bernstein, 2003) given the many pressures which faculties face when trying to ensure the doctoral candidate-supervisor relationship works (Taylor & Beasley, 2005).

Insights from studies that examine the success of under-represented doctoral students such as African Americans who benefitted from faculty mentoring also highlight the challenges of a lack of diversity amongst faculty leadership (Felder, 2010). In the USA, the phenomenon of Historically Black Colleges and Universities (HBCUs) also provides unique social capital (Palmer & Gasman, 2008). First-generation and students of colour gain access to social capital thanks to mentoring relationships (Smith, 2007). This matters because the relationship between a candidate and faculty members is a critical one for the quality of their experience (Noy & Ray, 2012). Initiatives such as support groups for international doctoral candidates can broaden their cross-cultural perspectives (Ku, Lahman, Yeh, & Cheng, 2008). However, we must stress that there is a lot of progress to make with respect to the mentorship of under-represented researchers, challenged not least by a lack of role model diversity in business schools where 'social hierarchy and gatekeepers reproduce inequitable practices' (Grier cited in Bohanon, 2022, p. 1).

Mentorship can be gained through a variety of sources (Zografou & McDermott, 2022), in groups (Manabe et al., 2018), informally as well as formally, beyond mentoring as pedagogy in business schools (George & Mampilly, 2012). In the USA, the American Accounting Association funds a PhD mentorship programme (American Accounting Association, 2023). In Germany, the Max Planck Institute (2003) provides mentoring programmes for women PhD students. In Australia, Canberra University (2023) offers a PhD Plus mentoring programme with alumni. Recognition of the value of mentoring of researchers in university contexts has gained momentum in recent years to support personal and/or professional growth or development. Although it can be time-consuming for faculty to mentor doctoral candidates, mentoring can help to reduce candidates' sense of isolation and improve retention (Mollica & Nemeth, 2014). Webb, Wangmo, Ewen, Teaster, and Hatch (2009) found that peer mentors are helpful in providing social support while academic staff mentors tend to offer direction. In another model, the Scottish Graduate School of Social Science (SGSSS, 2022) Career

Pathways Mentoring Programme pairs doctoral researchers with PhD alumni as mentors to gain relevant sector knowledge. King's College London (n.d.) operates a diversity mentoring programme for students to connect with alumni. We note that post-COVID a shift towards blended supervision and mentorship (Kessio, 2022) may have widened opportunities for doctoral candidates to access in-programme support to assist personal and professional growth.

Although business schools may be well positioned to enable changes to address gender and racial discrimination in corporations, research from Cambridge Judge Business School noted that top-ranked UK and USA business schools which boast about international diversity should not be using this as a 'proxy for racial diversity' (Ethier, 2022). PREDOC (n.d.) highlights the importance of mentoring students from diverse backgrounds before they apply for doctoral programmes, especially for prospective candidates who might not have considered doctoral study as an option. This is a real challenge to overcome homophily in graduate admissions (Posselt, 2016) and transparency in admissions processes (Cassuto, 2016). There is scope for business schools to collaborate to create new talent pools (He, 2018) and research networks (Schiavone & Simoni, 2011). Clearly, there are also issues about the racial/ethnic composition of faculty members and how search committees make hiring decisions to enhance diversity (White-Lewis, 2020) as we have noted in Chapter 2.

All parties in a mentoring relationship need to be clear about their roles and what successful mentoring looks like (Zografou & McDermott, 2022). At a sector level, the European Academy of Management (EURAM) offers a Doctoral Accelerator programme that brings together doctoral candidates and senior academics as well as industry practitioners (EURAM, n.d.). PhD candidates who are working in industry also benefit from industry mentors. Vauterin and Virkki-Hatakka (2021) adopted the Laurillard conversational framework to examine a mentor's experience of mentoring a group of industrial PhD candidates using hermeneutics to understand how subjective meanings are translated into transferable knowledge. We must be mindful, however, of horror stories from PhD students who felt belittled by their supervisors and mentors, particularly in male-dominated fields (Times Higher Education, 2017). The power of a mentor's advice is also open to question, at least in terms of perceived directive advice, as illustrated through an anonymous comment on the *Times Higher Education* post (2017, p. 1):

> I was thirty when I was awarded my PhD (this was before time constraints were imposed) after seven years of hard and dedicated work. My supervisor told me I was too old to apply for university posts. He was wrong; but I believed him, and so I didn't. Now sixty, I look back on a ruined and wasted life.

Mental Health and Well-Being and Diminished Capacity

Attention was first drawn to mental health problems in PhD candidates as a widespread issue in a European context by Levecque, Anseel, De Beuckelaer, Van der Heyden, and Gisle (2017). Since then, we note an increase in the number of doctoral candidates reportedly affected by poor mental health. This has captured the attention of policy makers and researcher developers. Vitae's (2018) pioneering UK research survey exploring well-being and mental health and associated support services for PGRs identified at-risk characteristics including having part-time status; balancing caring responsibilities; being a woman; and being an international researcher. Many of these characteristics are increasingly visible in business and management doctoral candidates.

Watson and Turnpenny (2022, p. 1975) identify PGRs as an 'at-risk population' in terms of mental health with challenges at individual, organisational and wider social/political levels. They argue that

> [f]ailure to attend to PGR wellbeing and the wellbeing of those working in the research sector more generally may result in losses to scientific advancement, significant costs and limit the supply of talent in the research workforce.

Therefore, the support of peer networks and open conversations with appropriate well-being interventions customised to doctoral candidates' needs are vital (Casey et al., 2022). University graduate schools can also help to support the supervisory relationship and sense of community spirit (Smith McGloin & Wynne, 2015) in addition to signposting non-academic support services (Waight & Giordano, 2018).

Doctoral supervisors are also at risk of poor mental health and well-being. This is a topic area that is under-explored. The role of the supervisor in supporting the emotional well-being of doctoral researchers has gained increased attention over the past five years. Moreover, mental health and well-being have become salient issues since the COVID-19 pandemic (Edwards, Martin, & Ashkanasy, 2021; Ryan, Baik, & Larcombe, 2022), and the notion of doctoral supervisors as some kind of 'academic superheroes' (Pitt & Mewburn, 2016) raises questions about their own well-being. However, Wang (2022) has identified performance appraisal-related factors and PhD candidate-related factors to be stressors in Chinese doctoral supervisor experiences. In a UK context, Clegg and Gower (2021, p. 1) have observed the appearance of difficulties in supervision 'when supervisors try to implement broad strategies in the context of other responsibilities and the specific and individual needs of candidates' and have highlighted implications for supervisor ability to contribute to a positive research culture. It is striking that in a UK-wide survey that captured the views of 3,435 doctoral supervisors

> Only a third (33 per cent) of respondents reported no difficulty in managing their own well-being suggesting that two-thirds are feeling the strain and worryingly 61 per cent disagreed that their institution adequately supports them in terms of being a work/life balance role model for their candidates. (Clegg & Gower, 2021, p. 1)

We have witnessed reports of four in ten academics considering leaving UK universities frustrated by 'frequent rejection and loss of control' (Fazackerley, 2019, p. 1) and, more recently, a higher percentage of UK academics demoralised by pay, working conditions, and pensions (Lough, 2022). In Australia too, diminished joy and increased burnout amongst academic staff have been high-lighted (Whitsed & Girardi, 2022). The implications of this for the capacity to deliver doctoral education must be appreciated.

In the context of business schools, we have already noted particular cultural and environmental characteristics that contribute to a working environment described as 'often aggressive and harmful' (Coriat, 2021, p. 102). Questioning of the disciplinary status of business and management is ongoing. Indeed, O'Doherty and De Cock (2017, p. 462) describe management as 'a discipline haunted by aporia and incoherence' whereas other commentators argue for the status of management science. Bothello and Roulet (2019, p. 854) note how passion and aspiration to contribute to a greater good may be quashed by a 'peculiarly single-minded focus on theory'. This results in a particular propensity for the imposter phenomenon to manifest in graduate school education and entrance into business and management academia. Linked to the idea of feeling like an imposter arising from frustrations around the representation of self in academic life, Harley (2019, p. 286) has observed a crisis of confidence in management studies in relation to how academic success is assessed and 'an apparent lack of practical or academic impact from most published research'. Perceptions of value relating to research and the researcher, embedded in the research and innovation environment, appear to be core contributors to a sense of esteem, worthiness, and levels of confidence. Building on this theme, Wickert, Post, Doh, Prescott, and Prencipe (2021) acknowledge a need to broaden their understanding of what constitutes impactful research for business and management scholars who are seeking to 'make a difference' to society. The 2022 *Academy of Management Learning & Education* special issue on impact points to a growing interest in the impact agenda.

Capabilities as Opportunities to Enable Being or Doing

There are ongoing discussions internationally about what skills and knowledge doctoral graduates should have. If we think about capabilities more broadly as 'the abilities of an individual to function, to use opportunities, to make choices, and to take actions' (Dorjsuren & Palmer, 2018, p. 60), we might look beyond conventional doctoral skills training agendas to identify how business school doctorates contribute beyond being or doing to 'real freedoms or opportunities to facilitate or enable being or doing' (Dorjsuren & Palmer, 2018, p. 61). This perspective aligns well with a social justice agenda from which higher education, business, researcher development, and doctoral education are not exempt.

We have earlier noted track record as a measure of capability in relation to the intellectual measures of applicants and the completions of supervisors. Equity of opportunity is, however, uneven. In their review of a body of published work based on the practice of developing researchers in the UK and Australia, Bromley and Warnock (2021) identified research gaps in research governance, work-life balance, engagement influence and impact training, and creativity and innovation training. These aspects may be mapped to the Vitae Researcher Development Framework (RDF) cited in Chapter 4. The ambitions of this tool in describing 'the knowledge, behaviour, and attributes of successful researchers' (Vitae, 2023, p. 1) are noted. We also acknowledge the relevance of ongoing developments such as the EU's Research Competency Framework (Almerud, Ricksten, & O'Neill, 2022) to the identification of doctoral capabilities.

Access to the acquisition of knowledge and the development of behaviours and attributes depend on researcher development provision. This is often governed by institutional (resource-based) decisions and, as we have noted in Chapter 3, socialisation and integration into learning communities. Sun and Trent (2020, p. 422) draw our attention to the need to appreciate 'the nature of becoming a doctoral student'. Considering capabilities requires us to extend our focus beyond this to appreciate the nature of becoming a researcher.

Lin (2021) has proposed that there is merit in examining the spill-over effects of sharing research knowledge from faculty on the research lives of graduate students in the context of Japan. Building on this idea, we recognise that there is scope to explore further how researchers at an early career stage, including doctoral researchers, build capabilities through experiential learning opportunities. We have already acknowledged mentoring as a means of supporting the development of business school doctoral researchers.

We observe that structured experiential learning opportunities for business and management researchers are not widely available. In Chapter 4, we highlighted Norges Bank's salaried PhD internship programme (Norges Bank, 2020) as an example of innovative practice. In 2016, Blessinger and Stockley's identification of *Emerging directions in doctoral education* spotlighted the private USA higher education provider Antioch University as operating a PhD in Leadership and Change that presented a 'model of doctoral education that focuses on preparing students as scholar-practitioners and stewards of society' (Blessinger & Stockley, 2016, p. 17). It is apparent that further attention needs to be paid to opportunities to enable business school doctoral candidates to develop as researchers. This also requires consideration of academic workplace research opportunities for DBA candidates.

Nevertheless, we must not overlook where knowledge sits in terms of the characteristics of doctoral learners. There are candidates who come to the doctorate with a wealth of experience and talents developed through the workplace and continuing professional development (CPD) activities and who have the propensity to contribute to a culture of reciprocity in skills development. There are also business schools that have closer ties with commercial institutions and appear to be more readily able and/or willing to explore innovative capabilities.

Connectivity

Business doctorates involve a multitude of dimensions linked to the concepts of connectivity, networks, and webs of relationships. We note the multifarious nature of the term 'connectivity' and recognise rich and varied connotations in relation to the business school doctorate. In Chapters 1 and 2, for example, we noted making connections and collaboration as a capacity-building strategy. Chapters 2 and 3 acknowledged the importance of networks to assist candidate integration into doctoral communities. Chapters 3 and 4 drew attention to supervisory and workplace relationships. A common theme thus far is that stronger connections are possible and desirable – especially between business schools and industry, across business schools, and amongst PhD and DBA researchers. These connections are contingent on the extent to which networks are 'open' or 'closed' in terms of membership and operate in exclusive or inclusive spaces (Palmer, 2022). We note some entrenched conventions about who works together, when, how, and why.

During the COVID-19 pandemic, we noticed an appetite for EFMD business schools to increase the sharing of practice and voiced hope that 'new ways of working and collaborating within business school doctoral communities will continue to provide inspiration as we move towards realising intentions for more blended offerings in doctoral education', observing that 'New technologies have brought us closer together at a distance' (Davies, Palmer, Braccia, Clegg, & Smith, 2021, p. 1).

We also stated our optimism that doctoral education would be prioritised in business schools in the face of multiple public health, economic, social, and climate challenges (Davies et al., 2021). Contemporary challenges facing business schools include the need for transdisciplinary research (Rashid, 2021) to address the United Nations' Sustainable Development Goals yet doctoral structures make this difficult. There are also issues of white hegemony in terms of knowledge production which candidates of colour must grapple with (Masta, 2021), especially challenges in knowing where and how to publish in peer-reviewed academic journals (Rowley, 2023).

Interdisciplinarity and Team Science

Manathunga, Lant, and Mellick (2006) call for re-imagining doctoral pedagogy as interdisciplinary to address twenty-first century challenges through Mode 2 knowledge production. In the UK, Pizzolato (2023) provides an example of the DProf (Doctorate in Professional Studies) offered at Middlesex Business School. The DProf is a transdisciplinary programme for candidates who research across different disciplines and sectors. He highlights the 'interstitial way' (Lindvig, Lyall, & Meagher, 2019) delivery mode with activities incrementally woven into the programme to mitigate candidates' resistance to the notion of interdisciplinarity. He emphasises the importance of relational sociology (Donati, 2010) which sees the social world as a network of ties and interactions of various types and scales which form actors in the interactions, for instance through communities of practice, special interest groups, annual doctoral research away days across disciplines. Pizzolato (2023) also stresses that learning during interactions *in situ* (Lattuca, 2002), include physical and virtual spaces that are not disciplinary silos. Furthermore, contamination between disciplines where management researchers on doctoral programmes learn research methods such as ethnography from other disciplines like anthropology can be very creative with transformational opportunities to synthesise different forms of knowledge beyond monodisciplinary perspectives. Ryan and Neumann (2013), however, comment that national research assessment exercises tend to emphasise and reinforce disciplinary silos. This is despite an increasing focus on research impact case studies in countries like the UK in national research evaluation policy and rankings such as the *Times Higher Education* impact rankings.

Collaboration is important for doctoral candidates' socialisation in learning to publish in peer-reviewed publications (Larivière, 2012). As the number of co-authors on academic papers increases and research impact becomes more important in national policies such as the Research Excellence Framework (Blackburn et al., 2023), what might business schools learn from big science where team science, that is, collaborative research (Cooke & Hilton, 2015), is more common than in social sciences?

Team science requires appropriate organisational support structures, team building, and professional research administrators and managers to deal with conflict resolution. Falk-Krzesinski et al. (2010) emphasise the value of the field of Science of Team Science (SciTS) to understand enablers and barriers. The European Commission has driven the principles of Open Science and Responsible Research and Innovation to disseminate knowledge using digital and collaborative technologies. We note the potential to strengthen research capability through working in diverse and collaborative environments. We also are aware that other disciplinary fields have successfully brought together the realms of industry, research, and policy through scientific collaboration that builds relationships for knowledge integration. Business schools possess a wealth of knowledge resources but weak internal and external knowledge-sharing practices impact on value creation (Ranjan, 2011) alongside a traditional, hard-to-shift preoccupation with scientific rigour above other forms of knowledge (Bennis & O'Toole, 2005).

Looking to the Future of Business School Doctorates

The AACSB and EDAMBA (2021) report highlighted variability in business doctoral programmes globally and the need to understand better the potential for greater innovation. It called for re-imagining the purpose of doctorates beyond traditional academic careers, capacity-building, expanding access, assuring quality, and developing doctoral ecosystems. In addition, we need to revisit doctoral supervisory models, programme structures, and expectations of research/thesis outputs as the aspirations of doctoral candidates and supervisors shift. It is helpful to understand the different supervisory models and assessments in various cities (Joannidès de Lautour, 2023), countries, and institutions following the COVID-19 disruptions to the responsible management education agenda (Falkenstein, Hommel, & Snelson-Powell, 2022). We look forward to ongoing dialogue in the academy and beyond, gaining much needed perspective from multiple stakeholder viewpoints. There is a need to spotlight individual candidate characteristics, backgrounds, lived experiences and ambitions within our attempts to design and deliver generic business doctorate awards. We need to consider the ant and the helicopter acknowledged in our Preface. It is important to strive to innovate and professionalise business school doctorate education beyond the sake of the future business school academic workforce and talent management.

Summary

In this final chapter, we have considered national and institutional contingencies and identified how context and culture in different countries might influence doctoral research in business and management. The concepts of research environment and culture can be viewed as dynamic and amorphous, incorporating many intangible dimensions. They are also open to multiple interpretations. Nevertheless, we have emphasised the importance of creating environments that are conducive to supportive research cultures, various paradigms, mentoring and social capital, and capacity development activities. Specifically, we have highlighted the importance of a relational approach, ensuring trust and research integrity to enable equity, diversity, inclusion, and a sense of belonging (DEIB).

We note some inter-related observations on the chapter theme of research environment, culture, capacity, capabilities, and connectivity. In particular:

- For under-represented or minoritised doctoral candidates mentoring offers a means to gain social capital and can assist in capacity-building and capacity development. However, this depends on role model diversity and sensitivity to candidates' attributes and needs that are often not fully considered and explored in business school strategic planning.
- Mental health and well-being challenges may diminish doctoral education capacity. There is a need for greater recognition of how these challenges relate to the academic climate, research environment and context. Strategies to tackle structural and disciplinary causes rather than treat (or even dismiss) symptoms are necessary.
- Equity of opportunities to enable being or doing must be considered.
- Isolation of programmes and candidates frustrates knowledge exchange. A lack of connectivity may negatively impact on efficacy in relation to doctoral and business school goals.
- The value of collaboration versus individual-based competition should be emphasised. There is scope to capitalise on the wider benefits of team-based science approaches.

Questions you might like to consider:

- What are the key elements of a productive and supportive research environment?
- How do we ensure an inclusive and collaborative research culture in practice?
- How can competency frameworks such as Vitae's Researcher Development Framework be applied across all business school doctoral candidate journeys?
- How can supervisors support mental health and well-being challenges among doctoral candidates <u>and</u> themselves?
- What can supervisors do to enable connectivity to the United Nations' Sustainable Development Goals, conference networks, and other relevant communities of practice linked to responsible business education agendas?
- Why are mentors so important? Are we fully clear about the value that they add to business school doctoral candidate experiences?
- What can you do to ensure diversity, equity, inclusion, and belonging in business doctoral programmes?

Final Reflections

One of the starting points in writing this book was to think about 'what makes doctorates in business and management different?' We have noted some key characteristics of the business school context as fundamental in the shaping of the nature of provision, expectations, experiences, and outcomes. Practices and behaviours are inevitably reflective of the history and evolution of the business school and business and management education. We have also identified challenges that cut across the management of doctoral education *per se* and the doctoral candidate's lifecycle in terms of positioning, status, recruitment, throughput, and impact. Responses to these challenges are to some extent dynamic and linked to oscillating influences but they may also be read more generally as static and improvident, reflecting attachments to entrenched norms and traditions in doctoral education. As we reach the end of this book we reflect on many unanswered questions, not least in terms of the future shape of business school doctorates worldwide and the absorptive capacity for doctoral graduates in business, academia, and beyond. Our exploration remains a work-in-progress.

References

AACSB. (2021). Our commitment to diversity, equity, inclusion, and belonging. Retrieved from https://www.aacsb.edu/about-us/advocacy/diversity-and-inclusion/. Accessed on March 2, 2023.

AACSB & EDAMBA. (2021). Mapping the global landscape of business doctoral programs. Retrieved from https://www.aacsb.edu/-/media/publications/research-reports/aacsb-edamba-doctoral-education-report.pdf/. Accessed on March 2, 2023.

Ajjawi, R., Crampton, P. E., & Rees, C. E. (2018). What really matters for successful research environments? A realist synthesis. *Medical Education, 52*(9), 936–950.

Almerud, M., Ricksten, M., & O'Neill, G. (2022). Using a competence-based approach for career development in academic and beyond. In L. Núñez & A. De Coen (Eds.), *Knowledge ecosystems in the new ERA*. Publications Office of the European Union. https://data.europa.eu/doi/10.2777/150763

American Accounting Association. (2023). MAS PhD student mentorship program. Retrieved from https://aaahq.org/MAS/PHD-MENTORSHIP-PROGRAM. Accessed on March 23, 2023.

Antunes, D., & Thomas, H. (2007). The competitive (dis) advantages of European business schools. *Long Range Planning, 40*(3), 382–404.

Armstrong, J. S., & Sperry, T. (1994). The ombudsman: Business school prestige—Research versus teaching. *Interfaces, 24*(2), 13–43.

Austin, A. E. (2002). Preparing the next generation of faculty: Graduate school as socialization to the academic career. *The Journal of Higher Education, 73*(1), 94–122.

Baden-Fuller, C., Ravazzolo, F., & Schweizer, T. (2000). Making and measuring reputations: The research ranking of European business schools. *Long Range Planning, 33*(5), 621–650.

BAM. (n.d.). The doctoral journey: Your route to excellence. *Webinar*. Retrieved from https://www.bam.ac.uk/events-landing/ems-event-calendar/the-doctoral-journey-your-route-to-excellence.html. Accessed on April 10, 2023.

Becker, T. E., Kernan, M. C., Clark, K. D., & Klein, H. J. (2018). Dual commitments to organizations and professions: Different motivational pathways to productivity. *Journal of Management, 44*(3), 1202–1225.

Bennis, W. G., & O'Toole, J. (2005). How business schools have lost their way. *Harvard Business Review, 83*(5), 96–104.

Berdahl, L., Malloy, J., & Young, L. (2022). Doctoral mentorship practices in Canadian political science. *Canadian Journal of Political Science/Revue Canadienne de Science Politique, 55*(3), 709–720.

Bernstein, B. (2003). *Class, codes and control: The structuring of pedagogic discourse* (Vol. 4). London: Psychology Press.

Berry, D., & Davidson, P. (2022). Building an inclusive and supportive research environment. Retrieved from https://ref.ac.uk/about-the-ref/blogs/building-an-inclusive-and-supportive-research-environment/. Accessed on March 3, 2023.

Blackburn, R., Dibb, S., & Tonks, I. (2023). Business and management studies in the United Kingdom's 2021 research excellence framework: Implications for research quality assessment. *British Journal of Management.* https://doi.org/10.1111/1467-8551.12721

Bland, C. J., Center, B. A., Finstad, D. A., Risbey, K. R., & Staples, J. G. (2005). A theoretical, practical, predictive model of faculty and department research productivity. *Academic Medicine, 80*(3), 225–237.

Blessinger, P., & Stockley, D. (Eds.). (2016). *Emerging directions in doctoral education.* Leeds: Emerald.

Bohanon, M. (2022). Business schools need to serve as better role models of workforce diversity. *Insight into Diversity.* Retrieved from https://www.insightintodiversity.com/business-schools-need-to-serve-as-better-role-models-of-workforce-diversity/. Accessed on March 2, 2023.

Bothello, J., & Roulet, T. J. (2019). The imposter syndrome, or the mis-representation of self in academic life. *Journal of Management Studies, 56*(4), 854–861.

Bromley, T., & Warnock, L. (2021). The practice of the development of researchers: The 'state-of-the-art'. *Studies in Graduate and Postdoctoral Education, 12*(2), 283–299.

Bryan, B., & Guccione, K. (2018). Was it worth it? A qualitative exploration into graduate perceptions of doctoral value. *Higher Education Research & Development, 37*(6), 1124–1140.

Bui, H. T. (2014). Student–supervisor expectations in the doctoral supervision process for business and management students. *Business and Management Education in HE, 1*(1), 12–27.

Canberra University. (2023). PhD Plus. Retrieved from https://www.canberra.edu.au/research/graduate-research/current-research-students/uc-phd-alumni-mentoring-program/. Accessed on March 25, 2023.

Carter, S., Blumenstein, M., & Cook, C. (2013). Different for women? The challenges of doctoral studies. *Teaching in Higher Education, 18*(4), 339–351.

Casey, C., Harvey, O., Taylor, J., Knight, F., & Trenoweth, S. (2022). Exploring the wellbeing and resilience of postgraduate researchers. *Journal of Further and Higher Education, 46*(6), 850–867.

Cassuto, L. (2016). Inside the graduate-admissions process. *The Chronicle of Higher Education,* January 31.

Chapman, K. J., Davis, R., Toy, D., & Wright, L. (2004). Academic integrity in the business school environment: I'll get by with a little help from my friends. *Journal of Marketing Education, 26*(3), 236–249.

Chen, L. H. (2006). Attracting East Asian students to Canadian graduate schools. *Canadian Journal of Higher Education, 36*(2), 77–105.

Chen, Y., Gupta, A., & Hoshower, L. (2006). Factors that motivate business faculty to conduct research: An expectancy theory analysis. *Journal of Education for Business, 81*(4), 179–189.

Ching, G. S. (2021). Academic identity and communities of practice: Narratives of social science academics career decisions in Taiwan. *Education Sciences, 11*(8), 388.

Clance, P. R., & Imes, S. A. (1978). The imposter phenomenon in high achieving women: Dynamics and therapeutic intervention. *Psychotherapy: Theory, Research & Practice, 15*(3), 241–247.

Clarke, T., Dameron, S., & Durand, T. (2013). Strategies for business schools in a multi-polar world. *Education+Training, 55*(4–5), 323–335.

Clegg, K., & Gower, O. (2021). PhD supervisors need better support, recognition and reward. *WONKHE,* October 8. Retrieved from https://wonkhe.com/blogs/phd-supervi sors-need-better-support-recognition-and-reward/. Accessed on March 23, 2023.

Colombo, L. A. (2023). Civilize the business school: For a civic management education. *Academy of Management Learning & Education, 22*(1), 132–149.

Cooke, N. J., & Hilton, M. L. (2015). *Enhancing the effectiveness of team science.* Washington, DC: National Academies Press.

Coriat, A. M. (2021). The interplay between policy and funding. In A. Lee & R. Bongaardt (Eds.), *The future of doctoral research: Challenges and opportunities* (pp. 101–109). Oxon: Routledge.

Cowling, M. (2017). *Happiness in UK postgraduate research.* Higher Education Academy. Retrieved from file:///N:/Downloads/happiness_in_uk_post-graduate_research_in_uk_heis_2013-2015_v1.1.pdf. Accessed December 12, 2019.

D'Aveni, R. A. (1996). A multiple-constituency, status-based approach to interorgani-zational mobility of faculty and input–output competition among top business schools. *Organization Science, 7*(2), 166–189.

Davies, A., & Berry, D. (2022, June 24). Will an individual circumstances process still be needed in any future REF? Retrieved from https://www.ref.ac.uk/about-the-ref/ blogs/will-an-individual-circumstances-process-still-be-needed-in-any-future-ref/

Davies, J., Palmer, N., Braccia, E., Clegg, K., & Smith, M. (2021). Supporting doctoral programmes during a global pandemic: Crisis as opportunity. *EFMD Global Focus, 1*(15). Retrieved from www.globalfocusmagazine.com

Davies, J., Thomas, H., Cornuel, E., & Cremer, R. D. (2023). *Leading a business school.* Abingdon: Routledge.

Davies, J., Yarrow, E., & Syed, J. (2020). The curious under-representation of women impact case leaders: Can we disengender inequality regimes? *Gender, Work & Organization, 27*(2), 129–148.

De Angelo, H., DeAngelo, L., & Zimmerman, J. (2005). *What's really wrong with U.S. business schools?* Working Paper. University of Southern California, Los Angeles, CA.

Dias, P., Freedman, A., Medway, P., & Par, A. (1999). *Worlds apart: Acting and writing in academic and workplace contexts* (1st ed.). Oxford: Routledge.

Dinham, S., & Scott, C. (2001). The experience of disseminating the results of doctoral research. *Journal of Further and Higher Education, 25*(1), 45–55.

Dorjsuren, A., & Palmer, N. (2018). Equity in tourism development: Procedural (in)justice and distributive justice in Mongolia, East Asia. *Asian Journal of Tourism Research, 3*(1), 58–87.

Donati, P. (2010). *Relational sociology: A new paradigm for the social sciences.* Oxford: Routledge.

Dubois, S., & Walsh, I. (2017). The globalization of research highlighted through the research networks of management education institutions: The case of French business schools. *Management, 20*(5), 435–462.

Eagan, M. K., Jr, Jaeger, A. J., & Grantham, A. (2015). Supporting the academic majority: Policies and practices related to part-time faculty's job satisfaction. *The Journal of Higher Education, 86*(3), 448–483.

Edwards, M. S., Martin, A. J., & Ashkanasy, N. M. (2021). Mental health and psychological well-being among management students and educators. *Journal of Management Education, 45*(1), 3–18.

Espino, M. M. (2014). Exploring the role of community cultural wealth in graduate school access and persistence for Mexican American PhDs. *American Journal of Education, 120*(4), 545–574.

Ethier, M. (2022). B-schools: Leading or struggling on gender & race diversity?*Poets& Quants.* Retrieved from https://poetsandquants.com/2022/03/21/b-schools-leading-or-struggling-on-gender-race-diversity/. Accessed on March 22, 2022.

EURAM. (n.d.). EURAM Doctoral Accelerator. Retrieved from https://euram.academy/euram?service=info&p=hq_DoctoralAccelerator. Accessed on March 26, 2023.

Eury, J. L., & Treviño, L. K. (2019). Building a culture of honor and integrity in a business school. *Journal of Management Education, 43*(5), 484–508.

Ezeh, A., & Lu, J. (2019). *Transforming the institutional landscape in sub-Saharan Africa: Considerations for leveraging Africa's research capacity to achieve socioeconomic development.* Washington, DC: Center for Global Development.

Falk-Krzesinski, H. J., Borner, K., Contractor, N., Fiore, S. M., Hall, K. L., Keyton, J., …, Uzzi, B. (2010). Advancing the science of team science. *Clinical and Translational Science, 3*(5), 263–266.

Falkenstein, M., Hommel, U., & Snelson-Powell, A. (2022). COVID-19: Accelerator or demolisher of the RME agenda? *Journal of Global Responsibility, 13*(1), 87–100.

Fazackerley, A. (2019). 'It's cut throat': Half of UK academics stressed and 40% thinking of leaving. The Guardian Education. Retrieved from https://www.theguardian.com/education/2019/may/21/cut-throat-half-academics-stressed-thinking-leaving/. Accessed on March 26, 2023.

Felder, P. (2010). On doctoral student development: Exploring faculty mentoring in the shaping of African American doctoral student success. *Qualitative Report, 15*(2), 455–474.

Fleming, P. (2022). 'Never let a good crisis go to waste': How consulting firms are using COVID-19 as a pretext to transform universities and business school education. *Academy of Management Learning & Education.* https://doi.org/10.5465/amle.2022.0217.

Gardner, S. K. (2010). Keeping up with the Joneses: Socialization and culture in doctoral education at one striving institution. *The Journal of Higher Education, 81*(6), 658–679.

George, M. P., & Rupert Mampilly, S. (2012). A model for student mentoring in business schools. *International Journal of Mentoring and Coaching in Education, 1*(2), 136–154.

Gough, M. (2019). PGR supervisor development at the University of Liverpool: A review and the next steps. Retrieved from https://livrepository.liverpool.ac.uk/3143153/1/PGRSupervisorDevReportSept2019.pdf. Accessed September 1, 2019.

Green, P., & Bowden, J. (2012). Completion mindset and contexts in doctoral supervision. *Quality Assurance in Education, 20*(1), 66–80.

Greener, S. L. (2021). Non-supervisory support for doctoral students in business and management: A critical friend. *The International Journal of Management Education, 19*(2), 100463.

Grove, J. (2021). UKRI to review 'one principal investigator per grant' rule. *Times Higher Education,* May 19.

Gupta, U. G., & Cooper, S. (2022). An integrated framework of UN and AACSB principles for responsible management education. *Journal of Global Responsibility, 13*(1), 42–55.

Hall, J., & Martin, B. R. (2019). Towards a taxonomy of research misconduct: The case of business school research. *Research Policy, 48*(2), 414–427.

Harley, B. (2019). Confronting the crisis of confidence in management studies: Why senior scholars need to stop setting a bad example. *Academy of Management Learning & Education, 18*(2), 286–297.

Hauss, K. (2021). What are the social and scientific benefits of participating at academic conferences? Insights from a survey among doctoral students and postdocs in Germany. *Research Evaluation, 30*(1), 1–12.

He, Y. (2018). *Enhancing international students' experience in the UK through the development of a higher education co-opetition framework: An examination into Welsh universities' international collaboration and student recruitment activities.* Ph.D. thesis, Cardiff Metropolitan University, Cardiff.

Heng, K., Hamid, M., & Khan, A. (2020). Factors influencing academics' research engagement and productivity: A developing countries perspective. *Issues in Educational Research, 30*(3), 965–987.

Hogan, O., Kortt, M. A., & Charles, M. B. (2020). Standing at the crossroads: The vulnerabilities of Australian business schools. *Education+ Training, 62*(6), 707–720.

Horta, H., & Li, H. (2022). Nothing but publishing: The overriding goal of PhD students in mainland China, Hong Kong, and Macau. *Studies in Higher Education*, 1–20. https://doi.org/10.1080/03075079.2022.2131764.

Huet, I., & Casanova, D. (2022). Exploring the professional development of doctoral supervisors through workplace learning: A literature review. *Higher Education Research & Development, 41*(3), 774–788.

Ignite Adaptive. (2017, June 17). EP22-How Business School Lausanne reinvents itself with Dr. Katrin Muff. Retrieved from https://www.youtube.com/watch?v=py6sOlZ_Tss/. Accessed on March 26, 2023.

Jack, A. (2019). UK business schools fear faculty exodus post-Brexit. *The Financial Times*, June 17. Retrieved from https://www.ft.com/content/758da392-70e3-11e9-bf5c-6eeb837566c5. Accessed on March 24, 2023.

James, H., & Mihov, I. (2023). Transformative change starts with responsible research. *Times Higher Education*, February 28. Retrieved from https://www.timeshighereducation.com/blog/transformative-change-starts-responsible-research. Accessed on March 26, 2023.

Joannidès de Lautour, V. (2023). Academic partners in a city-wide doctoral ecosystem. Special supplement: Towards healthy doctoral systems in business schools. *Global Focus, 2*(17), 16–21.

Johnson, G., Scholes, K., & Whittington, R. (2011). *Exploring strategy: Text and cases* (9th ed.). London: Financial Times/Prentice Hall.

Jørgensen, T. E. (2012). *CODOC, cooperation on doctoral education between Africa, Asia, Latin America and Europe.* European University Association.

Kessio, D. K. (2022). Effective strategies of doctorate students' blended supervision and mentorship at school of education, Moi University, Kenya. *US-China Education Review, 12*(6), 220–226.

King's College London. (n.d.). *Diversity mentoring programme.* Retrieved from https://www.kcl.ac.uk/business/connections/alumni/diversity-mentoring-programme/. Accessed on March 26, 2023.

Ku, H. Y., Lahman, M. K., Yeh, H. T., & Cheng, Y. C. (2008). Into the academy: Preparing and mentoring international doctoral students. *Educational Technology Research and Development, 56*(3), 365–377.

Kuvaas, B., Buch, R., & Dysvik, A. (2017). Constructive supervisor feedback is not sufficient: Immediacy and frequency is essential. *Human Resource Management, 56*(3), 519–531.

Larivière, V. (2012). On the shoulders of students? The contribution of PhD students to the advancement of knowledge. *Scientometrics, 90*(2), 463–481.

Lattuca, L. (2002). Learning interdisciplinarity. *The Journal of Higher Education, 73*(6), 711–739.

Lekhetho, M. (2022). Postgraduate students' perceptions of support services rendered by a distance learning institution. *International Journal of Higher Education, 11*(7), 1–24.

Levecque, K., Anseel, F., De Beuckelaer, A., Van der Heyden, J., & Gisle, L. (2017). Work organization and mental health problems in PhD students. *Research Policy, 46*(4), 868–879.

Lin, J. (2021). *Two birds with one stone? Spillover effects of faculty's research knowledge sharing on students' research lives.* Unpublished data. Department of Education, University of Hong Kong, Hong Kong.

Lindsay, S. (2015). What works for doctoral students in completing their thesis? *Teaching in Higher Education, 20*(2), 183–196.

Lindvig, K., Lyall, C., & Meagher, L. R. (2019). Creating interdisciplinary education within monodisciplinary structures: The art of managing interstitiality. *Studies in Higher Education, 44*(2), 347–360.

Löfström, E., & Pyhältö, K. (2020). What are ethics in doctoral supervision, and how do they matter? Doctoral students' perspective. *Scandinavian Journal of Educational Research, 64*(4), 535–550.

Lough, C. (2022). Nearly two thirds of academics set to leave HE sector. Evening Standard, March 25. Retrieved from https://www.standard.co.uk/news/uk/university-and-college-union-universities-uk-b990387.html. Accessed on March 26, 2023.

Manabe, Y. C., Nambooze, H., Okello, E. S., Kamya, M. R., Katabira, E. T., Ssinabulya, I., … Sewankambo, N. K. (2018). Group mentorship model to enhance the efficiency and productivity of PhD research training in Sub-Saharan Africa. *Annals of Global Health, 84*(1), 170–175.

Manathunga, C., Lant, P., & Mellick, G. (2006). Imagining an interdisciplinary doctoral pedagogy. *Teaching in Higher Education, 11*(3), 365–379.

Marder, B., Oliver, S., Yau, A., Lavertu, L., Perier, C., Frank, M., & Cowan, K. (2021). Impression formation of PhD supervisors during student-led selection: An examination of UK business schools with a focus on staff profiles. *The International Journal of Management Education, 19*(1), 100453.

Masta, S. (2021). Classroom counterspaces: Centering Brown and Black students in doctoral education. *Teaching in Higher Education, 26*(3), 354–369.

Max Planck Institute. (2003). Mentoring programs for female PhD students. Retrieved from https://www.mpipz.mpg.de/phd-program/mentoring/. Accessed on March 26, 2023.

McKiernan, P., & Tsui, A. S. (2019). Responsible management research: A senior scholar legacy in doctoral education. *Academy of Management Learning & Education, 18*(2), 310–313.

McPherson, C., Punch, S., & Graham, E. (2018). Postgraduate transitions from masters to doctoral study: Managing independence, emotion, and support. *Stirling International Journal of Postgraduate Research SPARK, 4*, 1–24.

Mejlgaard, N., Bouter, L. M., Gaskell, G., Kavouras, P., Allum, N., Bendtsen, A. K., … Veltri, G. A. (2020). Research integrity: Nine ways to move from talk to walk. *Nature, 586*(7829), 358–360.

Mogaji, E., Adamu, N., & Nguyen, N. P. (2021). Stakeholders shaping experiences of self-funded international PhD students in UK business schools. *The International Journal of Management Education, 19*(3), 100543.

Mollica, M., & Nemeth, L. (2014). Outcomes and characteristics of faculty/student mentorship in PhD programs. *American Journal of Educational Research, 2*(9), 703–708.

Mtwisha, L., Jackson, J., Mitchel, A., Aikins, A. D. G., Kebirungi, H., Outtara, K., & Viney, C. (2021). Early-and mid-career transitions to research leadership in Africa. *Wellcome Open Research, 6*, 74. https://doi.org/10.12688/wellcomeopenres.16540.2.

Nerad, M., Bogle, D., Kohl, U., O'Carroll, C., Peters, C., & Scholz, B. (2022). *Towards a global core value system in doctoral education* (pp. 290). London: UCL Press.

Noy, S., & Ray, R. (2012). Graduate students' perceptions of their advisors: Is there systematic disadvantage in mentorship? *The Journal of Higher Education, 83*(6), 876–914.

O'Doherty, D., & De Cock, C. (2017). Management as an academic discipline? In A. Wilkinson, S. J. Armstrong, & M. Lounsbury (Eds.), *The Oxford handbook of management* (pp. 461–480). Oxford: Oxford University Press.

Oviatt, B. M., & Miller, W. D. (1989). Irrelevance, intransigence, and business professors. *Academy of Management Perspectives*, *3*(4), 304–312.

Palmer, N. (2022). Contesting boundaries: Researcher networks as inclusive and exclusive spaces. *Vitae Blog*, August 17. Retrieved from http://www.Vitae.ac.uk/news/Vitae-blog/contesting-boundaries-researcher-networks-as-inclusive-and-exclusive-spaces/. Accessed on March 26, 2023.

Palmer, R., & Gasman, M. (2008). 'It takes a village to raise a child': The role of social capital in promoting academic success for African American men at a Black college. *Journal of College Student Development*, *49*(1), 52–70.

Parker-Jenkins, M. (2018). Mind the gap: Developing the roles, expectations and boundaries in the doctoral supervisor–supervisee relationship. *Studies in Higher Education*, *43*(1), 57–71.

Pasupathy, R., & Siwatu, K. O. (2014). An investigation of research self-efficacy beliefs and research productivity among faculty members at an emerging research university in the USA. *Higher Education Research & Development*, *33*(4), 728–741.

Pearson, M., & Brew, A. (2002). Research training and supervision development. *Studies in Higher Education*, *27*(2), 135–150.

Pfeffer, J., & Fong, C. T. (2002). The end of business schools? Less success than meets the eye. *Academy of Management Learning & Education*, *1*(1), 78–95.

PhD Project. Retrieved from https://phdproject.org/

Pitt, R., & Mewburn, I. (2016). Academic superheroes? A critical analysis of academic job descriptions. *Journal of Higher Education Policy and Management*, *38*(1), 88–101.

Pizzolato, N. (2023). Four dimensions of an interdisciplinary doctoral ecosystem. *Global Focus*, *2*(17), 16–21.

Posselt, J. R. (2016). *Inside graduate admissions: Merit, diversity, and faculty gatekeeping*. Boston, MA: Harvard University Press.

Pouza, L. (2022). EFMD behind the scenes: Conversation with Jean-Alexis Spitz (JAS). *EFMD*, March 18. Retrieved from https://blog.efmdglobal.org/2022/03/18/efmd-behind-the-scenes-conversation-with-jean-alexis-spitz-jas/. Accessed on March 18, 2022.

Pratt, M., Margaritis, D., & Coy, D. (1999). Developing a research culture in a university faculty. *Journal of higher Education Policy and Management*, *21*(1), 43–55.

PREDOC. (n.d.). Mentoring best practices. Retrieved from https://predoc.org/mentoring. Accessed on March 3, 2023.

Pyne, D. (2017). The rewards of predatory publications at a small business school. *Journal of Scholarly Publishing*, *48*(3), 137–160.

Ranjan, J. (2011). Study of sharing knowledge resources in business schools. *The Learning Organization*, *18*(2), 102–114.

Rashid, R. (2021). Updating the PhD: Making the case for interdisciplinarity in twenty-first-century doctoral education. *Teaching in Higher Education*, *26*(3), 508–517.

Reeves, J. (2022). New beginnings or same old ending for researcher development? In M. L. Österlind, P. Denicolo, & B. M. Apelgren (Eds.), *Doctoral education as if people matter* (pp. 140–154). Leiden: Brill.

Robeyns, I. (2019, December 29). *Time for PhD supervision*. Retrieved from https://crookedtimber.org/2019/12/29/time-for-phd-supervision/. Accessed on July 23, 2023.

Rowley, J. (2023). Getting published in peer reviewed academic journals in business and management: Perspectives for doctoral and early career researchers. *Management Research Review*, *46*(2), 306–319.

Rui, G., & Chao, L. (2022). University leadership styles in the 'new normal'. *Times Higher Education*. Retrieved from https://www.timeshighereducation.com/campus/leadership-styles-work-new-normal. Accessed on March 10, 2023.

Ryan, N., & Mulligan, D. L. (2023). A comparative autoethnographic lens on the doctorate as told by a supervisor and a doctoral candidate. In E. A. Anteliz, D. L. Mulligan, & P. A. Danaher (Eds.), *The Routledge international handbook of autoethnography in educational research* (pp. 137–147). Abingdon: Routledge.

Ryan, S., & Neumann, R. (2013). Interdisciplinarity in an era of new public management: A case study of graduate business schools. *Studies in Higher Education, 38*(2), 192–206.

Ryan, T., Baik, C., & Larcombe, W. (2022). How can universities better support the mental wellbeing of higher degree research students? A study of students' suggestions. *Higher Education Research & Development, 41*(3), 867–881.

Ryazanova, O., & McNamara, P. (2016). Socialization and proactive behavior: Multilevel exploration of research productivity drivers in US business schools. *Academy of Management Learning & Education, 15*(3), 525–548.

Sambrook, S. (2016). Managing the psychological contract within doctoral supervisory relationships. In P. Blessinger & D. Stockley (Eds.), *Emerging directions in doctoral education (innovations in Higher Education Teaching and Learning)* (Vol. 6, pp. 61–87). Leeds: Emerald Group Publishing Limited.

Saxena, D. (2021). Contextual factors shaping the student–supervisor relationship: A cross-country perspective. In A. S. Zimmerman (Ed.), *Handbook of research on developing students' scholarly dispositions in higher education* (pp. 298–313). Hershey, PA: IGI Global.

Schiavone, F., & Simoni, M. (2011). An experience-based view of co-opetition in R&D networks. *European Journal of Innovation Management, 14*(2), 136–154.

Scottish Graduate School of Social Science (SGSSS). (2022). SGSSS career pathways mentoring programme. Retrieved from https://www.sgsss.ac.uk/mentoring/sgsss-career-pathways/

Smith, B. (2007). Accessing social capital through the academic mentoring process. *Equity & Excellence in Education, 40*(1), 36–46.

Smith McGloin, R., & Wynne, C. (2015). Structural changes in doctoral education in the UK: A review of graduate schools and the development of doctoral colleges. Litchfield: UKCGE.

Stremersch, S., Winer, R., & Camacho, N. (2021). Faculty research incentives and business school health: A new perspective from and for marketing. *Journal of Marketing, 85*(5), 1–21.

Sun, X., & Trent, J. (2020). Ongoing doctoral study process to live by: A narrative inquiry into the doctoral identity construction experiences—A Chinese case. *Frontiers of Education in China, 15*(3), 422–452.

Taylor, S., & Beasley, N. (2005). *A handbook for doctoral supervisors.* Abingdon: Routledge.

The Association of Commonwealth Universities. (2020). Developing the next generation of researchers: International perspectives. Retrieved from https://www.acu.ac.uk/news/developing-early-career-researchers-international-perspectives/. Accessed on March 24, 2023.

Thomas, H., & Thomas, L. (2011). Perspectives on leadership in business schools. *Journal of Management Development, 30*(5), 526–540.

Times Higher Education. (2017). Of monsters and mentors: PhD disasters, and how to avoid them. *THE*, June 1.

Trkman, P. (2019). Value proposition of business schools: More than meets the eye. *The International Journal of Management Education, 17*(3), 100310.

Tsigaris, P., & Teixeira da Silva, J. A. (2020). Reproducibility issues with correlating Beall-listed publications and research awards at a small Canadian business school. *Scientometrics, 123*(1), 143–157.

UKCGE. (n.d.). Good supervisory practice framework. Retrieved from https://supervision.ukcge.ac.uk/good-supervisory-practice-framework. Accessed on March 25, 2023.

UKRIO. (2023). What makes a good working environment for researchers? Retrieved from https://ukrio.org/news/what-makes-a-good-working-environment-for-researchers/. Accessed on March 25, 2023.

Vauterin, J. J., & Virkki-Hatakka, T. (2021). Mentoring PhD students working in industry: Using hermeneutics as a critical approach to the experience. *Industry and Higher Education*, *35*(3), 252–263.

Vidaver-Cohen, D. (2007). Reputation beyond the rankings: A conceptual framework for business school research. *Corporate Reputation Review*, *10*(4), 278–304.

Vitae. (2018). Exploring wellbeing and mental health and associated support services for postgraduate researchers. *Higher Education Funding Council for England*. Retrieved from https://www.vitae.ac.uk/doing-research/wellbeing-and-mental-health/HEFCE-Report_Exploring-PGR-Mental-health-support/view. Accessed on March 27, 2023.

Vitae. (2023). About the Vitae Researcher Development Framework. Retrieved from https://www.Vitae.ac.uk/researchers-professional-development/about-the-Vitae-researcher-development-framework/. Accessed on March 26, 2023.

Waight, E., & Giordano, A. (2018). Doctoral students' access to non-academic support for mental health. *Journal of Higher Education Policy and Management*, *40*(4), 390–412.

Wang, X. (2022). Occupational stress in Chinese higher education institutions: A case study of doctoral supervisors. *International Journal of Environmental Research and Public Health*, *19*(15), 9503.

Watson, D., & Turnpenny, J. (2022). Interventions, practices and institutional arrangements for supporting PGR mental health and wellbeing: reviewing effectiveness and addressing barriers. *Studies in Higher Education*, *47*(9), 1957–1979.

Watts, J. H. (2010). Team supervision of the doctorate: Managing roles, relationships and contradictions. *Teaching in Higher Education*, *15*(3), 335–339.

Way, S. F., Morgan, A. C., Larremore, D. B., & Clauset, A. (2019). Productivity, prominence, and the effects of academic environment. *Proceedings of the National Academy of Sciences*, *116*(22), 10729–10733.

Webb, A. K., Wangmo, T., Ewen, H. H., Teaster, P. B., & Hatch, L. R. (2009). Peer and faculty mentoring for students pursuing a PhD in gerontology. *Educational Gerontology*, *35*(12), 1089–1106.

Wellcome Trust. (2020). *What researchers think about the culture they work in*. London: Wellcome Trust.

Weybrecht, G. (2022). Business schools are embracing the SDGs–But is it enough?How business schools are reporting on their engagement in the SDGs. *International Journal of Management Education*, *20*(1), 100589.

White-Lewis, D. K. (2020). The facade of fit in faculty search processes. *Journal of Higher Education*, *91*(6), 833–857.

Whitsed, C., & Girardi, A. (2022). Where has the joy of working in Australian universities gone? Retrieved from https://theconversation.com/where-has-the-joy-of-working-in-australian-universities-gone-184251. Accessed on March 24, 2023.

Wickert, C., Post, C., Doh, J. P., Prescott, J. E., & Prencipe, A. (2021). Management research that makes a difference: Broadening the meaning of impact. *Journal of Management Studies*, *58*(2), 297–320.

Wilkinson, A. (2015). The rules of the game: A short guide for PhD students and new academics on publishing in academic journals. *Innovations in Education and Teaching International*, *52*(1), 99–107.

Wisker, G., & Robinson, G. (2013). Doctoral 'orphans': Nurturing and supporting the success of postgraduates who have lost their supervisors. *Higher Education Research & Development*, *32*(2), 300–313.

WONKHE. (2021). Generative AI can change assessment for the better. *WONKHE*, April 11.

Woodhouse, J., & Wood, P. (2022). Creating dialogic spaces: Developing doctoral students' critical writing skills through peer assessment and review. *Studies in Higher Education, 47*(3), 643–655.

Wright, P. M. (2016). Ensuring research integrity: An editor's perspective. *Journal of Management, 42*(5), 1037–1043.

Zografou, A., & McDermott, L. (2022). Mentorship in higher education: The keys to unlocking meaningful mentoring relationships. *GiLE Journal of Skills Development, 2*(1), 71–78.

Index